BASICS OF

GROWING

CHRISTMAS

TREES

BASICS OF

GROWING

CHRISTMAS

TREES

Treehaven Evergreen Nursery
981 Jamison Road
Elma, New York 14059

This report was authored by Donald B. Hilliker, Jr. in colla-
boration with his wife, Joan, owners and managers of Treehaven
Evergreen Nursery, Elma, New York (near Buffalo, New York) and
Hill Top Acres Christmas Tree Plantation, Yorkshire, New York,
to assist new and prospective Christmas Tree growers in the
planning and early action stages of establishing a tree plantation.

BASICS OF GROWING CHRISTMAS TREES

Published by: Treehaven Evergreen Nursery
                 981 Jamison Road
                 Elma, New York 14059-9536

Copyright (c) April, 1993
Revised Printing
Printed in the United States of America

Library of Congress Catalog Card Number: 92-93374

        ISBN: 1-878755-02-1
              Price: $24.95

Information contained in this publication has been carefully
compiled from sources believed to be reliable, but the accuracy
of the information is not guaranteed. This report is sold with
the understanding that the authors are not engaged in rendering
legal, taxation, employment, accounting, or other professional
service. If legal advice, or other expert assistance is
required, the services of a competent professional should be
sought.

ACKNOWLEDGEMENTS

This book would not have been possible without the cooperation and unselfish assistance of many individuals, companies, and organizations throughout the United States.

Our early inspiration, knowledge, and assistance came from men like Fred Winch, Jr., Alex Dickson, and Claude E. Heit. We thank William Ballagh, Guy Cockburn, and the late Cleland Cook (New York). They are well-known for their cultural techniques regarding Balsam fir, Douglas fir, and blue spruce respectively. We thank Darwin Pound (Ohio CTA) and Bernard Douglass (Northwest CTA) for their cultural work with Fraser fir and Douglas fir respectively.

Others providing material herein are:
...Alvin A. Alm, Marvin E. Smith, and Carl D. Wegner, Univ. of Minnesota and John M. Ahrens, Conn. Exp. Station, S. Windsor, Conn., a tree grower, himself, whose work with herbicides has benefited all tree growers.
...Herbert Attaway, Lake City, Florida, a long-time grower and National Director. His guidance has helped many to become successful tree growers in the S.E.
...Turner Davis, Griffin, Ga., forester, tree grower and inventor. His untiring efforts have contributed greatly to the establishment of tree growing in the South.
...Warren T. Johnson, author, Dept. of Entomology, Cornell Univ., Ithaca, N.Y. His recent efforts have been to develop methods to control pest insects in ways friendly to our environment.
...Larry J. Kuhns, Penn State Univ., University Park, Pa. has contributed to sections on vegetation control and plant nutrition.
...Gregory Passewitz, Resource Devel., Ohio State Univ. Extension for his suggestions about marketing.
...David W. Taber, Susan J. Richa, W. Shaw Reid and George L. Good, Cornell Univ., and Donald H. Bickelhaupt, Syracuse Univ., for their writings on Christmas Tree fertilization.
...Earl Becker, Treehaven Evergreen Nursery, Elma, N.Y.
...Michael R. Hall, Treehaven Evergreen Nursery, Elma, N.Y.
...Lehmann Bros., Arthur & Henry, Springville, N.Y. for 35 years of loyal service.
...Larry & Jackie Cavaletto, Noel Christmas Tree Farm, Santa Barbara, Ca.
...A.R. Gilmore, Program Associate & tree grower, Auburn Univ., Ala.
...Thomas A. Green, Pest Management Supply, Amherst, Mass.
...Thomas J. Nichols, Kellogg Forest, Michigan State Univ., Augusta
...Ronald Restum, Pure Gro Co., W. Sacramento, Calif.
..."Sky" & Joan Weller, Sky View Acres, Scotia, N.Y.
...Our thanks to all the others mentioned in various sections of the contents.
...Our thanks to Allied Signal, Inc. (formerly Allied Chemical) - Nitrogen Div. for permission to reprint (The History of the Christmas Tree). This 1966 book entitled "Arcadian Technical Manual for Christmas Tree Farmers" was authored by Lester E. Bell and Dr. Donald P. White of Michigan State Univ.

...Our appreciation to many Cooperative Extension Universities and our U.S. Department of Agriculture-Forestry Service for all the good works that have enabled us to be successful.

THE HISTORY OF THE CHRISTMAS TREE

In America today there is no greater traditional symbol than the Christmas Tree. The use of decorated evergreen trees during the Christmas season provides the focal point for American families to celebrate the birthday of the Christ child. It is the living symbol of everlasting life. It is our link to the freshness and the fragrance of the forest.

The legends which surround the origin of the first Christmas tree are many. Some historians trace it to St. Boniface in the 8th Century when he decided at Odin that a young fir tree, a child of the forest, should be the holy tree. Others say that Martin Luther (1483-1546) was responsible for developing the custom of celebrating the Christmas season with a decorated evergreen tree.

History records that Martin Luther, while thinking of the story of the nativity, strolled into the German countryside on Christmas Eve. He was impressed with the beauty of the starlit heavens, the twinkling of the frost particles on the trees and the beautiful blanket of snow on the landscape. He was especially taken with the snow flecked beauty of a tiny fir tree. As he returned to his home he was so elated by what he had seen that he tried to reproduce the winter scene inside his house for his family. He therefore brought a small fir tree into the house, decorated it with lighted candles and christened it a "Christmas Tree".

It appears that this custom prevailed along the Rhine River and throughout Germany for many years before being accepted elsewhere. Historians relate that the use of a Christmas Tree in America dates back to the Hessian soldiers who were British mercenaries during the American Revolution (1778).

The first use of the Christmas Tree in England as an accepted house decoration for the Yule season is attributed to Prince Albert in the 1840's, although a few trees were used for this purpose earlier. Prince Albert brought a Christmas tree to Windsor Castle in 1841.

Today's Christmas Tree with blinking lights, tinsel, plastic baubles, artificial snow, and flocking may be a far cry from Martin Luther's tree but the custom is now traditional in most Christian countries of the world.

DEDICATION

To my father, Donald B. Hilliker, 1905 - 1982. His dedication to
growing Christmas Trees was borne from his farming family background in Delevan, New York. In 1947 the land on "Blue Hill" was
acquired and Christmas Trees planted soon thereafter. The entire
family became involved. His perseverance through the bad times,
as well as the good, provided the knowledge and desire needed to
have Hill Top Acres the sustaining business it is today.

To my wife, Joan Mary Schultz Hilliker, whose family background
was farming and growing Christmas Trees on "Homer Hill" on the
N.W. slopes of Olean, New York. She has a natural devotion that
evolved to make Treehaven Evergreen Nursery and Hill Top Acres
Christmas Tree Plantation a successful combined venture. Her
bountiful energy and continuous effort has brought respect and
good fortune to our undertaking. It is through her inspiration
and teamwork that we are able to present this book to you.

PREFACE

Treehaven Evergreen Nursery had its beginning 25 years ago, in a suburb of Buffalo, NY not far from our location today. Early on we had progressed far enough with Christmas Tree growing to realize a major key to success was in the quality of the planting stock from the best possible seed sources. Most nurseries, years ago, had little or no knowledge of the parentage of the seed they sowed and the seedlings they planted. Several very successful Scotch Pine plantings we had made could not be repeated because the suppliers no longer offered those seedlings. Little or no field studies had been undertaken to find out what grew best where.

Today we have provenance studies (seed source) in progress for Douglas Fir, Concolor Fir, Blue Spruce, Austrian Pine, Ponderosa Pine and Scotch Pine. We are growing lesser known varieties such as: Turkish Fir, Alpine Fir, Bristlecone Fir, Spanish Fir and several other firs.

During the years, Joan and I pursued our careers, hers as an executive and medical secretary, mine in chemical sales. In 1985 we reached a crossroads - to develop the nursery or give it up. The work load at our family "Hill Top Acres" location (wholesale) was beyond "part-time" as well. At this point, we retired from our outside business activities to devote 100% of our time to our nursery and Christmas tree plantation.

In our nursery activities we strive to provide tree growers with the richest quality and freshest planting stock possible. We want to assist you in your efforts to have a successful Christmas tree operation. Growing seedlings is entirely different than growing Christmas trees, so our discussions will be confined to helpful information that will enable you to produce the best quality trees.

This book is intended for new and prospective growers who need guidance. Those already entrenched in their own practices and prejudices, we hope, will benefit by improving their performance from ideas herein.

In 1987 we published our first edition of "Basics of Growing Christmas Trees". This edition has been expanded and up-dated to help tree growers everywhere. Some subjects herein are in a constant state of change. Tax laws, pesticide use, various fields of technology are constantly changing. The Cooperative Extension and other sources given herein will help you keep up to date. Many other sources of information and assistance are available to you. Other tree growing suppliers, trade publications, meetings and seminars, and books (library) are a few. You will need all the help you can get to compete with the artificial Christmas tree.

Last, but not least, we were motivated to write this for those with a profit objective in mind and not for the hobbyist. We are income and profit oriented, which means, we are competitive in our thinking and actions. We take that to be the same as "success" since this brings a reward of personal satisfaction, as well as monetary gain.

CONTENTS

INTRODUCTION

This might have been titled "Share the Wealth" (enjoyment), or "Get Rich with Trees" (experiences), but instead we decided to tell you what it is really about - farming! Christmas Tree Farming! To us growing Christmas trees is fun.

You will find Christmas tree growing both challenging and rewarding. It takes dedication to your ideas and objectives because the planting to harvest cycle is so long. Many growers have accomplished their goals far beyond their original expectations, both in personal satisfaction and in financial reward. In recent years the financial reward has been especially satisfying.

The Christmas tree growing commitment on a national scale began to take shape in the late 1940's and has continued to attract and excite more and more people ever since. Christmas tree growers come from every age and walk of life.

The marketing trend has changed dramatically from cut trees on a corner lot to the "Come Out And Cut Your Own At Our Farm". This marketing trend (U-Cut, Choose and Cut, Cut Your Own) has led to the greatly expanded industry that it is today. This process of getting the family Christmas tree has become a family event for the whole family. It is a day or partial day of family enjoyment.

From the grower's standpoint it usually involves all members of the grower's family, and provides income to all who participate in the planting, mowing, shearing and marketing efforts. Some growers sell wholesale entirely or sell part wholesale and part retail. Many just have a "Cut Your Own" retail business.

People are motivated to get into Christmas Tree growing for a variety of reasons. It may be needed funds for a college education, for retirement income, for another crop in their farming activity, and some people have land and don't know what else to do with it. Some people, like us, live entirely off the income as a livelihood. For most growers, however, it is additional income.

Other facets of retailing are frequently included in the tree growing activity or is taken up as a side line business. That includes wreath making, operating a (seasonal) gift shop, retail nursery/garden center, landscaping, even snowplowing. There are many other activities as well.

Many of you who are reading this now are undecided. You don't know what to do or how to go about doing it, or how much work and commitment is really involved. We hope to give you some basics for determining the answers from the material presented in this book. Many other sources of information are also available to you.

Once you have made the decision to grow trees, don't put off starting. Remember we are involved with a growing cycle that will span a period of years. It doesn't start up suddenly, or end abruptly either. Also, most established growers, just like us, alter our thinking from year to year. For example, as Fraser Fir became known, and its acceptance certain, we included this as one of our principal varieties (after some trial plantings). If we find weaknesses or deficiencies in the seed source of a particular variety, we change. Belgium Scotch is an example, it shows signs of early yellowing in the fall, so we are discontinuing growing the seedlings and the trees.

A couple pointers here will keep you on the right track. "Make small mistakes not big ones", and my father used to say "Investigate before you invest" (Dad was in the stock and bond business). These same guidelines should be followed by the new Christmas Tree Grower. Gather facts and information that will help you make a decision with the least risky consequences. The objective of this book is to help you do just that. Let me hasten to add, however, we do not have all the answers. For one reason, we are in an ever changing business, just dealing with mother nature provides a never ending set of circumstances.

While plantings in many states have been heavy in the past five to eight years (Especially New York State), the whole eastern seaboard provides a market that has never been filled by the tree growers in the northeastern U.S. Many trees are still "imported" from other parts of the U.S. as well as from Canada. Canada and our own west coast growers ship millions of trees annually into what should be your markets. Most local market areas still provide opportunities especially for a "Choose and Cut" business. Do some investigation on your own. Ask yourself that all important question: "Who will buy my trees?" and "Do I have competitive advantages?" "Can I grow them better than what is around now?" "Can I grow trees economically even if a favorable factor turned against me?" (Lower selling price, etc.).

One major factor turned against all of us with the passage of the the 1986 tax laws (begins taking effect in 1987). We discuss this later in the book. Consider all the factors before reaching the decision of "Should I or Shouldn't I". The final chapter will comment on the market situation and the industry.

While other growers can be very helpful in your decision making process, only you live with the mistakes. Avoid the "monkey see, monkey do" tendency. What someone else does doesn't necessarily mean that it is the thing you should do. Although another grower may appear to be successful, they may in fact be doing many things that could be improved upon. Your objectives may be different, your resources may be very much different: your land, your planting sites, your equipment, your time and energy resources; these and many other factors will be different. You will not eliminate mistakes.

Our own preferences and prejudices are expressed in the chapters that follow since we are relating our experiences. Under even slightly different circumstances we might do something differently. Many materials and products are available today that may not even be referred to in this book, but this omission does not mean they are not worthy. Since this writing is not sponsored or supported by any company, organization or group, we have not been so influenced. Some portions and entire sections, herein are dated material. You should verify the accuracy of some practices and procedures before implementing them. The section on "Pesticides and Toxicity" is an example. Products and procedures are under constant change as well.

Finally, you will not eliminate mistakes! Profiting by them is what Christmas tree growing is all about.

It is a great learning experience!

It can be a lot of fun!

PLANTATION LOCATION

If you are still in the thinking stage and have not acquired land, or may have decided to purchase another parcel of land, then some very important elements of Christmas tree growing and marketing need to be considered.

It will take you eight to ten years to really get into the business and possibly another ten years to get back your investment and make some money. The point I am making is that, if you don't intend to spend twenty years at tree growing, then you should consider investing your money (and time and energy) elsewhere.

People today will travel considerable distance for the Family Event of selecting a Christmas tree. You do not have to be located at the city limits to draw customers. On the other hand, you must be relatively easy to reach by good roads. Under adverse weather conditions people are not inclined to go very far to cut their own tree. They will go to a nearby cut tree lot.

Land within reasonable proximity to a major market area can be very expensive (as are taxes), yet it could also appreciate in value as the years go by. Read the business consideration section for a cost guide. Choose and cut plantations may readily wholesale trees but a wholesale plantation is usually much less adaptable (or impossible) to adapt to a sizable retail business.

Because recovery of expenditures is long-term, objectives should be established prior to land purchase. Don't buy a piece of land and then decide what to do with it. Be patient and purchase a planting site that will result in a high probability of success.

Don't rule out buying an established plantation. If it is at or near a productive level, it may be able to pay its own way. (Create income to pay mortgage, etc.) You may, also, buy 10 years of time. (Wish I could do that!)

Land already "in hand" usually means living with the conditions that exist or making changes that can only be justified on the basis of income. (Sometimes you can purchase adjoining land that would be more productive).

In this day of high labor costs, machinery, taxes, etc., it may be better to abandon the idea of trying to "recover" a land area that requires excessive effort and cost. Simply, the projected return for all the effort may not justify the land reclamation required. You may be better off purchasing land better suited, and usable, to your purpose. Remember the old adage, "you can't make a silk purse from a sow's ear". I'll say it again, land preparation cost is money spent and not recovered for a period of years.

This same cost consideration should be given to land requiring drainage tile, waterways, etc. Measures can be undertaken sometimes such as ditching with a tractor and plow, etc. to avoid a greater outlay of capital.

Nearby conditions or facilities might present unforeseen obstacles such as quarry operations, adjoining brush land, dumps that could contaminate water and soil and manufacturing plants that discharge residue.

Some other considerations need to be investigated prior to any land purchase. A reputable realtor should prove helpful. Most cities, towns and townships today have zoning codes. Ordinances governing all types of behavior will dictate what you can or cannot do. Although ordinances can be changed, it can be a lengthy and costly event. Find out what the permits/restrictions are before you decide to set yourself up in business. On street/off street parking; permits to sell; sign restrictions; high taxes and many others can be deterrent factors. Land classification may deter a retail farming activity and preclude you from taking advantage of things such as the agricultural value assessment. Some farm land can receive partial exemption from real property taxes in New York State. For more information about this you can contact the nearest Soil Conservation office, or write:

Agricultural Unit
N. Y. State Div. of Equalization & Assessment
Agency Bldg. #4
Empire State Plaza
Albany, New York 12223
Tel. No. (518) 474-1694

Other States may have similar tax relief. Contact your State property tax department.

A retail "cut your own" location should not be so far away from a population center that it discourages travel; also, it must be able to accommodate traffic and have areas to handle parked cars. Some townships have restrictions to parking along the road. It may be inconvenient as well as dangerous. The parking accommodations should be proportional to the volume of trees being sold. For example, the second weekend in December may account for 1/3 or 1/2 of your entire volume of business and the volume of traffic (vehicles) can become unmanageable. Traffic control from your local police may be needed.

Parking areas must be readily accessible and free of obstacles and potential problems. Wet, rough and soft soil areas are to be avoided. Handicapped parking must be provided. Roadways within the plantation must accommodate the means by which your customers will enter and leave your plantation. If tractors and wagons are going to be used, wider roadways will be needed. Spacing between trees is usually greater to allow people to pass between them, etc. No less than 6' by 6' is considered practical. Room must be allowed if replanting is being done on a seasonal basis.

Some common sense about the geographic conditions of the land you are considering is necessary. Steep slopes, swampy or perpetually wet areas, poor roads to your plantation are all very negative factors. These problem situations can take all the joy out of an otherwise fun activity.

Your land and its soil is your most essential resource; the more your know about it the better.

To find out more about the land you are considering purchasing, or have already purchased, go to the nearest Soil Conservation office (or inquire through your Cooperative Extension office). Ask to see the aerial map of the area under consideration. These maps chart all the land within a county with subsequent identity of the major soil types. (See portion of map and soil descriptions in "Soil" chapter).

A description of the soil type(s) will tell you what you have to work with. Keep in mind that the soil type does not tell you slope and other site situations, although certain soil types are indigenous to site situations. The soil type does not necessarily reveal fertility, although certain soil types have a characteristic. Your Soil Conservation office will be invaluable in guiding you. A soil sample and analysis is essential. The more you can learn about a piece of land you want to buy, the better.

A few dollars invested in soil samples is well worth avoiding serious mistakes. Lime and fertilizer use and subsequent cost to compensate for seriously deficient soil can easily exceed a bargain-land price. Other soil characteristics are important to know. The section on soils will be helpful. Read the partial list of problems associated with planting sites in the chaper that follows. One or more of these negative factors might alter your decision to purchase or utilize a specific plot of land.

Close-up of container grown loblolly pine. International Forest Seed Co., Odenville, AL.

"Bare root" beds ready for lifting Treehaven Evergreen Nursery, Elma, N.Y.

SITE PREPARATION

Site preparation means to prepare the area to be planted. Many situations may exist, but usually few are recognized by the beginning farmer. For people who have a background in farming, this is different. It is a matter of recognizing land problems before planting a crop - in our case, Christmas Trees. It is very important to rectify a problem before planting because you may have to live with it for eight, ten or twelve years or longer, until that particular growing cycle is complete. (Putting in drain tile is an example.)

Common problems associated with planting sites are:

- The soil itself should be evaluated. (Read chapter on soil.)
- Low areas which become frost pockets on a year-to-year basis. (Poor air drainage).
- Excessively wet areas over a major part of the year. (Growth of marsh grass and other signs are evident).
- Unfavorable ground cover that will hinder crop. (Goldenrod, milkweed, bracken fern and brush).
- Establishment of brush, poplar and other difficult to control vegetation.
- Eroded land, rough land, ditches and ruts make mowing and spraying very difficult. (Some land should be worked prior to any planting).
- Prior crop - Alfalfa can overrun and kill off evergreen seedlings.
- Stony or rocky land. A rock picker may be effective; otherwise, other procedures may need to be employed to avoid problems later. (Breakup of brush hogs, Roof-type mowers, etc.). Abandonment of an area may be in order or else it could be randomly planted and managed accordingly.
- Land near heavy tree/brush cover provides a favorable browsing situation for deer and other wildlife (wide open land would be better).
- Water runoff areas. Poor ditches or no ditches may allow roadway drainage and adjoining property to drain across your land. Evaluate springs/localized trapped areas. A spring area may need to be opened up to provide controlled drainage; that is, do not allow it to spread over the land where trees can be or are planted.
- General land clearing. (Large to mature trees). Forget any such notions of recovering this land. Perimeter clearing may be in order but general land clearing usually cannot be justified from a cost standpoint. Lease land and joint venture are options that you could explore.

The layout of your plantation should be done on paper first. Quadrille paper, as found in the Appendix, can be used. First, a topographic map or an aerial photo of your property can be very helpful. Your area Soil Conservation office should be helpful. The larger the land area involved, the greater the necessity for layout and planning.

Most land has features that provide a guide to its layout. Streams, wooded areas, ditches, slopes, and roads all provide a basis for laying out the block or areas of trees. For many cultural reasons, all of one specie are usually planted in the same area, but that is not a firm rule. Certain varieties should not be planted in proximity to each other. (Douglas Fir and Blue Spruce is an example).

Roadways usually go around the perimeter of an area. Sometimes that area is bounded by trees or woods. Conifers, generally, do not tolerate shade. (Grand Fir is an exception). Perimeter roadways usually work out well. We put in a roadway every 16 to 22 rows of trees, depending on where we run out of one lot of seedlings, or where we switch from one variety to another, or one seed source to another, etc. Whether a retail or wholesale operation, it is not desirable to drag trees a long distance.

Sometimes just a mowing of the area to be planted will suffice to clear random brush. A tractor-operated brush hog can accomplish this. We have found it better, sometimes, to hire services rather than accumulate debt in buying equipment (if it isn't equipment used regularly). It may be seven years or longer before the first dollar/income comes in to offset costs.

Let's go back to getting the land prepared. There are situations where plowing, disking and seeding (cover crop) of the land is in order. Such action will save a lot of grief later, in terms of mowing, shearing, spraying, harvesting, etc.

Ground that is rough, rutted, eroded, has outcropping rock or has considerable young brush coming in should probably be worked before any planting is done. Woodchuck holes should be treated with gas cartridges and all entrances sealed. They should be checked several weeks later to be sure the dens are rendered inactive. A twisted ankle, broken leg, a mower out of control, or a similar event, will dramatize the importance of this action. Frequently there are one or more mounds of dirt and stone that need to be leveled off, so this is added reason to work an area before planting. Recent cropland is usually satisfactory, however.

After the land has been prepared, a cover crop is usually desirable. A recent study on this subject, specifically for Christmas tree producers, was undertaken by Dr. Larry Kuhns, Dept. of Horticulture, The Pennsylvania State University, State College, PA. This information should prove helpful. Part of what Dr. Kuhns has to say in his booklet titled "Permanent Cover Crops For Christmas Tree Plantings" is given in the following section.

"Fruit and grape growers have used cover crops as part of their production systems for many years. Cover crops can prevent soil erosion and limit loss of pesticides and fertilizers to streams, ponds, and ground water. They provide a firm surface to walk or drive equipment on. This helps prevent soil compaction and promotes water penetration rather than runoff. The roots and leaf clippings add organic matter to the soil and help support beneficial soil microorganisms. Areas planted in a carefully selected cover crop have few problem weeds and require less maintenance than "wild" areas.

The cover crops that have traditionally been used in orchards and vineyards have rapid growth rates and have required a higher level of maintenance than desired. At Penn State we are trying to find plants that will provide all the benefits listed without requiring high maintenance. We would like to find a plant or plants that have as many of the following desirable characteristics as possible:

1. Rapid establishment.
2. Dense enough to crowd out weeds.
3. Slow vertical growth and lateral spread.
4. Tolerant of drought and poor soil.
5. Low fertility requirements.
6. Withstands traffic.
7. Will not support rodents.

Based on research conducted at Penn State, the following covers were selected for further evaluation. Combinations would be recommended over pure stands to minimize the risk of one insect or disease problem affecting the entire stand.

1. Hard fescue - Reliant, Waldina, Biljart, Aurora.
2. Chewings fescue - Jamestown or Shadow.
3. Sheeps fescue - Bighorn or Covar.
4. Creeping red fescue - Ensylva.
5. Perennial ryegrass - Turf type (i.e. Pennfine, Palmer, Manhattan).
6. Canada Bluegrass - Reubens.
7. White clover.
8. Hard fescue (95%) + white clover (5%).
9. Hard fescue (65%) + Ensylva red fescue (35%).
10. Chewings fescue (65%) + Ensylva red fescue (35%.)
11. Hard fescue (70%) + Canada bluegrass (30%).
12. Ensylva red fescue (70%) + Turf type perennial ryegrass (30%).

None of these covers have all of the desirable characteristics we would like. The hard fescue, sheep fescue and Canada bluegrass are slow to establish. The chewings fescue and creeping red fescue grow fast and "mat". perennial ryegrass grows fast and may be short-lived in cold areas. White clover is slippery when wet and its flowers attract bees. But compared to other readily available covers, these are the best we have worked with to date."

In addition to what we are doing at Penn State, some excellent work is being done at Oregon State University on cover crops. Dr. Ray William is leading the program there and is an excellent source of information for growers in the northwest part of the country.

One caution when using cover crops - they are competitive with trees if grown right up to the base of the trees. Maintaining a vegetation free strip 30 to 36" wide around the trees will minimize the effect of the covers on the trees and make mowing easy. Do not plant a cover unless your weed control program is good enough to assure the cover can be kept 15 to 18 inches away from the trees on both sides.

To establish a cover
follow these steps

1. Eliminate perennial weeds prior to planting. The slow growing covers do not compete well with perennial weeds during their establishment phase.
2. Have the soil treated and amended according to the needs of the crop. Apply 40 lbs. of nitrogen per acre at the time the cover is seeded.
3. Loosen the soil (plow, disk, or rotovate) prior to planting the cover.
4. Seed the grasses at a rate of 40 - 80 lbs. per acre. White clover should be seeded at 6-10 lbs. per acre. Spread the seed with a cyclone or drop spreader or grain drill. If a grain drill is used, disconnect the hoses at the seedbox. The light, fine seed of the recommended covers do not readily fall through the hoses, and distribution over the soil surface is better if the seed must fall several feet. After seeding drag, roll, or cultipack the field to make sure the seed is firmly placed in contact with the soil. A brillion-type seeder drops the seed and presses it into the soil with one pass.
5. The best time to seed is late September because the grass has two cool seasons in which to get established before it must compete with heavy weed growth. The next best time is mid-March to mid-May.
6. Limit weed competition the year of planting by mowing weeds before they reach 10 inches in height. Broadleaved weeds can be controlled with directed sprays of 2,4-D or triclopyr (Garlon). **The slow growing covers will not compete well with weeds the first growing season if spring seeded.**

Establishing a slow growing cover between the rows of your trees will provide all of the benefits previously mentioned, reduce the time you spend mowing, and limit the establishment and growth of weeds.

Land in recent use for pasture or cropland is usually ready for planting. (Atrex, Atrazine recently-treated land can usually be planted on (if moderate level of herbicides had been used) in the season that follows such application). If in doubt, consult your Cooperative Extension representative or other crop specialist.

Vegetation control can be initiated the fall before planting and this can also serve as a guide in planting. A boom spraying unit can quickly and effectively spray rows. A dye can be added to the tank mix to make rows more visible for the tractor operator, and/or it is done just prior to planting and the ground cover has not died off yet. Heavier brush and stumps can also be chemically treated to reduce or eliminate continued growth. This is especially true with poplar and shrubs that spread rapidly.

Sometimes you create a problem when you are trying to solve one. In rocky soil, plowing might necessitate a major rock-picking job. In the process of smoothing out the soil, weed seed, such as milkweed, can be brought to the surface and become established. The silk can blow into trees making them unsightly at harvest time.

Knowledge of the growing characteristics of each tree type will be especially helpful in site preparation. For example, spruce usually tolerates wetter areas than firs, hence, an area should be utilized accordingly.

Your desires involving a specific site condition may require changing it but, more often, a different tree specie and/or cultural practice is the better course to follow. Try to utilize a site condition in keeping with its inherent characteristics. Some conditions cannot be changed (i.e. frost pockets). The chapters ahead will provide a guide as to site utilization.

For computation purposes, these area and distance measures may be helpful:
     1 acre = 43,560 sq. ft. = 4,840 sq. yds. = 160 sq. rods
     1 sq. rod = 272-1/4 sq. ft. = 30.3 sq. yds.
     9 sq. ft. = 1 sq. yd.
     1 sq. ft. = 144 sq. inches

     1 rod = 16.5 feet = 5.5 yards.
     1 mile = 5,280 ft. = 1,760 yards = 320 rods = 80 chains
     1 chain = 66 feet = 22 yards = 4 rods = 100 links
     1 inch = 2.54 centimeters = 25.4 millimeters
     1 foot = 30.5 centimeters
     1 meter = 39.37 inches

Use of spacing for planting and, trees per acre chart, is in the chapter on planting. The rule for determining the number of trees per acre is:

Multiply the distance in feet between the rows by the distance the trees are apart in the rows. The product will be the number of square feet for each tree. Divide the number of square feet in an acre (43,560) by the square feet per tree to determine total number of trees per acre.

PLANTING STOCK

BARE ROOT SEEDLINGS AND TRANSPLANTS

We will dwell at some length about the planting stock and planting procedures since that is a critical part of our income producing activity, the same way it will be for you in terms of producing high quality Christmas trees in a competitive market place.

Planting stock is referred to by its time in the ground, for example:

       1-0   One growing season in seed bed
       2-0   Two growing seasons in seed bed
       3-0   Three growing seasons in seed bed

When a 3-0 seedling is transplanted for one growing season it is designated as a 3-1 transplant (actually 4 years old from seed). A seedling might also be transplanted in a pot or other container, and/or transplanted a second time, (3-1-1).

This is only an indication of age, not size or overall quality or development. For example, one seed source of Douglas Fir as a 2-0 might actually be larger in size than another seed source as a 3-0. One year in a transplant bed usually results in more root growth than proportionate top growth (the usual reason for transplanting). A 3-0 pine might be larger than a 3-0 spruce, etc.

Size per se is not the determining factor of a plant's quality. Many growers look for a good "root to top" ratio. This is a balance of good root development to good top development. Good root development means a better chance of survival when planted in the field.

"Caliper" is another reference used to indicate quality or character of the plant. A larger caliper means larger diameter of stem thickness.

Low density seed beds assure better caliper of the seedlings because they get more sunlight and nutrition. Larger caliper planting stock can tolerate more stress than thin, meager seedlings. For this reason, Treehaven Evergreen Nursery has gone to all low density beds.

Experiments with very low density 4-0 Douglas Fir beds produced large plants equivalent to some 2-2 transplant stock. These may be sold at around $.25 each, rather than $.40 each or more, for transplant stock, since the costly transplanting procedure has been avoided. We will develop this procedure more in the future. The under-cutting of the bed (root pruning) helps to develop fibrous roots.

Price alone is no measure at all of seedling/transplant quality. Success or failure (degree of success) and ultimate field performance is a measure of the value of one's planting stock versus another. (Handling and planting procedures are very important too.)

Poor performance of a particular seed source may simply mean it is not best suited to the site, soil and/or other growing conditions of your farm (or area of your farm). Trying another seed source of that same specie might be in order. With the exception of Fraser Fir and Grand Fir, we field plant more than one seed source of every specie. Simply, one seed source may do better than another.

Actually, there are variations in Fraser and Grand Fir sources, also, because we plant new specific seed collections (portions of a seed zone). With Fraser Fir a seed orchard collection may be planted versus a general collection such as Roan Mt., or Mt. Mitchell, hence a selective seed source that should perform better.

We are constantly on the search for better seed sources.

This equates to dollars when you consider that one variety of Scotch Pine may start to come to market in six years while another might take seven or eight years. If the wholesale price is the same for either one (same quality) then the $12.00 "on the stump" price is divided by eight years instead of six. That is, each year of growth is worth $2.00/year at six years in the field versus $1.50/year at eight years. For example, this can become a very important factor in a low acreage "choose and cut" business because sale of sizable trees usually cannot keep up with demand. Therefore, if trees can reach salable size in six years instead of eight years, it means a great deal more income to you, the grower.

A tree grower owes it to himself to find out from his own experience what does best on his land. We do now, and will continue to, grow a variety of seed sources of all possible specie, thus affording you the opportunity to evaluate for yourself.

Each seed source has very specialized features that make it uniquely different from its "cousin". The chart later on Scotch Pine points this out.

There are seed sources and there are seed sources! Many growers plant at least some Douglas Fir with the seed origin of Lincoln National Forest (LNF). (State of New Mexico), "The Lincoln" extends almost 200 miles north and south and more than 50 miles wide (east of Alamagordo). Elevation may vary from 3,000' to almost 10,000'. This is a vast area where seed might be collected, selectively, or non-selectively, by many people. We purchase seed collected from several very select areas, as near to pure stands as possible. These have proven to be superior sources over the years. Many of the national forest areas are large in square miles, hence, our careful consideration of cone collectors who can fill our precise needs. This is why we have confidence in our planting stock and you can, also.

12

Most seedling growers became established because they were a nursery operation in some form or other, and gravitated to growing Christmas Trees because of excess planting stock or other reasons. Treehaven Evergreen Nursery was just the opposite. After 20 years of growing Christmas Trees, we saw the need to make improvements at the very beginning, the plant stock.

Some of our objectives are:

1) Find seed sources better acclimated to our soil and climate.
2) Find seed sources with faster growth characteristics.
3) Find seed sources with better insect and disease resistance.
4) Find seed sources that respond better to cultural practices (shearing, etc.).
5) Find seed sources that give us any competitive advantages over other tree producers.
6) Overall, provide a better return on investment.

We could add, "Find a seed source where the tree does it all without our help".

The planting stock we produce are either "bare root" seedlings or transplants. "Bare Root" seedlings are just that - most of the soil has fallen from the roots when lifted from the seed beds they were grown in. The procedure we use is to start growing from seed (in raised beds) outdoors, allowing nature to dictate survival according to climatic conditions and soil. When the seedlings are two to three years old (sometimes four years old), we "lift" or "undercut" the beds with a bed lifter of our own design. Our bed lifter (see photo) does not have a shaker as most commercial units do because we do not want to expose the roots to the air, even for a very brief period. We actually lift them by hand (after the undercutting) and place them in crates, wheelbarrows, etc., where they go to the cool, damp grading room.

We remove them from the soil only as we can process them in a grading room. They do not lay in the sun to bake as in some commercial nurseries who cannot process them immediately.

They are graded for size. All injured and deformed seedlings are thrown away, as they are those below the standards. The seedlings are counted and usually tied in bundles of 25, 50, or 100. This number varies depending on the size, age or caliper of the stock. The bundles are placed in cartons. They are kept damp at all times. We have found that this painstaking procedure insures almost 100% healthy stock when picked up or shipped.

A moist medium such as sphagnum moss, is placed between bundles and layers of bundles inside the waterproof-lined carton. The carton is then placed in a walk-in cooler with the temperature set at 35 degrees to maintain dormancy of the seedlings (holding life processes in limbo).

It is paramount that the person getting the stock follows these same careful procedures. This will be discussed further in the "planting" section.

Occasionally, we sell a bed of seedlings "bed run". That means we lift and pack, without grading, and the count is estimated since the carton is packed right in the field. You usually always get an overrun with this procedure. The grading must be done by you since it is not wise to plant everyone of these seedlings in the field (at random) due to the extreme size variation (possibly 4" to 16"+) as with Blue Spruce in a 3-0 bed. This would result in a growing/harvest cycle that is undesirable no matter how you sell your trees. Since you would be doing the grading, you can grade them in any way or size that you prefer. The smallest size would be lined-out or transplanted for another year or two, even three, to get them up to a desirable size for field planting. You might even want to do some potting. By doing your own grading (and even if you re-grade graded stock) you can plant seedlings of approximate size and, hence, reduce the growing cycle in the field.

Choose and cut plantations are usually replanting constantly, but it is still desirable, sometimes, to completely recycle a tree area. In the wholesale production of trees, this growing cycle is of much concern since the cycle needs to be controlled and the area or section cycled on a pre-determined schedule. In fact, without establishing a plant or projection prior to the harvest (income), your profit/loss projection cannot be established. In other words, you must have some fairly accurate means of measuring income with regard to the growth period of any crop in order to determine whether your investment (time, labor and expenses) will prove to be profitable. This will be discussed further as we go along.

The nursery activity comes into the picture when you decide to improve the size/quality of the plants you take to the field (out-plant). It is much easier to provide the care and attention to the smaller seedlings when they are in a more carefully controlled area and environment. Losses are minimal and cost and care factors can be carefully monitored (weeding, watering, fertilizing, etc.).

We prepare transplant beds for resale by replanting the small seedlings in beds that have been specially prepared for them. Seedlings of varying size can also be potted and allowed to grow for a year or two and then field planted. If this is done on a significant scale (and on a regular basis), then an auger may be a desirable tool to use, either hand operated or operated off a tractor (3 point hitch).

Since transplantings, whether in a bed or into pots, is labor intensive, this is where you can control cost and/or benefit most by utilizing your own time and energy. Here at Treehaven Evergreen Nursery we produce transplants by popular demand, not because it is a big money making venture. Actually we would rather encourage you to grow your own transplants from our high quality 2-0 or 3-0 seedling stock.

The following is our procedure for producing transplants. Bed/soil preparation is the key factor. That is, you must have a workable place to do it advantageously. It makes a very good son/daughter project for profit. Use a garden area that is well-drained and manageable. Develop "tilth" of the soil with old sawdust/peat moss/old manure, etc. One of these sources can usually be found nearby at a reasonable cost and delivery method. Your own "compost" pile is fine. Whatever your organic medium, be sure it is relatively free of weed seed and undesirable insect/disease elements. Steam or chemical sterilization of the potting soil is very beneficial.

"Plugs" or containerized seedlings are a more recent entry in the planting picture. This method of production was introduced in the northeast twenty or more years ago. They are grown in blocks of "cells" in a carefully controlled greenhouse environment. They are removed and "hardened off" so as to prepare them for the "cruel world". They are usually more expensive than a comparable bare root seedling. It is a cost effective way for timber companies (mostly) to produce a two-year equivalent seedling in about six months. They may provide more uniformity of seedling size but various studies in the northwest have not shown them to have any better survival than most bare root seedlings grown in outdoor beds.

Hi.Ho.Hi.Ho...
It's off to the tree lot we go!

15

VARIETIES TO PLANT - Northern States

Dramatic changes have been taking place, countrywide, in the past 15 years with regard to tree varieties as well as quality. Some changes of trend are evident in the Northeast with more emphasis to Fraser Fir and White Pine. Red Pine and Norway Spruce have tended to fall out of favor, at least here in New York State. Although Balsam Fir is still favored, it is being replaced by Fraser Fir in areas outside its natural range.

The principal varieties you should consider as a new grower are as follows:

Scotch Pine	White Spruce	Douglas Fir
White Pine	Blue Spruce	Fraser Fir
Austrian Pine	Norway Spruce	Balsam Fir

Others for consideration are:

S.W. (Mexican) Border Pine

Serbian Spruce	Concolor Fir	Black Hills Spruce
Englemann Spruce	Grand Fir	Noble Fir

Those with the most favorable ornamental qualities are:

Austrian Pine	Blue Spruce	Serbian Spruce
Black Hills Spruce	Englemann Spruce	Douglas Fir
And All true Firs		

Trees and other plants having Christmas-related value are:

Potted Trees
Dwarf Alberta Spruce
Black Hills Spruce
Blue Spruce
And a host of others can be cultured for potting.

Foliage: Holly, Bayberry, Boxwood; grape vines are also used for wreath-making. Plants and trees for foliage may include any or all of the above mentioned trees as well as the following:

Norway Spruce is used to some extent in outdoor sprays, grave blankets, wreaths and, also, as a potted tree.

Foliage we are most familiar with are:

Noble Fir	Concolor Fir	Grand Fir
Douglas Fir	Balsam/Fraser Fir	White Pine
Scotch Pine	White Cedar	Juniper and Yews

All other True Fir Foliage, including exotic ones like:

Greek Fir	Turkish Fir
Korean Fir	Nikko Fir

The above exotic firs have a market that is limited only by lack of supply.

I'm sure the column "Approximate Years to Harvest" will draw
the most comment from the veteran growers. Let me say, those
figures are not necessarily from my experience. They are from
many others' experiences since we recognize that some of our tree
areas have considerably less optimum conditions to produce the
trees we planted. The chapter on planting stock provided
considerable insight as to why growing time can vary so greatly
from the same group of seedlings under site conditions. All the
soil, site and cultural factors, plus seed genetics, influence
growth.

Some seed suppliers sell seed from indiscriminate collections;
i.e., cones might be collected from every coning tree within a
selected area regardless of the tree's inherent characteristics.
Some seed is collected from squirrel caches. Although squirrels
are smart (sometimes smarter than people) in regard to cones
containing viable seed, they don't care much about the
characteristics of the trees they cut the cones from!!! In
observing a 2-0 seedling we can't always tell what the adult
characteristics will be. This chart will acquaint you with the
tree types by general characteristics and environmental
preferences.

THE PINES (Pinus)

Scotch Pine (Scot's Pine) (Pinus Sylvestris): Worldwide it
occupies natural habitats larger than any other pine from Scotland
to Siberia and from Norway to Spain. There are a great number of
variations because they grow in a wide range of soil, climate and
environmental conditions. They are found south of the Equator
only because man took it there. It is the least fussy of any
Christmas Tree with regard to soil and fertility. It is still
the #1 Christmas Tree in many areas of the country. The different
seed sources show much variability on growth rate, foliage color,
needle length, susceptibility to disease, stem straightness and
other characteristics. It grows on infertile sites but does best
on moist well-drained soils. Color is yellow-to-blue with every
hue of green in between. Needles are in two's (fascicles) with
needle length generally from 1" to 3" in length. Its form, shape
and rate of growth can vary greatly.

Most nurseries grow only two or three sources - those
preferred by their customers. We grow various sources in order to
satisfy the need you have to try different ones. Ask other
growers with similar soil, site and climatic circumstances what
does best for them. Don't be afraid to evaluate other sources,
however, you may have a situation where one source may be much
better than the "standard" ones.

Eastern White Pine (Pinus Strobus): This graceful, blue-green
tree is growing in popularity. A traditional, desirable Christmas
tree in New England, East Coast States and Midwest States. Grows
rapidly on well-drained loamy sites. Requires yearly shaping, as
do other pines, and has the excellent needle-retention
characteristic of pines. Foliage is desirable for floral use.
Disease tendencies can be controlled but can be a problem in some
areas, however. Avoid wet planting sites. Due to its soft
foliage it is a nice tree for families with young children. Has
increasing ornamental appeal. It can even be sheared and shaped
for a hedge or windbreak effect. (See picture).

Wherever you are located, you should find out the most popular four or five tree varieties that sell best in your area and compare their characteristics as closely as possible to the soil and sites you have to work with. Many other considerations are discussed as you read the book.

You may not want to just consider what is in demand in your immediate area but, also, in areas more distant from your immediate market should you have an excess production of your trees. Some degree of pioneering spirit is essential in the tree-growing-enterprise but you must grow the varieties that present the least risk, be it growing, culture or marketing. A new grower should plan wisely and start with standard varieties.

The trees on the comparison chart that follows are those with a history and following in the Northeast and Midwestern States; of course, many of these are not only popular but native to other areas of the country. Tree growing in the Southern half of the country, from the Carolinas and Florida to New Mexico, has been undergoing the most dramatic changes in the past 15 years or so. Our Northern markets will be affected by that, especially in the next five to ten years. Many tree varieties being cultivated there are unsuitable in our harsh Northern Climates. (Afghan Pine (Pinus Eldarica), Monterey Pine (Pinus Radiata), etc. You should keep in mind that some of the other Southern grown trees compete in our Northern market (White Pine, Fraser Fir).

A few footnotes to the characteristics chart that follows are in order. This data is presented as a guide only, not as gospel. Many descriptive words are used as a matter of judgment and you might evaluate a specific characteristic differently. There are cultural varieties that could affect your tree development and, therefore, your judgment of the trait description. For example, many people buy a Norway Spruce for their Christmas Tree, yet it has a reputation for poor needle retention. House temperatures of 75 degrees rather than 65 degrees could make a big difference as to its continued freshness. Late cutting (closer to Christmas) improves freshness. A tree mounted in a water stand will definitely stay fresh longer no matter what specie is involved. These are just three factors that would give a different image of a specific tree in light of these variations, we have tried to follow a "relative" evaluation, i.e. how one tree type compares with the others.

Noble fir being harvested at Drake's Crossing Nursery, Silverton, OR. 50,000 trees a year are harvested-many transported by helicopter.

Top left: Specimen Colorado Blue Spruce - Treehaven "Super Blue" Strain, Elma, N.Y.
Top right: Premium quality Scotch pine at Hill Top Acres - Delevan, N.Y.
Above: Virginia pine (bottom to top of photo) - newly planted, one-year old, two-year old, three-year old. Photo courtesy Turner Davis, Spalding County, Georgia.

SELECTED CHARACTERISTICS

Specie	Trunk/Stem	Stifness of Branch	Needle Retenion	Freedom From Pests
Scotch Pine *	F - E	VG - E	E	P - VG
Austrian Pine	G - E	E	E	G - E
Southwestern W. Pine	G - E	G	E	G
Eastern W. Pine	G - E	F	E	F - VG
Red (Norway) Pine	G - E	E	E	VG
Western W. Pine	G - E	F - P	E	VG
....				
White Spruce	E	VG - E	G	G
Black Spruce	VG	VG	F	G
Blue Spruce	E	G	G - VG	VG
Black Hills Spruce	E	E	G	G
Serbian Spruce	E	F - G	G	G - VG
Norway Spruce	VG	G	F	G
Englemann Spruce	E	E	G - VG	VG
....				
Douglas Fir (Blue)**	E	VG	E	G - VG
Douglas Fir (Grn/Grey)	E	VG	E	E
Balsam Fir	E	VG	VG	G - VG
Fraser Fir	E	E	E	VG
Concolor Fir	VG - E	VG	E	E
Grand Fir	VG - E	VG	E	E
Noble Fir	VG - E	E	E	VG

....

E	=	Excellent	
VG	=	Very Good	
G	=	Good	
F	=	Fair	
P	=	Poor	

VS = very short
VL = very long
L = long
S = short
M = medium
Shrp = sharp
Sft = soft
NSS = not so sharp

Fragrance	Color/Color Retention	Needle Length	Approx. Yrs. to Harvest***	Comments
F	P – E	VS/VL	6 – 8	Still # 1 in production
F	VG – E	L – VL	7 – 10	Becoming more popular-durable
F	VG – E	L	7	Has advantages over E.W. Pine
F	G – E	L	7 – 8	Increasg Pop.-Pine Shoot Moth
F	G – E	VL	7 – 8	Nice foliage – limit planting & away from other pines
F	E	L	7 – 8	Ex. foliage color-possibly more disease resistant
G	VG	S	8 – 10	Most popular spruce in N.E.
F	G	VS	10	Limited to northern most N.E.
F	F – E	S/Shrp	8 – 10	G demand-shrp ndls-ornamental
F	G	VS	10 – 12	Excellent as ornamental
F	E	S/Sft	8 – 10	Sft ndls/branchs-nice color-better as ornamental
G	E	S	7 – 9	Fast grower-better for U-cut
F	VG	S/NSS	9 – 12	Softer ndls than B.Spruce- good as ornamental
E	G – E	M	8 – 12	High value/good demand – needs proper site
E	E	S – M	8 – 12	Same as above – also needs vegetation control
E	VG – E	S	8 – 12	Trad. tree-Fraser replacing
E	E	S	8 – 12	Gaining popularity-very desire-able characteristics
E	G – E	M	8 – 12	Lovely tree-should grow more
E	E	M	9+	" " " " "
E	E	M	10+	Outstanding foliage – pick site very carefully

*See detailed chart for Scotch pine in "Addendum".

**See detailed chart for Douglas Fir in "Addendum".

***Best from 3-0 seedling to 7' treeon good site & soil.

21

Austrian Pine (Pinus Nigra): A long, stiff, green-needled straight stem tree with wide form. This tree has strong-upright form and will tolerate heavy decoration. Popularity is increasing due to its disease-resistance and road-salt tolerance (ornamental use in highway plantings). Very early shaping is needed to develop adequate branching as it matures. Does best on well-drained soils where lime content is high. Takes about two years longer to market than Scotch Pine. Adaptable to wide range of planting sites. Ornamental use for windbreaks and sound barriers should be encouraged. Treehaven is investigating seed sources to find more desirable characteristics such as lighter branches/trunk and more prolific bud formation and, possibly, better winter color.

Red Pine (Norway Pine) (Pinus Resinosa): Long, dark green needles give this tree a lovely graceful appearance. Although sturdy-branched, it is very susceptible to snow injury because heavy melting snow will pull branches out of their sockets. Grows on a wide range of soils with rapid growth like Scotch Pine. Early shaping is necessary to avoid gaps. Should not be planted in Northern New York State or in Scleroderris Canker Quarantine area or in surrounding areas. Foliage is desirable for floral use. Best soil type is well-drained loamy, but stays moist between rains. Cool North and East slopes are preferred. Level land protected on South and West by tall trees may also be suitable. South and West slopes generally not recommended due to excessive drying by wind and sun. Alternate variety is Fraser Fir or White Spruce. The further the distance from natural areas, the more suitable Fraser Fir might be. Austrian Pine is now frequently planted instead of Red Pine.

Mexican Border Pine (S.W. White Pine) (Pinus Strobiformis): Hardy, high elevation tree native to Arizona and New Mexico. Nice blue-green color with stiffer branches than our Eastern White Pine. Believed to have better disease resistance than Eastern White Pine. Does well on well-drained semi-fertile loamy sites. Very nice form with good growth characteristics. Prune and shape early. Gaining in popularity. Trunk is straight with smooth bark. Very good "keeping" character-istics. Do not confuse with Limber Pine which has slow growth and less favorable characteristics. Southwestern White Pine should be more widely planted. See article in C.E. Heit Series, "Propogation From Seed".

Ponderosa Pine (Yellow Pine - Western Yellow Pine (Pinus Ponderosa): Native to wide range in Western U.S. with many variations depending on locale. Needles in bundles of two's and three's with five to eleven inches in length. Grows best on moist, well-drained soils and has good drought resistance. Needs full sunlight to do well. A fast grower. Little experimentation has been conducted, either in nursery or field trials, for Christmas Tree culture in the Eastern U.S. Trials at Treehaven Evergreen Nursery are being initiated in 1986 and 1987 with more than 25 seed sources to determine if any sources are promising for Christmas Tree culture in the Northeastern U.S. Disease resistance, winter color and hardness are a few of

 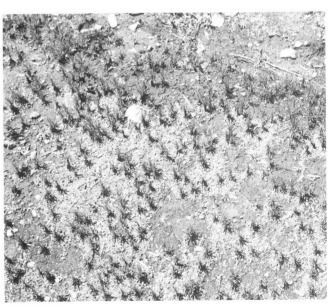

Upper left: Potting area - "Sky" & Joan Weller's Sky View Acres Tree Farm, Scotia, N.Y.
Upper right: Low density beds with uniform-size seedlings grown at Treehaven Nursery;
              assures uniform tree production.
Lower left: Spruce seeded too dense to produce vigorous seedlings.
Lower right: 2-month-old, low density Concolor fir bed at Treehaven.

the traits we want to evaluate. Because of its widespread natural habitat, it may prove suitable on soils and sites marginal for other trees. Contact us if you want to participate in field trials. In some areas out west it is cultured for Christmas Trees.

Japanese Black Pine (Pinus Thunbergii): Good green color with needle length 3 - 5" like Eastern White Pine. Grown like Austrian Pine. Relatively fast grower along Northeastern coast of the U.S. May have high mortality in harsher winter areas of New York State and northern New England. Native to Japan, responds well to shearing. Other than the Long Island area, New York State growers should plant on trial basis only. Japanese Red Pine appears more winter hardy. We have had varying experiences with Japanese Black Pine.

Himalayan Pine (Pinus Griffithi - Pinus Wallichiana): A soft-needled White Pine with long, whitish needles and the appearance of drooping branches. It makes an excellent ornamental and is used for landscape planting. It is very tolerant to air pollution. It won't replace the Eastern or Southwestern White Pine, however. An exotic pine.

Balkan Pine (Macedonian Pine) (Pinus Peuce): This is a narrow, conical, straight pine of nice natural quality. It is native to mountain areas of Albania, Yugoslavia and Greece - probably cross-pollinated with Corsican and/or Austrian Pines in some geographic regions. The needles are five to a sheath, 3 to 4-1/2 inches long and bluish-green. Warrants more evaluation.

Japanese Red Pine (Pinus Densiflora): Similar to traditional Scotch Pine but having lighter green foliage. The needles are soft like White Pine, dull green and 2 to 4-1/2 inches long. It tends to develop double stems and frequently grows twisted and crooked. It shapes well and makes a good ornamental. Native to Japan. It is found to be winter hardy here. It has been cross-bred with Austrian Pine to achieve the best traits of both parents. This new seedling stock will be available in Spring, '88, from Treehaven Evergreen Nursery.

Japanese White Pine (Pinus Parviflora) - (Pinus Himekomatsu): It has wide spreading branching and dark green foliage. It has promise, mostly as an ornamental. It is cultivated in dwarf form for use as Bonsai. A hardy and handsome pine.

Other pines that could be evaluated in your own situation are: Western White Pine (Pinus Monticola), Corsican Pine (Pinus Nigra, var. Poiretiana), Calabrian Pine (Pinus Brutia), and Korean Pine (Pinus Koraiensis).

FIRS

Douglas Fir (Pseudotsuga Menziesii): Not a true fir. It has steadily increased in popularity over the past twenty-five years as more growers plant it and consumer acceptance increased. This tree has all the favorable characteristics a family looks for in a Christmas Tree - straight trunk, nice fragrance, good needle-retention, soft foliage and green color. Response to accepted cultural practices makes this tree desirable to growers when planted on proper sites. Some growers don't have favorable soil and site conditions, however. Well-drained, sloped sites are best because they usually have good water and air drainage. Good air flow reduces chances of severe late spring and early fall frosts. Three types of Douglas Fir are recognized, each type with its own characteristics which differ from each other. Because of these, sometimes subtle, differences we have prepared a chart indicating these variations. These differences suggest that cultural practices and techniques, timing of them, may be modified to your own area and site. This chart has been incorporated in the new book, "Addendum", which contains more detailed information. The Blue "Glauca" strains come principally from the states of Colorado, Arizona and New Mexico. The comparison chart identifies national forest areas within the states where favorable trees are situated. (These same national forest areas may yield very favorable seed sources for Concolor Fir, Ponderosa Pine and other tree types). These Blue types are usually fast growers, have green to blue-green foliage and are from high elevations. They tend to be more susceptible to aphid and needle diseases.

The "Grey" sources are generally considered to be from Montana, Utah, and Idaho. They tend to be slower growers with foliage not so deep green. They grow on varying soil types and grow at elevations and latitude more closely matched to our Northeast. They are less susceptible to some diseases.

The "Green" types are those generally associated with the states of Washington and Oregon. The province of British Columbia, Canada has Douglas Fir in large areas as well. Most Douglas Fir west of the Cascades, as well as lower elevations in the Puget Sound area, are not winter hardy in Northeast climates. Christmas trees from those areas shed their needles readily when exposed to our cold climate (cut trees).

Douglas Fir, and all True firs, respond to sunlight and fertile soil. A marketable tree is possible in ten years from a 3-0 seedling on favorable sites. This growing time can be reduced significantly by optimum soil, site and cultural practices.

Additional evaluation of Douglas Fir seed sources is available in Part #17 of C.E. Heit's Series, "Propagation From Seed".

Austrian, red, Scotch & white pines

Left to right: Norway, blue, white, Engelmann and Sitka spruces

Left to right: White spruce, Engelmann spruce, Douglas fir, grand fir, Scotch pine & lower right, white pine

Top left to right: Concolor fir, fraser fir, Douglas fir

Bottom left to right: Grand fir, noble fir & silver fir

Inside building at Itasca Greenhouse, Inc., Cohasset, MN. Controlled environment with 24 hours/day growth cycle produces plants (plugs) in fraction of time required for outdoor beds.

Leyland cypress, Leighton Green cultivar. A full-size tree is produced in 3 to 4 yrs. at Christmas-Tree-Land, Lake City, Fl. by Herb Attaway.

Grand Fir

Grand fir produced by the Kaylor's of Fantasy Farms Nursery, Peck, ID. Lush, bright-green, fragrant foliage identify this specie.

TRUE FIRS (ABIES)

Balsam Fir (Abies Balsamea): This "original" Christmas Tree was the only one most people were acquainted with until plantation-grown trees began to evolve in the early 1950's. Higher quality plantation-grown trees started to displace the Balsam Fir in the Northeast U.S. The traditional fragrance, straight stem, deep green (sometimes bluish) color and good needle retention made this tree the popular tree it is to this day. Plantation-grown Balsam of high quality are still grown by the millions today - many from Nova Scotia, New Brunswick and Quebec as well as from New York, New Hampshire, Vermont and Maine.

This tree responds well to shearing and other cultural practices. The branches (called brush) remain in great demand for wreath making and other decorating purposes. Balsam tolerates wetter soil sites and withstands the harshest of winters. Some disease problems are associated with this specie. The farther a grower is from the native tree areas in New York and the upper New England states, the more likely that Fraser Fir (Southern Balsam) is being grown instead.

Fraser Fir (Abies Fraseri): Its birthplace and home is in the high elevations of the lush, cool mountains of Western North Carolina. Its strong branches, wonderful aroma, excellent needle retention and suitability to a wide range of Northeastern soils was contributed to its rapid acceptance as a Christmas Tree, by grower and consumer alike. Roan Mt. and nearby Mt. Mitchell are the sources of all seed that produces Fraser Fir seedlings. A good seed crop is available only every six to eight years causing a high demand for the seed. Seed orchards are helping to meet the demand. Fraser Fir likes a fertile soil and is slow to start in the field. One key biological advantage over Balsam Fir is its late bud break. Bud break that might result in injury due to late frost in the spring rarely bothers Fraser Fir. It will bud two to three weeks later than Balsam Fir and most other varieties. It is one of the few specie that will survive otherwise frost-prone areas. Transplants or large 3-0 stock are frequently planted. This tree commands a price equal or higher than Douglas Fir and definitely a higher price over Balsam Fir.

Concolor Fir (White Fir) (Abies Concolor): It has the widest geographical range of all true firs. Depending on the seed source, color ranges from a light green to a deep blue, with several sources, a silver blue. Tends to be slow to start but generally does well on Douglas Fir-type soils and sites in New York State. Successfully grown on all slopes. Foliage is soft with 1" or longer wide flat needles. It is very seldom affected by frost and free of most diseases even those associated with Balsam, Fraser and Douglas Firs. It responds well to fertilizer. Heavy shearing is not usually necessary. It is aromatic (citrus) and is long-lasting in the home. More field evaluation is needed as newer, favorable seed sources have become available in recent years. Lincoln, San Juan, Rio Grande and Cibola National Forests are faster growers; Santa Fe

National Forest good for color and growth rate; Kaibab (Arizona) source has excellent color but a slower growth rate. No California source has shown promise. Various evaluations are in progress, including our own. Date of bud break, tolerance to frost, response to fertilization and shearing/shaping techniques are questions being investigated through these studies. Ornamental use of foliage would be more widespread if it were available. See photograph of decorations. It could be used much more for landscape purposes due to its graceful form and minimal maintenance.

Grand Fir (Abies Grandis): It has a straight trunk, deep green foliage of long, wide flat needles on heavy branches and a fragrance of citrus/oranges that sells this tree in the marketplace. Most Cascade sources are not sufficiently winter hardy in Northeastern U.S. Clearwater drainage area (Idaho) is the best general source with fast growth traits found in select areas. Grows well on moist but fairly well-drained loam sites. Preferably not in direct harsh western or north windy slopes as windburn can result. Keeps well. Will tolerate some shade and responds on lower slopes and somewhat poorer soils than Noble and Shasta Firs. Usually frost injury free, relatively little disease but is rust susceptible – it shouldn't be planted near bracken fern. Retailers have found that a Grand Fir customer is always a Grand Fir customer. Like Concolor Fir, it has much potential for decorative uses as well as ornamental plantings. Although this tree is slower growing compared to Balsam or Fraser Firs, it is almost problem free with minimal cultural demands. Like Concolor and Silver Firs, we have never had deer or other predator problems.

Other More Exotic True Firs might be propagated more for ornamental or floral purposes. Some of these include, Veitch Fir (Abies Veitchii), Nikko Fir (Abies Homolepsis), Nordmann Fir (Abies Nordmanniana), Turkish Fir (Abies Bornmuelleriana), Sakhalin Fir (Abies Sachalinensis) and Greek Fir (Abies Cephalonica). They are typically slow to establish, but have good-to-poor growth rate characteristics in the order listed. They enjoy relatively moist, well-drained sites with good fertility. Cultural practices (as with all true firs) have a lot to do with their growth rate, form and general development. All of these firs are known to be winter hardy in the Northeastern U.S. Although none are native here. Veitch (much like Balsam), Nikko and Sakhalin are native to mountain areas of Japan. Nordmann is native to Armenia, Turkish Fir to Turkey and Pakistan. Several more firs will become better known in the future; they include Ernest Pindrow and Farges Firs (native to mainland China) and Momi or Japanese Fir (native to Japan). All foliage is beautiful. They should be used more for ornamental plantings, as well as for floral and decorative purposes, as the foliage is valuable. Consult bibliography and other texts for more information. "Addendum..." has source information on Concolor Fir as well as Douglas Fir.

White pine 2-2 transplants
ready for potting/sale, or
field planting.

Seedlings transplanted
into pots. May be
allowed to grow two
years in pots, then
sold or field planted.

Transplants field planted
at the Ferguson plantation,
Warsaw, N.Y.

30

VARIETIES TO PLANT (continued)

SPRUCE (PICEA)

In general, they are all short needled as compared to pines and shorter than most Douglas Fir. Needles are sharper than most firs. Serbian Spruce (Picea Omorika) would be an exception. Most spruce are stiff branched and retain color well under the coldest conditions as are several oriental spruces. Needle retention varies from very good to poor. Spruce are frequently associated with less well-drained soil, primarily because other tree types cannot tolerate these conditions as well. Spruce do better, however, on better-drained sites and loamy soils. Its woodsy fragrance is appreciated by many tree buyers plus the fact that the many branches can support many ornaments. The descriptions that follow will help you to evaluate the ones you want to grow.

White Spruce (Picea Glauca): Generally, spruce have a conical shape, compact busy growth and are almost immune to snow damage. A long-time Christmas Tree favorite and native of the Adirondacks. A bluish-white tree with a typical woodsy odor. Needle retention is better than most spruces. This specie does well in areas less suitable to Balsam or Douglas Fir. It is tolerant of a wide range of soils. Once established the rapid growth will produce a marketable tree in ten years or less. Some disease pests may appear.

Norway Spruce (Picea Abies): A native of Europe with best native stands in Germany - now widely grown in the U.S. A fast-growing spruce, usually marketable as a seven foot tree in seven to nine years with shaping necessary. A lovely tree when cultured. Poor needle retention is a negative factor so far as wholesale tree growers are concerned. It is considered suitable as a "choose and cut" variety. Susceptibility to disease but less so than with other spruces. Will tolerate less than ideal sites. Many people like the fragrance of the tree. A water well in the tree stand helps to prolong the freshness.

Blue Spruce (Colorado Blue Spruce) (Picea Pungens): The desirable blue foliage, ornamental form and best needle-holding quality of all common spruces keeps this tree on demand and in a high price range. Needles are very sharp and branches stiff, resists snow damage. Minimal shaping is necessary even though the seedling is slow to start. A strong ornamental market is a plus factor as well as the desire of some buyers to purchase the tree potted or balled, for planting after Christmas, outdoors. Insist on a good blue color seedling/seed source. Kaibab National Forest (Arizona) and San Juan National Forest (Colorado) are two recognized sources. We are evaluating several other sources that western researchers say have good blue color and fast growth. Rio Grande National Forest has fast growth characteristics but foliage tends to be green in color. Other national forest areas have exhibited a wide range of color and other characteristics. In two years we will offer two new sources, one native and one hybrid. Both have exceptional blue color and growth rate.

Engelmann Spruce (Picea Engelmann):   Variation of Blue Spruce with generally slower growth characteristics. Frequently confused with Blue Spruce, but needles not as sharp and has characteristic bluish-purple cast. Needles give off a rank odor when crushed. Grows best on richer and deeper soils than other spruce and will accept moist and shaded sites. Considered, also, as an ornamental specie.

Black Hills Spruce (Picea Glauca Densata):   Native to Black Hills of South Dakota. Very similar to White Spruce but with some distinct variations. A slower grower with better density and excellent form. An excellent ornamental, also. A prize-winning Christmas Tree variety. Does well on typical spruce sites. Seed in recent years from faster growth sources.

Serbian Spruce (Picea Omorika):   Native to Yugoslavia. A graceful tree with soft, light-to-deep blue needles. Fast grower once established on loam soil and drained sites. Holds needles poorly, although branches are much more limber than White Spruce. A fine ornamental.

Red Spruce (Picea Rubens):   Native to Northern New York State and New England States as well as Canada. Seldom plantation grown due to site limitations and consumer preferences for other varieties.   It is an accepted Christmas Tree in its native areas.

Black Spruce (Picea Mariana):   A faster growing spruce native to higher elevation Northern New England climate. Poor form as a Christmas Tree. Restricted to natural growing sites. Like Red Spruce it does not respond well to plantation culture.

Several Other Spruces merit further evaluation since they have shown to be winter hardy in Northeastern U.S. Sitka Spruce (Picea Sitchensis), native to the Northwest and Alaska; Koyama Spruce (Picea Kayomai), native to Japan; Sakhalin Spruce (Picea Glehnii), native to Sakhalin and Hokkaido, Japan; Oriental Spruce (Picea Orientalis), native of Asia Minor and Southern Russia; and Dragon Spruce (Picea Asperata), native of Western China. The Oriental ones have exceptional ornamental quality.

Hemlock (Canadian, Carolina): A Christmas tree in a few areas along the East Coast. A slow grower in many places outside its native range. This lovely tree has wispy limbs, weak branches, and poor needle retention as a cut tree. There is some use in wreath and floral decorations but it is more desirable as an ornamental; not a good candidate for plantation planting except in its natural area.

Arizona Cypress: Has many varieties; native to Arizona, southern Texas, and northern Mexico. A relatively fast grower. A medium size tree with non-prickly foliage; usually blue-green in color and quite aromatic. It needs shaping to develop width, but otherwise a dense-like foliage. Grows best on well-drained soil but over a wide pH range. It is recognized as an ornamental for foundation plantings and hedges and as a Christmas tree in some areas of the Southwest. Experience in our western New York State nursery has been unfavorable due to severe windburn.

Serbian spruce (picea omorika): Native to Yugoslavia. A fast-growing graceful tree with soft, light-to-deep blue needles. It adapts itself to well-drained soils with a pH of 6 or higher. It is hardy in harsh climates such as in Nebraska. Christmas tree growers report poor needle retention as drying occurs readily after cutting. This fine tree is better suited, and more valuable, for ornamental plantings.

Top row left to right: Yew, arborvitae, red cedar

Bottom row left to right: Hemlock, American boxwood, hybrid holly

Tree Varieties for Temporate United States

The following plant descriptions are more specific to southern climates. Some descriptions and photographs follow.

Sand pine   Red cedar
Virginia pine   White pine
Spruce pine   Leyland cypress
Afghan pine   Several other pines

Arizona cypress for Christmas tree or ornamental.

White pine sheared to form a hedge.

Sand pine (pinus clausa): Natural range is limited to a small area of Florida, but had to be adapted to sites in several other southeastern states. This dense, long-needled tree has good drought resistance and better tolerance in regard to fusiform rust. It has poor tolerance to cold and wet areas and is susceptible to some diseases, such as, littleleaf disease and mushroom rot.

Virginia pine (pinus virginiana): A pine native to the south but grows in more than 5 states. It grows at elevations from 100 to 2500' above sea level and in a precipitation range of 35 to 55 inches. Virginia pine has withstood temperatures ranging between 25° and 110° F. It will not tolerate poor drainage. It grows well on clay, loam, or sandy-loam soils but poorly on shaley or very sandy soils. It does not tolerate shade. Plant selection has been undertaken by Kimberly Clark and other propagators to produce planting stock desirable for Christmas trees. This tree, when cultured, will reach market size in 3 to 5 years.

Spruce pine (pinus glabra): Native to Louisiana with some volume planted in the 1970's for Christmas tree culture. This long-needled tree responds favorably to shearing which usually begins the third season in the field in less fertile soil. It responds to fertilization, and vegetation around it can be controlled with Roundup and Simazine. It grows best on well-drained or terraced soils, but will do better in poorly-drained soils than Virginia pine. This specie tends to dry after cutting so it is most suited to a "choose-and cut" operation where it would be cut closer to Christmas.

Afghan pine (pinus eldarica): Prior to 1961 this fast-growing Far East native was never grown in the United States. The first seed came from southern Afghanistan, in or near the town of Laskargah. Trial planting with irrigation yielded 6 foot Christmas trees in 2 to 3 years. It lends itself well to ornamental use and was recognized early as a favorable live-tree market prospect. Prospective Christmas tree growers in the Southwest should investigate this specie. Studies continue with this unusual specie at New Mexico State University, Las Cruces. Investigation of seed origins and tree improvement has been undertaken by other interests also.

Eastern red cedar (Juniperus virginiana): A medium-size tree that grows fast in the form of a teardrop. On ideal sites, two foot of growth in one growing season is not unusual. It has prickly scale-like leaves only 1/16th inch long except on leading shoots up to 3/8 inch. Foliage is mostly green to blue-green during growth period and gradually turns to dull rust-brown. Foliage has a pleasant aroma. There is much variation in the growth, form, color, and disease resistance, however. It grows best on loamy sites with a pH around 6. It has a dense, tight natural form compared to pines. It is known in the Northeast as an ornamental for hedge and corner plantings; a Christmas tree type in the mid-to-deep South. Some disease problems are encountered.

Eastern White Pine (pinus strobus): This graceful, blue-green tree is growing in popularity. A traditional, desirable Christmas tree in New England, East Coast States and Midwest States. It grows rapidly on well-drained loamy sites; requires yearly shaping as do other pines, and has excellent needle retention characteristic of

pines. The foliage is desirable for floral use. Disease tendencies
can be controlled, but can be a problem in some areas, however. Avoid
wet planting sites. Due to its soft foliage it is a nice tree for
families with young children. It has increasing ornamental appeal.
It can even be sheared for a hedge or a windbreak effect.

Leyland cypress (cupressocyparis leylandii - member of the family
cypressaceae): This specie is relatively new on the Christmas tree
scene. Its very fast growth and adaptability to soils and sites
makes this clean, deep blue-green colored tree a fine choice in a
Christmas tree. Developed as a hybrid of C. nootkatensis (Alaska
cedar) and cupressus macrocarpa (Monterey cypress) in England in
1888. This tree captured the traits of both its parents. Branching is distinctive with the many branched twigs and small-paired
scalelike leaves arranged in fernlike sprays. It has nice density
and its lack of falling needles and excellent keepability further
adds to its desirability. It does not have significant fragrance,
however.It is often used for windbreaks, ornamental plantings, and
hedges because of its beauty and variety of form.

Scotch pine "turn-up" (stump culture).
Crooked branch on left would be removed
and branch on right trimmed to form a
new tree.

A bough orchard can be perpetuated
from established trees by allowing
new branches to form on trunk.

36

VIRGINIA PINE FOR CHRISTMAS TREES

The Texas SuperTree Nursery began growing Virginia pine for the
Texas Christmas Tree Growers Association in 1985 with a volume of
250,000 seedlings. Nursery production has expanded to 800,000 for
1992. We now sell to individual growers all over the South.
Customer satisfaction is our main concern and that is why we
attend annual fall association meetings to display seedlings and
talk to customers in person.

The Texas SuperTree Nursery's Virginia pine are genetically
improved, low density seedlings. Our seedlings are bareroot,
10" - 14" in size, and packaged 500 to a box. We have four
different varieties of Virginia pine available - Catawba,
Hiwassee, Hammermill, and the new Texas seed source (developed by
the Texas Christmas Tree Growers Association and the Texas Forest
Service).

Seedlings are conditioned for top performance and root pruning
plays a critical part. The Texas SuperTree Nursery uses a special
root pruning technique to help seedlings develop compact fibrous
root systems. Undercutting produces a stiff tap root which
reduces the chance of 'J' or 'L' roots. Pruning lateral roots and
stimulating high levels of food reserves cause roots to explode
with new growth as soil temperatures rise after outplanting. By
establishing the root system early on, the survival and growth of
the young seedlings are enhanced. If pruning is done after
seedlings leave the nursery, excessive root loss can result from
excess exposure to the elements and poor pruning practices. That
is why seedlings are pruned in the nursery so you don't have to do
it in the field.

Texas SuperTree Nursery Virginia pine seedlings are packaged in
unique TreePack boxes designed to provide maximum protection
from sun, wind, and physical injury during transport and storage.
Keeping seedlings fresh and undamaged will help insure good
survival and growth. We offer "to your door" delivery by UPS to
meet your planting schedule. For more information contact Elaine
Perdue, 800-642-2264, or write International Paper, Route 1, Box
314-A, Bullard, Texas 75757.

"Jelly roll" of 25 Swift's Silver Concolor fir. Plugs grown at Itasca Greenhouse, Cohasset, MN. for Treehaven. Maximum uniform production of seedlings from scarce seed is one reason for this type of propagation. (This size plant is then transplanted).

Noble fir, lightly shaped is on display at Oregon State University for Summer Meeting.

Joan shaping Silver fir at Hill Top Acres; although a slow grower, this tree is unsurpassed for beauty.

Machine planting at Rowell's Hemlock Haven Tree Farm, Sandy Creek, NY. Note guide bar to assure even spacing between rows.

Close-up of machine planter showing channel where seedlings are placed. Rear packing wheels under seat close up the trench.

"Two-man" team hand planting (with planting bar) using 2-line system. Several "two-man" teams get the job done quickly.

I believe many other conifer species might be cultured in the mid-south region and in other areas of the country with related weather/climate conditions.

Some lesser known true firs:

Turkish fir (abies bornmüeller)
Pindrow fir
Algerian fir
Spanish fir
Japanese (Momi) fir

Pines:

Japanese red pine
Japanese black pine
Corsican pine
Meyers spruce and
others native to Far East

The experimentation that may have been done in this regard either hasn't become known or lacks documentation; therefore, not much background data and information to go by. Growers in the mid-south and south will have to put forth considerable evaluation effort to find new varieties to consider for Christmas tree cultivation.

Different areas of the country employ their own native plant material. What may be popular in New York may not be in California. Native grown tree types tend to dominate the market.

In addition to the plant description given, the following are specific or are being cultured in the west.

Douglas fir
Monterey pine
Monterey/Knobcone hybrid
Western white pine
Ponderosa pine
Arizona cypress

Grand fir
Shasta fir
Noble fir
California red fir
Sitka spruce
plus many Eastern varieties

Turkish fir (abies bornmuelleriana) growing in Wayne Co., Indiana (left) and Tompkins Co., N.Y. (above). Photos courtesy Ed Cope, Cornell Univ.

Trees of the Future

Many exciting events will take place in the years ahead. The past 10 years have provided improved seed from seed orchards of many tree varieties. Some of these are Scotch pine, Virginia pine, blue spruce, Fraser fir, balsam fir, Afghan pine, and many more.

Another way of developing improved tree types for both Christmas tree grower and nurseryman has been by hybridizing, or crossbreeding, two types to produce one with (hopefully) the preferred traits of both parents. Examples are: hybrid Austrian pine (Austrian pine X Japanese red pine); Spartan spruce (blue spruce X white spruce); hybrid Monterey pine (Monterey X Knobcone pine) and in Nature Bornmüeller fir (abies) - (Greek fir X Nordmann fir). Since abies (true firs) tend to hybridize easily, many of these variations of parentage are believed to exist. This is especially apparent right now as many firs native to China are being "identified" and described.

Genetic improvement, such as cloning and tissue culture, are progressing and many advances will be made in this direction in the next 5 to 10 years. Producing a field of Douglas fir, all identical in form and feature, is something only dreamed about 20 years ago, or even 10 years ago.

Very little is known about many tree types in other areas of the world. As more becomes known, other tree prospects should emerge for commercial development in the United States.

Various means of genetic improvement are being conducted by Forestry Services, Companies, and Universities. Forestry Canada, Georgia-Pacific Co., and Oregon State University are examples.

Note variation in size/development of Grand fir - all planted at the same time in early 1970's in Cattaraugus Co., N.Y. Select area seed collections from higher quality trees has contributed to more uniform growth. Seed orchard collections are the way of the future.

PLANTING

There are "good" springs and "poor" springs. Excessive rain, freezing cold and very dry weather conditions are examples of poor planting situations. Moist soil is vital to a successful plant (low mortality). Since conditions vary dramatically from one year to the next, successive planting will usually provide a favorable average over a period of years.

Planting survival should be 80% or better to be considered successful. Planting stock under stress, poor handling and holding of the stock, poor soil conditions and bad weather conditions can greatly affect survival rate.

Most growers plant every year, for various reasons. Yearly planting to replace the previous year's harvest and/or losses makes good sense and insures continuing production.

Time and labor factors favor yearly planting since many growers are "part-time", hence do not have days or weeks to do a large planting.

Springtime is more predictable weatherwise and rains and warm soil favor the successful establishment of a seedling.

Predators, such as mice and rabbits, are less likely to contribute to the mortality since they have ample food sources in the spring.

Fall planting is practiced by some growers. They do so to space out their work load or to make room for other spring activity. Initial fall planting should be done on a small scale. Land lacking adequate drainage will result in frost heaving of the seedlings. Fall planting occasionally results in drowning of the stock, such as occurred in some areas of New York state in the fall of 1986.

From a nursery standpoint we discourage fall planting because the root growth that develops in the fall can be disrupted and cause stress and possible injury to the plant. In the spring, since we try to lift or undercut as soon as the frost is out, the roots have not yet had a chance to "sprout" new growth, hence minimal injury.

Plan your planting activity prior to the day you intend to do it. Plan your field layout ahead of time and have all needed materials at hand. If you need to hire help then you must have your act together in order to avoid paying them for "standing around".

Materials needed include: planting bar/dibble/spade/shovel, plastic buckets, plenty of water or a source of water available, sphagnum, peat moss, leaves to keep roots damp, shovels to trench seedlings, if necessary; planting line (a reel makes handling the line(s) much easier). Stake out the ends of the rows in advance to avoid loss of time and confusion on planting day; also, dress according to work and weather conditions.

Planting is the most important part of the Christmas tree business. If you don't have a successful planting season you will have to replant or settle for a partially productive area. We always replant the following first or second season if survival is not atleast 85%.

Most hand planting is done with a "two-man" procedure. One person carries the pail with wet mulch around the roots of the seedlings. Your pail/pails should contain enough seedlings to plant down on one row and back on the next row. If stock is large, place buckets at other ends of the rows so enough stock is ready to get back to the other end. The person carrying the stock sets the seedling in the "cut" or hole made by the second person who carries the planting bar or spade.

"Steps in Hand Tree Planting" follow: (Our thanks to Mr. Phil W. Jones, National Director from Shelton, Conn. for his contribution).

STEPS IN HAND TREE PLANTING BARE ROOT STOCK

1. Trees to be planted should never be allowed to let their roots dry out. Wind and sunshine on bare seedling roots can kill or seriously injure their vitality in one minute. Stronger and older transplant trees are tougher but drying roots are injuring the tree all the while they are exposed.

2. When ready for planting, carry trees in pail or bucket with soupy mud of very moist mulch surrounding roots. Keep moist, out of the sun and wind while waiting to be planted.

3. Dig holes deep enough and large enough so roots are not crowded and twisted into a cramped wad or ball. Do not dig holes much ahead of planting time. Dirt can dry out rapidly in the sun and wind. Exception would be cloudy, damp or rainy days. Get one side of the hole straight so tree placed against straight side will stand up straight when planted and packed in. Exception: Auger Holes - place trees in center and fill in with moist dirt from edges.

4. Repeat - don't crowd roots. Spread them out as they grew in the nursery. Many larger transplant trees will have a small root ball of earth attached. Don't shake it off. Plant it without disturbing the roots if possible.

5. When digging holes do not throw dirt away from the hole. The dirt has to go right back in around the roots. Do not fill hole in with leaves, grass or sticks. Push the dirt in around roots with your heel. Tree must be as tight as it was in the nursery or tighter. Take care not to scrape the bark off the tree, bend and crack the trunk, etc. Figure out your best method of packing in so tree

stands up straight. Crooked trees will have a crooked stem. If there are old leaves, needles or duff near the planted tree, kick or scrape it over the fresh dirt to act as mulch. It will help a great deal to prevent the newly planted tree from drying out.

6. Make sure roots are all in the hole with root ends not bent up or sticking out of the ground. Work around stones. Some may have to come out. Usually very few have to be slaved over.

7. Do not plant too deep, burying live branches. This upsets tree top and root balance. Tree may either die, or stunt its growth.

8. Pack the dirt in properly. Empty space and air pockets will prevent roots from taking hold. Small rocks can be replaced along with dirt and packed back in the hole. Rocks left out on top will be a hazard to stumble over and be in the way of mowers.

9. If a rock is in the way and too large to pop out with your shovel, jab around it until you locate the spot to plant the tree. From the marked planting spot you can probe a foot away in a circle until finding the hole spot. If unable to properly plant within that two foot circle move on to the next spot. Very few planted trees will live planted in shallow holes over big rocks.

10. In some areas where small trees are planted a shovel slit hole will be okay. Push shovel in to depth roots should go. Push shovel to open up root cavity hole. Open up enough so roots can be snapped in, properly placed and spaced and then tamped in good with your heel or tamp stick.

Correct and Incorrect Depths

Correct
At same depth or ½" deeper than seedling grew in nursery.

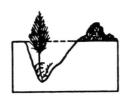

Incorrect
Too deep and roots bent.

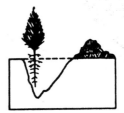

Incorrect
Too shallow and roots exposed.

44

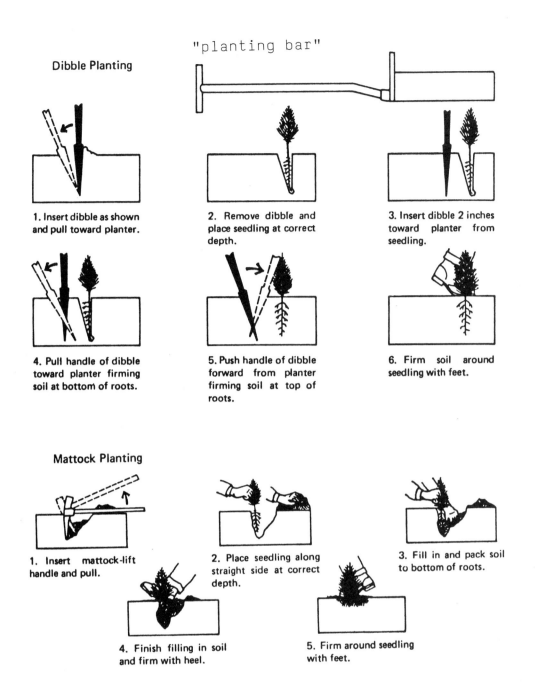

Dibble Planting

"planting bar"

1. Insert dibble as shown and pull toward planter.

2. Remove dibble and place seedling at correct depth.

3. Insert dibble 2 inches toward planter from seedling.

4. Pull handle of dibble toward planter firming soil at bottom of roots.

5. Push handle of dibble forward from planter firming soil at top of roots.

6. Firm soil around seedling with feet.

Mattock Planting

1. Insert mattock-lift handle and pull.

2. Place seedling along straight side at correct depth.

3. Fill in and pack soil to bottom of roots.

4. Finish filling in soil and firm with heel.

5. Firm around seedling with feet.

Here are a few additional suggestions:

A slurry of water and peat moss (like pea soup) is a good way to keep stock in the bucket you are carrying or tray of your machine planter; don't soak or drown the roots.

If roots are excessively long and/or are very difficult to cope with, then root pruning is in order. While still in bundles, hold upright, and with your fingers, gently straighten out roots so they hang freely. Cut not more than 1/3 of the root length with sharp scissors or lay flat on a wooden block and cut crosswise with a sharp knife - avoid tearing roots.

Spruce seedlings suffer greatly when planted too deep. The seedling will grow very little since a whole new root system has to be established on the trunk/stem portion that is below the surface of the soil. A seedling may be stunted by 2, 3, or 4 years. Sometimes the weakened seedling will die.

If a stone has to be removed from the ground to enable the seedling to be planted, do not leave the loose stone in the aisleway or a mower or other piece of equipment will be obtructed by it.

If you cannot complete you planting that day (or weekend, etc.) you must take extra care to avoid stress to the seedlings. The kitchen refrigerator is usually not large enough. Find a cool, wet, shaded and sheltered place, out of the wind and sun, and dig a trench or bed deep enough to accommodate the roots and long enough that the bundle or handful of seedlings can be placed tightly side by side (but not double layered) along the length of the trench. Dig so that the soil can be rolled back or placed back in the trench to tightly seal soil against the roots. Trench should be wet enough for water to form in the trench, but purged when soil is replaced. (Along a drainage ditch, a low wet spot, along lower edge of a spring, along the edge of a creek or pond area are all good locations.) Heal in the trench with your foot, water the trench if necessary, but be sure there is not standing water in the trench. For subsequent planting, simply pull the bundles of seedlings from the trench. If several thousand seedlings are involved, it may be necessary to make one or more lengthy trenches with a plow blade.

Planting stock should be covered lightly with evergreen branches, leaves or wet burlap to protect them. Don't cover with plastic or any heavy heat absorbent material. Plants will not survive suffocation. Covering your trench may be desirable as a deterrent to theft when you are not around. Stock can be held in this properly prepared trench for several weeks. Transplants can be treated as just described. If plugs are planted, they are best left in their containers. Almost daily attention might be necessary if extremely dry and hot weather is encountered. We are always happy when a heavy rain follows a weekend or several days of planting. A rain like this helps to "set" the plants and provides lifegiving water and nutrients to get them started.

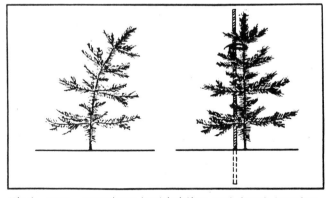

Wind, snow, premature herbiciding and frost heaving can result in bent seedlings and young trees. Staking into an upright position may become necessary if the tree is to develop into premium quality.

A hand planting procedure we have developed for large seedlings and transplant stock involves the use of a round-pointed, long handled shovel. It is a one-man procedure for sod covered ground.

Two cuts are made approximately 6" into the sod ground. When the second cut is made (the two cuts form a ⊢) the shovel is tilted back and the ground separates. The shovel is lifted up a little to allow the plant to be inserted into the ground underneath the bottom of the shovel. The shovel is then removed allowing two sections of sod to cover the roots. With your foot the sod is lightly pressed to establish the plant firmly in the ground. Make sure all the root is in the ground. Excessively long root systems can be pruned prior to planting.

PLANTING (continued)

A procedure using two (2) planting lines to reduce planting time follows:

The field to be planted should have been paced off and the number of seedlings needed determined prior to placing seedling order. (Determine distance between rows and spacing between trees and refer to chart). Decide what direction rows will run and place a stake at both ends of each row.

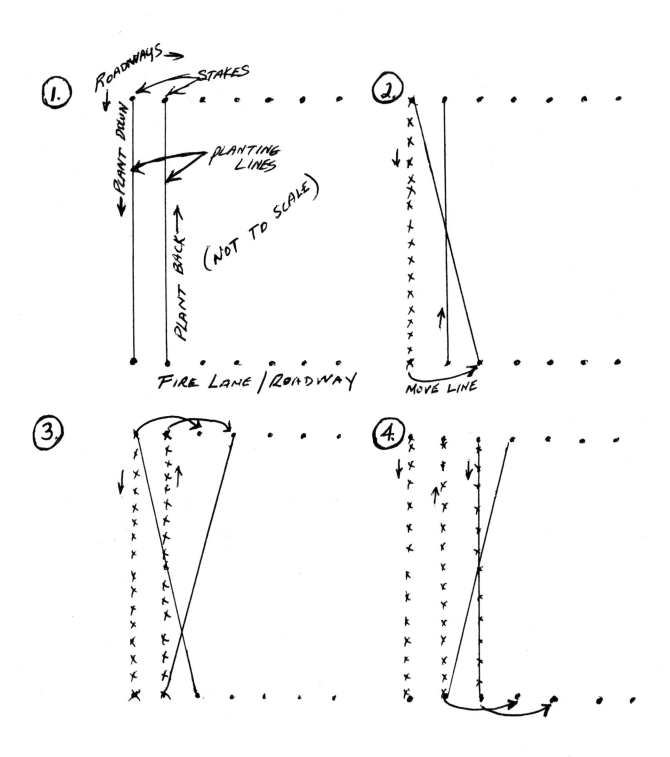

Prepare two (2) planting lines, each 200 feet long. You may have to tie two (2) 100 foot long plastic clothes lines together. On a flat surface mark off a 5 foot or 6 foot spacing or whatever spacing you intend to use between trees. Lay out your line and wrap a 1" to 2" colored tape around the clothesline between the selected spacing along the entire length (200 feet) of each line. This premarked line saves a great deal of time. A planting line much longer than 200 feet is difficult to move without a lot of fuss and lost time. This is also a good spacing to allow an aisle of roadway. (This 200 foot = 41 trees 5 feet apart). Place lines so rows #1 and #2 can be planted. Plant down row #1. When completed, move end of line #1 to row #3 and secure firmly. Plant back on line #2. When back at starting point, take other end of line #1 and move it to end of row #3. Straighten out the line and drive stake firmly into the ground. Move line #2 to line #4. Keep repeating this procedure until entire field is planted. Not having to run down and move planting lines in each row will save a great deal of time in the course of a day's planting.

Machine planting should be considered under these circumstances:

A. Planting 2,000 or more trees in a season and/or planting help is unavailable.

B. Where time doesn't permit prompt planting under favorable conditions, or planting time would be too extended.

C. Where hand planting has resulted in poor survival (even though soil and climatic conditions were favorable).

D. Where larger plants (especially transplants) create an excessive workload.

Limiting factors to machine planting:

A. Less than 500 foot length (too small an area takes excessive time turning around, etc.).

B. Stumps, brush, and other interferences are present.

C. Excessively rocky soil (may cause problems later and do a poor job of planting.

D. Cost of outlay of capital may be prohibitive.

E. Replanting in partially planted areas.

F. Unsuitable land conditions, i.e., too wet, frost, awkward shape of land, etc.

G. Should have more than 2,000 seedlings to be cost effective.

H. Some planting machines do not handle large seedlings or transplants satisfactorily.

I. Tractor driver must be able to drive a straight line.

You may want or need to have the work hired (which may involve moving tractor as well as planter). Some planters won't adapt to all tractors (even if the manufacturer says they do). A "crawler" gear is necessary for most planters to control travel speed of the planter.

Other planting procedures might be employed depending on labor and other factors.

One of the fastest ways to cycle a tree area is by planting potted transplants. An auger, either gasoline driven or attached to a 3 point tractor hitch, can be used. If replanting in a poorly accessible area or in a treed area, a tractor mounted auger is usually ruled out.

Manual augering allows planting by convenience and assures almost 100% survival. It is slow and labor-intensive. Large plantations usually cannot avail themselves to this kind of operations. They plant in larger numbers to allow for a longer growing cycle, which may only be a year or so.

Plugs are sometimes planted. They come in trays or "cell blocks" and are seedlings grown by acceleration in a controlled environment. Several studies conducted in the Northeast showed them to be easier to plant, but not necessarily superior in survival. After being removed from the "hot house" they must be allowed to "harden off". Sometimes the grower receives stock before that process is completed and the plug inadvertently may be subjected to stresses it is not ready for; i.e. use of fertilizer and herbicides. Both can burn roots and herbicides can harm foliage as well. A Dibble is usually used in planting plugs.

Number of trees on an Acre

FEET	2	3	4	5	6	7	8	9	10
1	21,780	14,520	10,890	8,712	7,260	6,222	5,445	4,840	4,356
1½	14,520	9,680	7,260	5,808	4,840	4,148	3,630	3,226	2,904
2	10,890	7,260	5,445	4,356	3,630	3,111	2,722	2,420	2,178
3	7,260	4,840	3,630	2,904	2,420	2,074	1,210	1,613	1,452
4	5,445	3,630	2,722	2,178	1,815	1,555	1,361	1,210	1,039
6	3,630	2,420	1,815	1,452	1,210	1,037	907	806	726
8	2,722	1,815	1,361	1,039	907	777	680	605	519
10	2,178	1,425	1,039	871	726	622	519	484	435

Rule: Multiply the distance in feet between the rows by the distance the trees are apart in the rows. The product will be the number of square feet for each tree. Divide the number of square feet in an acre (43,560) by the square feet per tree to determine total number of trees per acre.

"HEELING - IN"

Heeling-in is a temporary cultural practice used when plants cannot be planted immediately. The purpose of this technique is to return the plant to the soil until it can be field planted, potted, lined-out, etc.

Many tree growers are "weekend farmers". That is, they do their tree planting in between a regular job and they usually cannot complete their planting in one day or even in one weekend. Because many nurseries discourage partial shipments, and most tree growers lack adequate refrigeration facilities, trenching or heeling-in is the next best solution once the plants have been delivered.

Plants should be dormant when you pick them up at the nursery or receive them. This is _very_ _important_. Many nurseries have cold storage, but some do not. Ask your supplier if they do or don't. Unrefrigerated stock will not stay dormant, so the time span from digging to replanting should be as short as possible. If plants have begun to break bud or leaf out they should be planted as soon as possible, preferably by-passing the trenching procedure, as moving them a second time will only put more stress on the plants.

More growers are root-dipping their plants with a hydrophillic gel (water absorbing) to be sure plants' roots have access to moisture. Even the heeling-in trench can dry out (soil) so seedlings to be trenched should be root-dipped. It would be even better if this step was undertaken at the nursery; however, the critical points are to have the plants completely dormant and roots moist from lifting to replanting.

If more than a few hundred plants are to be trenched, a tractor and plow blade to open a furrow will be preferred over hand digging the trench. We have areas on our farm where seedlings are trenched and the trench can be used from year to year.

Coarse sphagnum moss is a good water-absorbing material and this can be put nearest the roots before the soil is moved back into the trench.

Even fine peat moss can be poured into a half part of water and made into a slurry. The roots of the bundles can be dipped in that. It would be wise to use the gel or slurry dip procedure even if plants are being held overnight.

The most ideal site for heeling-in is a sheltered, moist, gently sloping spot out of the sun and wind, and preferably shaded by evergreen trees. The edge of a drain-off ditch or along the edge of a spring is ideal.

If the best site you have is exposed to sun and wind, make sure the trench is always shaded by using evergreen branches or even a lean-to structure of cardboard or canvas. Absolutely _no_ _plastic_! Air must be allowed to circulate freely.

If in the digging process moisture begins to seep in, you have a good spot. Replacement of the soil and sod will displace any excess moisture. You can be assured of this by extending the low end of the trench well beyond the seedlings with the end open to permit excess water to drain out; no standing water should be in the trench.

A few additional pointers about heeling-in:

- Make sure the bundles are opened up and spread along the back of the trench.
- Be sure soil is loose and/or the back side of the trench is in contact with the roots of the seedling (no air pockets).
- Dig trench deep enough so that roots are straight down, not bent or J-rooted.
- Do not root prune seedlings/transplants (if necessary) until you are ready to plant them.
- Spraying or watering the tops of the plants can help restore/retain tissue moisture since leaves do absorb water as do the roots.
- Don't take delivery (or pick up) if you know you can't get the plants in the ground - at least a portion of them.
- If anything appears out of order with your plants, inform your supplier immediately. Any claims against a supplier usually must be made at the time you take delivery not a week or 6 mos. later.
- Unpack cartons, boxes as soon as you receive them.
- Never leave plants in water overnight (this will cause drowning and loss of the plants).
- A heeling-in trench is not the plant's best or natural environment; hence, all steps should be followed very carefully.

Many growers will have less than the best conditions with which to hold their plants until they can be planted, but the key points set forth must be followed. If you do not have a damp/sheltered place to hold the plants you either have to refrigerate them (35° best) or find a nearby place that does have a good site (neighbor, nearby farmer, etc.)

Refrigeration is best. A nearby florist may have extra refrigeration space or a deli or grocery store with a cooling room. Be sure to moisten the plants' tops and roots (upright position) before putting them in a cooler. Coolers have air circulating constantly and this will draw moisture from everything.

A root cellar is usually less than ideal because the temperature is not low enough. Mold and possible disease spores are everywhere; therefore, the other options we discussed should be employed first.

Condition of Plants. There are healthy-looking plants and not so healthy-looking plants. You must develop the awareness of the difference since "sick" plants are sure to die when planted in the "wilds".

Signs of sick plants:
- Dried out.
- Pale color, different from normal color of foliage.

- Browned needles (don't confuse with wind burn).
- Needles falling off (not the lower needles). You can test this by gently pulling on the twig or stem. Needles should remain firm.
- Mold on top and bottom of plant. Mold is everywhere and will grow on plants kept in storage. Wash off and try needle holding test.
- Any sign of underside browning, presence of insects or mottled spots, or puncture on needles.
- Broken needles/stem.
- Splitting of bark on seedling.

Suggestion if mold is present on plants: wash off, preferably with hose under moderate pressure. Inspect, and if apparently free of mold, plant immediately. Mold and mold spores usually die when exposed to sun and outdoor air circulation. If plants are heavily molded, make a solution (50-50) of acetic acid (vinegar and water in a pail or small drum and dip them until completely drenched. Allow plants to remain wet for 15 minutes before hosing off with water under moderate pressure (garden hose). Wash them for several minutes. The effectiveness of this procedure can be improved if the bundles are untied first. This has been reported to promptly kill the mold. Usually a completely defoliated plant will die so you will have to make the decision as to whether or not it is worth spending the time and labor to plant these seedlings.

Signs common to fresh plants.

- General freshness (like fresh lettuce at the grocery store.
- Green, usual shiny color, and moist foliage.
- Firm needles on twig/branch.
- Free of windburn/herbicide injury, etc. (both conditions put stress on seedling).
- Slight swelling of buds indicating "life" in seedling.
- Excess swelling denotes life, but immediate planting or transplanting is required.
- Tiny white shoots of new growth on roots. (these plants are "alive" and should be planted immediately).
- Pliable needles and stems.
- No mold or dried skin/bark on plant.
- By scraping on stem of one plant and observing green tissue is sign of health. (generally indication of the whole lot).

FOUR BASIC STEPS FOR HEELING-IN PLANTS

Dig a V-shaped trench that
is deep enough to accom-
modate roots in moist,
well drained soil.

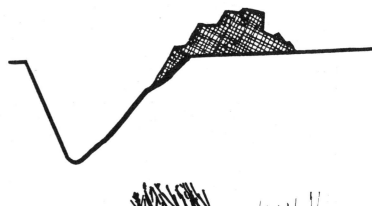

Open bundles of seedlings
and spread them out evenly
against one side of the
trench.

Fill trench with loose soil.
Water trench and plants.

Complete filling in soil
around roots and press with
foot. (Sod clumps can be
turned upside down over
loose soil)

Cover plants & trench lightly with evergreen branches. Water plants
and trench every 2 or 3 days. Allow excess water to drain out. The
best place to heel-in is in a usually moist-sheltered area out of
the sun & wind. Bunches of trees can be dug up and field planted
as opportunity allows. All planting, however, should be done during your normal planting period in your region.

54

WHY A TRANSPLANT BED?

The use of transplants in field planting has been gaining in popularity in the past 10 to 15 years. This trend seems parallel to that of choose and cut production and marketing of Christmas trees. Once into production the "cut your own" tree lots tend to thrive and soon more trees are being harvested than trees coming to size. This reality prompts a grower to seek every way possible to reduce the growing cycle. Planting larger plants is the first step.

Because transplants may cost 3 or 4 times that of seedlings, plant costs increase greatly. Growing their own transplants was a natural step for many growers. Pretty soon new growers realize that they can accelerate their growing cycle and get some money coming back in. Transplant size trees are also in demand for windbreaks, hedges, and general landscape plantings.

Having your own transplant bed provides other advantages. You have the flexibility of digging and replanting at a time of your own choosing. Movement of the plants can usually be done with less stress and mortality than if they had to be transported or shipped from a nursery. Sick or poorly formed seedlings will die or be graded out; hence, only the best plants will end up in your field.

If a shipment of seedlings has a wide range of sizes, it behooves you to regrade before field planting or potting to achieve more uniformity of field production. The smaller plants can then be transplanted and allowed to grow for 2 more years. The more evenly sized larger plants provide a more predictable growing cycle.

Small plants usually result in high mortality. The care small plants need to survive on their own is very difficult to give under field conditions. The time and cost of replanting a field where there is high mortality is good reason to regrade and transplant the smaller plants.

Most transplants should be removed from a bed after 2 years because they start to crowd each other and become much more difficult to dig if left longer. They can be field planted or potted.

Following is a typical procedure for establishing a transplant bed.

Steps in Preparing a Transplant Bed. Any garden area such as you would have for vegetable growing is usually adequate for a line-out or transplant bed.

It is strongly recommended that the area be replowed to loosen the soil in the 6-12" depth. If a new area is to be prepared the plowing, discing steps are essential. This step is not only to loosen soil but to kill unwanted grass and weeds.

Preparation of your nursery area could begin the year before you intend to plant it, thus allowing for several tillings or discings to further "work out" weed seed and some other undesirable

55

elements.

Nurserymen frequently add other materials to the soil (amendments) which usually provide nutrition (in addition to fertilizer), texture, and organic matter. Organic matter (compost, for example) usually provides beneficial organisms as well.

Your nursery area soil should be sampled for deficiencies, especially pH and potassium. Lime and potassium supplements should be added and tilled in, preferably the fall before.

Most nursery soils prefer the pH around 6. A range of 5.8 to 6.5 is usually satisfactory. Some plant types do better at either end of the range.

If your soil is not too acid, your soil analysis report will usually tell you how much lime is needed (per acre) to bring up the pH to the desired level.

Contact your nearest Cooperative Extension office or your Cooperative Extension University (see list Appendix A) to get instructions. You can also contact private soil testing laboratories.

The information you send with the soil sample should state that you have a conifer nursery. Usually the laboratory report will give recommendations based on that end use.

The fertilizer recommendation is frequently given so you know how much to incorporate into the soil prior to planting.

Most nurseries elevate the bed surface 2-4" to allow excess water to run out of the soil. This provides better aëration for the roots and reduces the chance of frost heaving during the winter months. Allowing excess water to drain out also reduces the chances of root diseases.

In a small nursery, the soil from the isles between beds, or the surrounding soil, is simply mounded to elevate the planting surface. Our beds never exceed 40" wide. We plant about 3" from the edge of the bed in case some erosion of the edges occurs.

Optimum soil preparation, including texture and moisture levels, are necessary for cost-effective transplant production. Detailed information about all aspects of seedling transplanting (lining-out, potting, etc.) can be found in Growing Conifer Seedlings, Transplants and Trees in an Outdoor Nursery - Books One and Two (Treehaven publications).

Depending on the size of the plants being transplanted, the spacing can be determined. Plants in the 3-6" size we usually plant in a 4" x 4" spacing. Plants such as 6-12" 3-0 seedlings are planted in a 6" x 6" spacing. Larger plants usually require a 1 foot by 1 foot spacing.

If you decide to grow landscape plants or live Christmas tree size (usually 3' to 5' size) then direct planting into a tilled area usually on 4' x 4' centers is practiced.

The larger you intend to grow the trees to be dug, the more space you must allow when planting. Most transplants and live trees in a nursery area are hand dug, hence a minimum of space is required. More space must be allowed if digging equipment is to be used.

As you proceed in the production of larger size trees, various techniques will become self-evident in keeping with your soil, site, and production conditions and objectives. Much more discussion can be found in nursery books one and two.

When 2-year transplants are ready to be field planted, the holes are dug ahead, either by hand or auger. If a lot of trees are to be planted, a power auger is usually employed. An auger operated off the PTO of your tractor can dig a lot of holes easily in a relatively short period of time. If you don't have the equipment, perhaps a neighbor or friend might. Check around ahead of time. (See photograph of Ferguson Tree Farm picturing a field of transplants).

The short-term transplant bed, if approximately 40" wide, permits easy hand weeding from both sides of the bed. Most nurseries employ chemical means of weed control. (See chapter on herbicides).

Weed control is essential if you are to produce healthy, vigorous plants.

Fraser fir seedling beds and transplant beds
at State Nursery, Linville, N.C.

SOIL

What is soil? It may be defined as the natural covering of planet earth, formed by the processes of nature, acting upon native rocks and vegetation throughout the ages. Several things we do know about it. It is a complex material; which nature's processes took centuries to accomplish. It is our most valuable asset. Best of all, we can make it better for our own purposes.

To give you a better understanding of soil, you should know something about its makeup. Soils vary greatly in their structure and composition. For our discussion we can refer to them as mineral soils, the nature of which is found on the average farm. The composition is sand, silt, clay and organic matter. These portions are referred to as "fractions" (i.e. sand fractions, etc.). These fractions came about through natural and chemical processes. Organic matter is composed of the residue of vegetable and animal matter deposited in the soil and is mainly responsible for its nitrogen producing capacity.

Sand and silt fractions occur in different proportions and serve as the main source of minerals used by the plant. These are phosphorus, potassium, calcium, magnesium, copper, manganese zinc, iron, cobalt, sulfur, sodium, chlorides, iodides, boron and others. Decomposition makes these available to the plant.

Clay is the sticky or colloidal fraction of the soil. It serves to give body and heavier structure to the soil. It binds and releases and exchanges mineral matter with soil, hence, has a stabilizing effect. The higher the clay fraction, the harder it is to work the soil. In the nursery (and vegetable garden) we alter the soil with various materials to make it easier to work (sand, peat, vermiculite, sawdust, leaves, manure, etc.). The last three not only condition the soil but add organic matter and nutrients.

Organic matter is that fraction which results from the decomposition of animal and vegetable matter through the action of bacteria. It is the natural home for bacteria (an essential part of plant life). In addition, its composition helps to retain water, carbon dioxide and other chemical components. The organic matter is a colloidal material and can be better understood if you visualize it as a coating around the soil particle in the top soil. This coating forms an active agent for exchange of mineral elements from soil to plant. Its preservation in the soil is vital. A good soil should have between 3% and 5% organic matter.

Due to the complexity of soils, classifying them for identification and study is complex. The table that follows provides names and descriptions of major soil types in New York State and a value rating as to crops use. A few basic soil characteristics are also given. For a more complete study, read "Soils of New York Landscapes", Information Bulletin 119 by M. G. Cline and R. L. Marshall, N.Y.S. College of Agriculture and Life Sciences, Cornell University. (See address in Appendix - cost $2.00). A general soils map of New York State with the respective symbols in the chart accompanies this 60-page bulletin. The N.Y. State county maps, however, are more specific in the land areas and soil types charted - that should be your primary source of information. (Your nearest Soil Conservation office). Other states have their soils classified so this information is available throughout most of the U.S. More detailed information about soil types will be found in the companion publication "Addendum to Basics of Growing Christmas Trees".

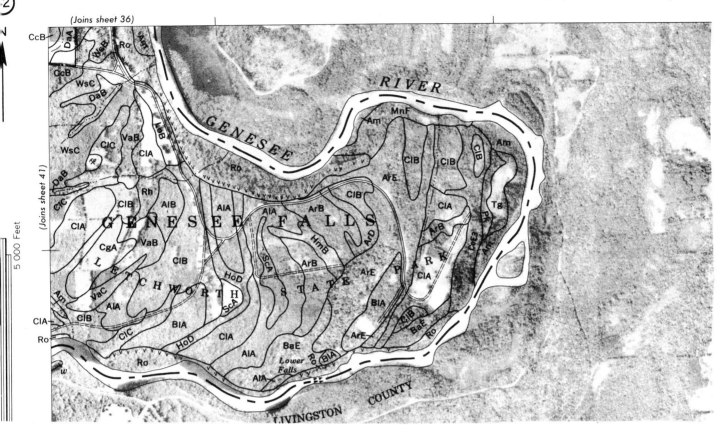

SYMBOL	NAME
Ad	Alden mucky silt loam
AlA	Allard silt loam, 0 to 3 percent slopes
AlB	Allard silt loam, 3 to 8 percent slopes
AlC	Allard silt loam, 8 to 15 percent slopes
Am	Alluvial land
AnA	Angola shaly silt loam, 0 to 3 percent slopes
AoB	Angola and Aurora shaly silt loams, 3 to 8 percent slopes
ApA	Appleton gravelly silt loam, 0 to 3 percent slopes
ApB	Appleton gravelly silt loam, 3 to 8 percent slopes
ArB	Arkport very fine sandy loam, 2 to 8 percent slopes
ArC	Arkport very fine sandy loam, 8 to 15 percent slopes
ArD	Arkport very fine sandy loam, 15 to 25 percent slopes
ArE	Arkport very fine sandy loam, 25 to 40 percent slopes
AtB	Arnot channery silt loam, 2 to 8 percent slopes
AtC	Arnot channery silt loam, 8 to 15 percent slopes
AuC	Aurora shaly silt loam, 8 to 15 percent slopes
BaA	Bath channery silt loam, 0 to 3 percent slopes
BaB	Bath channery silt loam, 3 to 8 percent slopes
BaC	Bath channery silt loam, 8 to 15 percent slopes
BaD	Bath channery silt loam, 15 to 25 percent slopes
BaE	Bath channery silt loam, 25 to 40 percent slopes
BlA	Bath-Valois gravelly loams, 0 to 3 percent slopes
BlB	Bath-Valois gravelly loams, 3 to 8 percent slopes
BlC	Bath-Valois gravelly loams, 8 to 15 percent slopes
BlD	Bath-Valois gravelly loams, 15 to 25 percent slopes
BuA	Burdett silt loam, 0 to 3 percent slopes
BuB	Burdett silt loam, 3 to 8 percent slopes
Ca	Canadice silty clay loam
CcA	Canaseraga silt loam, 0 to 3 percent slopes
CcB	Canaseraga silt loam, 3 to 8 percent slopes
CcC	Canaseraga silt loam, 8 to 15 percent slopes
CdA	Caneadea silt loam, 0 to 3 percent slopes
CdB	Caneadea silt loam, 3 to 8 percent slopes
CdC	Caneadea silt loam, 8 to 15 percent slopes
CeD3	Caneadea silty clay loam, 15 to 25 percent slopes, eroded
CeE3	Caneadea silty clay loam, 25 to 50 percent slopes, eroded
CgA	Castile gravelly loam, 0 to 3 percent slopes
CgB	Castile gravelly loam, 3 to 8 percent slopes
ChA	Castile channery silt loam, fans, 0 to 3 percent slopes
ClA	Chenango gravelly loam, 0 to 3 percent slopes
ClB	Chenango gravelly loam, 3 to 8 percent slopes
ClC	Chenango gravelly loam, 8 to 15 percent slopes
ClD	Chenango gravelly loam, 15 to 25 percent slopes
CmB	Chenango channery silt loam, fans, 3 to 8 percent slopes
CnB	Churchville silt loam, 2 to 8 percent slopes
CnC	Churchville silt loam, 8 to 15 percent slopes
CoB	Collamer silt loam, 3 to 8 percent slopes
CoC	Collamer silt loam, 8 to 15 percent slopes
CoD	Collamer silt loam, 15 to 25 percent slopes
CrA	Conesus gravelly silt loam, 0 to 3 percent slopes
CrB	Conesus gravelly silt loam, 3 to 8 percent slopes
CrC	Conesus gravelly silt loam, 8 to 15 percent slopes
DaA	Dalton silt loam, 0 to 3 percent slopes
DaB	Dalton silt loam, 3 to 8 percent slopes

ESSENTIAL MINERAL ELEMENTS

Certain mineral elements are essential for plant growth. Nine, called macronutrients, are required in relatively large amounts. Plants obtain carbon, hydrogen, and oxygen from air and water, nitrogen, phosphorus, potassium, calcium, magnesium, and sulfur are normally absorbed by the roots. The macronutrients are usually present in field soils, but their levels require careful management to obtain maximum growth.

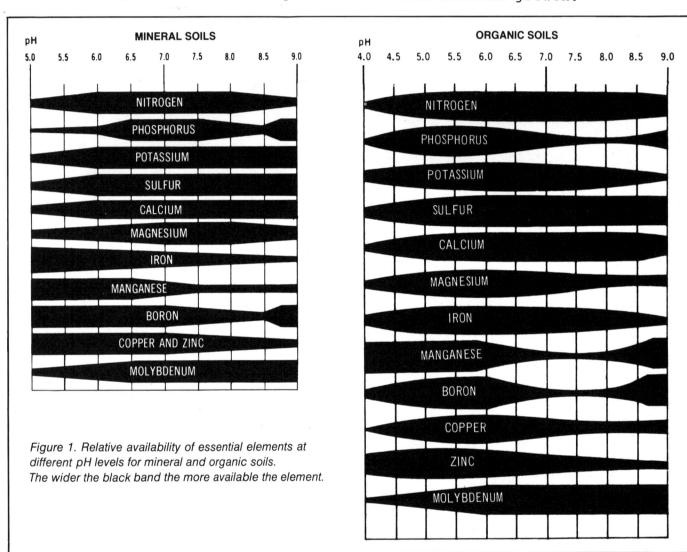

Figure 1. Relative availability of essential elements at different pH levels for mineral and organic soils. The wider the black band the more available the element.

Seven other elements, required in small amounts by plants, are called micronutrients. They include iron, manganese, zinc, boron, molybdenum, copper, and chlorine. Micronutrients are at low levels or totally lacking in most soilless media, so it is important to supply them when growing plants in such media. Micronutrients are rarely deficient in field soils, but may occur in chemical forms that some plants cannot use. Extreme pH conditions (either too acidic or too alkaline) are the most frequent cause of nutrients occurring in unavailable forms.

If plants absorb any of these essential elements in insufficient or excessive amounts, they will not achieve their maximum growth. Proper feeding and management of plants require knowledge and understanding of what plants need and how nutrients become available or unavailable because of conditions in the soil.

Nitrogen (N) is the element that most commonly limits growth in plants. Almost all plants respond to the addition of nitrogen fertilizers.

The amount of nitrogen available to plants in soil depends first on how much is present, then how much is added, and finally how much is used or lost.

Nitrogen becomes available to plants through:

- mineralization (decomposition) of organic matter by soil microorganisms
- addition of fertilizers
- fixation of nitrogen in the air by bacteria

Nitrogen in the soil becomes unavailable to crop plants through:

- absorption by weeds
- absorption by microorganisms decomposing organic matter low in nitrogen
- denitrification by soil organisms
- loss from the root zone by leaching

Except for the direct application of fertilizer, these processes are all influenced by the environment (temperature, moisture, soil aeration, pH, and microorganisms).

Several different chemical forms of nitrogen fertilizers come in a variety of formulations (liquid, granular, sulfur, coated, encapsulated, etc.). The nitrogen in most farm grade fertilizer is readily available to plants. In recent years several nitrogen products have been developed that delay or extend nutrient release over a period of time. These are "slow release" fertilizers.

Urea is a water soluble form of organic nitrogen that moves easily into the soil in the soil, urea converts first into ammonium nitrogen, then into nitrate. Significant quantities of nitrogen can be lost from urea by volatilization of the ammonia. These losses are accelerated by warm, moist soils, high pH, and surface organic matter. Losses are higher on soils with low cation exchange capacity (CEC) and sandy soils than on clay soils with a high CEC. Urea fertilizers should be applied in cool weather or incorporated into the soil by tillage or water movement. Urea is not recommended as a starter fertilizer because of the potential for ammonia toxicity to germinating seedlings or young roots.

Organic forms of nitrogen other than urea, either natural or synthetic, must be decomposed or transformed into more soluble forms to move into and through the soil to plant roots. The rate of decomposition or transformation is usually dependent on the forms of the material, temperature, soil moisture, and the abundance of soil microorganisms.

Phosphorus (P) exists in soils in both organic and inorganic forms. Mineral soils, especially those that are acidic, tend to fix or tie-up phosphorus in forms not readily available to plants. Calcium, iron, and aluminum ions and silicate clays may combine with phosphorus in low pH environments. An advantage of this soil fixation of phosphorus is that little, if any, phosphorus is lost by leaching.

Corrective applications based on soil test results should be made. Since phosphorus is not very mobile in the soil, it may move as little as one inch per year from the site of application. It is important to incorporate phosphorus prior to planting so that it is in the zone of root growth at the time of planting.

Single superphosphate (0-20-0) is preferred over triple superphosphate (0-40-0 or 0-46-0) because it supplies sulfur as well as calcium and phosphorus. Ammonium and potassium phosphates can also be used.

Although superphosphate can be added to soil at relatively high rates without directly injuring plants, soil levels of phosphorus exceeding five hundred pounds per acre should be avoided. In soils with higher phosphorus levels certain micronutrient deficiencies, particularly zinc or copper, may be induced.

In fertilization experiments, with a variety of ornamental plants, conifers have shown the greatest growth increases in response to phosphorus applications.

Potassium (K) or potash (K_2O) as it is known to many growers, is used in relatively large amounts by plants. It is the third of the macronutrients that is most likely to limit plant performance.

Potassium exists in the soil in three forms: nonexchangeable, exchangeable, and soil solution. Plants can absorb the exchangeable and soil-solution potassium with relative ease. As the exchangeable potassium is used by plants, it is partially replaced by nonexchangeable potassium. Nonexchangeable potassium is important because it can sustain plant growth over several growing seasons and thus alleviate the need for annual applications of potassium. Fields in which the potassium content is at a recommended level, may not need additional potassium for five years.

Potassium can be added as potassium sulfate, potassium chloride (also called muriate of potash), or potassium nitrate. The last formulation supplies both potassium and nitrogen.

Magnesium and calcium are positively charged ions that are strongly adsorbed by clay particles or organic matter. They must be applied to the root zone to be effective within a reasonable time. Preplant incorporation of fertilizers containing these elements is recommended.

Magnesium can be supplied in two forms - as magnesium sulfate (Epsom salts) or as dolomitic limestone (a mixture of calcium and magnesium carbonate). Selection of the form to be used depends on the soil pH. Magnesium sulfate is used in neutral or alkaline soils; dolomitic limestone under acid conditions. Magnesium sulfate can be broadcast on the soil surface, but dolomitic limestone must be incorporated into the soil to be effective.

As in the case of magnesium, selection of the calcium formulations added depends on the soil pH. Calcium sulfate (gypsum) should be applied to neutral or alkaline soils. Lime and limestone supply calcium and increase the pH of soils to which they are applied. Calcium nitrate can be used to add calcium and nitrogen to the soil.

In the soil, magnesium and calcium move from exchangeable forms into the soil solution as they are taken up by plants. In this way, they are maintained at adequate levels in the soil solution until the exchangeable sources are depleted. Therefore, one application of these elements may meet plant needs for several years.

Micronutrients - Iron and manganese are the micronutrients most often found to be deficient in plants. In almost all locations where plants show symptoms of iron or manganese deficiency, these elements are present in the soil in concentrations adequate to support normal growth. The deficiency occurs because the iron or manganese occurs in a chemical form that prevents its use by the plants. The situation is usually corrected by adjustments in soil pH. Plants in well-drained soils with a high pH are especially susceptible to this condition.

Nutrient-element balance - Plant growth is a function of both the total amount of nutrient elements available and the balance among the elements. Deficiency symptoms can develop in plants grown in soil in which all nutrients are present in adequate amounts, but not in the proper balance.

1. High levels of magnesium or calcium decrease the plants ability to obtain potassium
2. High levels of potassium, ammonium nitrogen, or calcium can induce a magnesium deficiency.
3. Conversely, high levels of magnesium can induce a calcium deficiency.
4. Very high phosphorus levels may induce certain micronutrient deficiencies, such as copper or zinc.
5. Conifers may show little or no response to increases in nitrogen fertility unless phosphorus levels are in balance with the nitrogen.
6. When nutrient imbalance is caused by too much potassium, plant levels are large, but relatively inefficient at photosynthesis. The resulting abnormally high concentration of nitrogen compounds compared to carbohydrates in the leaves makes the leaves more susceptible to fungal and bacterial diseases and drought stress.

The important point is that **fertilizer applications that are not based on soil test results may be a waste of money or may actually do more harm than good.**

Determining Nutritional Requirements - Plants often survive and appear to grow normally under a wide variety of soil conditions without the addition of any supplemental fertilizers. In almost all situations, the addition of one or more nutrients would significantly increase the growth of the plants. There are three ways of estimating how well the nutritional requirements of a crop are being met observing its growth, testing the soil, or testing the foliage.

Deficiency symptoms - The nutrient status of a plant can be determined by observing the length of shoot growth; leaf color, color pattern, and size; and time of leaf fall. A slight nutrient deficiency may reduce shoot growth without producing any other noticeable symptoms. The observer must have enough experience to know what constitutes "normal" growth. In more extreme cases, the visual symptoms may be difficult to interpret for several reasons. Deficiency symptoms of some elements are hard to distinguish. For example, deficiencies of iron or manganese produce an interveinal chlorosis on new leaves. Multiple deficiencies may be difficult to diagnose individually.

Problems not nutrient-related sometimes mimic deficiency symptoms. Bacteria or virus infections, overwatering, high soluble salts, or root damage may all cause symptoms resembling a nutrient deficiency. Therefore, considerable experience is needed to "read" a plant's nutritional status.

Perhaps the most important point to be remembered is that when a deficiency symptom is noticed, some damage has already been done. It is too late to make up the loss in growth and value. Any corrective actions taken only benefit future growth.

Soil reaction (pH) -The reaction of a soil, also called pH, represents its degree of acidity or alkalinity. It is measured on a scale of 0 to 14 with values below 7 considered acidic and values above 7 alkaline. The pH of a soil strongly influences the availability of the mineral elements needed for plant growth.

When the pH of mineral soil is 4.5 or below, aluminum, iron, and manganese are so soluble that they may become toxic to certain plants. Other mineral elements such as nitrogen, phosphorus, potassium, sulfur, calcium, and magnesium may become limiting for plant growth at low pH. In addition, the activity of bacteria is markedly reduced.

As the pH increases, ions of aluminum, iron, and manganese precipitate, and the availability of these elements decreases. If the Ph becomes alkaline, deficiencies of iron and manganese are likely to occur. Under alkaline conditions, phosphorus complexes with calcium to form insoluble calcium phosphorus.

A soil reaction between a pH of 5.5 and 7.5 is favorable for the growth of most plants. Within this range, the essential mineral elements are readily available to most plants, the microorganisms of the soil can carry on their beneficial functions, and aluminum toxicity is not a problem.

Terms commonly associated with pH are:

Term	pH Range
extremely acid	4.5
very strongly acid	4.5 - 5.0
strongly acid	5.1 - 5.3
medium acid	5.4 - 6.0
slightly acid	6.1 - 6.5
neutral	6.6 - 7.3
mildly alkaline	7.4 - 7.8

Usually neutral (unlimed) soils in Northeastern United States range in pH between extremely acid and mildly alkaline. Most plant species grow best in medium acid to neutral soils. Soil pH may vary slightly with soil moisture content and the time of year. Soil pH is usually lowest in mid summer when microbiological activity is the highest.

To prevent burning or damage to tender foliage, it is highly recommended that lime be applied only when the foliage is dormant and dry.

Lime may be purchased in bags or bulk quantities. Bagged lime is usually much more expensive than bulk purchase, but may be necessary in order to obtain small quantities. Lime purchased in bulk and spread by a commercial applicator usually requires the purchase of several tons and an application rate of at least one ton per acre. In 1985 the cost of bulk lime including the spreading fee was $25.00 to $40.00 per ton. The possibility of obtaining a commercial application of lime or fertilizer is greater if one plans ahead. Commercial applicators are likely to be more receptive to spreading small areas during periods such as mid summer to fall when they are not as busy with regular agricultural customers.

If soil pH is too low for optimum plant growth, it can be modified by applying limestone. The amount of limestone to be added depends on the amount of change desired, soil texture, organic-matter content, and form of limestone used. Various forms of limestone have different abilities to modify the acidity of soils. This difference in ability is referred to as the "neutralizing value". All forms of limestone are rated against the neutralizing value for pure calcium carbonate, which has been assigned a rating of 100.

If a soil is too alkaline, it can be acidified by the application of sulfur. The amount to be applied depends on the soil type and the degree of change desired. The approximate amounts of sulfur required to decrease the pH of silt-loam soils are listed in the table that follows:

Changing the pH of soils is best done prior to planting. The material should be spread evenly over the soil and thoroughly incorporated. The maximum amount of lime that should be applied in any season is 3 tons/acre. Nursery soils should be retested in one to three years to determine if additional lime is needed.

Soil Nutrition and Fertilization

Soil Analysis

Testing field soils reveals nutrient deficiencies or imbalances and provides an accurate basis for their correction. Some materials such as lime, sulfur, and phosphorus are most effective if incorporated into the soil, and this is much easier to achieve before the crop is planted. Soil samples should be tested and the required amendments incorporated the year prior to planting in order to allow time for them to produce their desired effect. If this is not practical, then the fertilizer bands around the tree should have the best formulation to correct the deficiencies.

Nitrogen is not regularly tested by most laboratories because of its unstable nature in soils. It is readily leached from the root zone area and is used in large amounts by plants.

If a recent soil test has not been conducted on your land, do so. Your nearest Cooperative Extension office can provide you with a kit for directions on taking the sample and having it processed. The cost amounts to about $5.00. Several other laboratories where a sample can be tested are as follows: (Fees are usually $25.00 or so). Some fertilizer suppliers offer laboratory analysis at a nominal fee.

Agricultural Consulting Services, Inc.
Richard F. Wildman, Pres.
139 Caroline Street
Rochester, New York 14620
Phone: (716) 473-1100

A & L Eastern Agricultural Labs, Inc.
7621 White Pine Road
Richmond, Virginia 23237
Phone: (804) 743-9401

Brookfield Farms Laboratory Assn., Inc.
New Knoxville, Ohio 45871
Phone: (419) 753-2448

W. R. Grace & Co.
Peters Soil Testing Laboratory
570 Grant Way
P.O. Box 789
Fogelsville, Pennsylvania 18051
Phone: (215) 395-7104

Soil Test Laboratory
Oregon State University
Corvallis, Oregon 97331
Phone: (503) 737-2187

If your test is conducted through your Cooperative Extension Program, their personnel can help you interpret the figures but, whatever lab you choose, they can provide additional assistance, such as, lime and fertilizer recommendation.

It might even be helpful to view (get a copy) of your soils chart and take more than one soil sample to coincide with distinct soil types. (The actual soil samples forming a composite from the same soil types rather than co-mingling soil types). Liming and fertilizing needs may differ, but the separate sampling may prove beneficial, since most fertilizing is banded around the individual tree rather than broadcasted.

Subsequent soil samples might be taken a year or two after a liming application has been done. If a fertilizing program is undertaken, (banded around trees), samples may be taken from the drip line area around randomly selected trees. (See section on fertilization.) Don't soil sample the same year you apply the fertilizer or results are sure to be erroneous.

Soil tests do not determine the actual quantity of plant nutrients available in the soil, but determine an index to that quantity such as very low, low, medium, high or very high. Soil properties, climate, and plant species, must also be known in order to convert that index to the quantity of plant nutrients available, and the resultant fertilizer recommendation.

A typical soil analysis will provide you with approximate numbers for the soil composition with comments about their level in the soil for what you want to plant. A cover letter then gives a specific fertilizer/lime recommendation.

FERTILIZER FOR SMALL AREAS

Metal 1 Lb. Coffee Can = 1 Qt.

Weight	Rate/100 sq. ft.	Material	Rate/Acre
30 ounces	1 quart	10-10-10	785 pounds
32 ounces	1 quart	33% ammonium nitrate	870 pounds
40 ounces	1 quart	ground limestone	1160 pounds

Caution! Over Fertilization is harmful.

It is relatively easy to apply too much fertilizer, especially on newly planted seedlings. There will be no response to fertilizer above a certain (usually modest) rate of application; and this rate will vary with species, available nutrients, and soil type. Some of the less nutrient demanding species such as the pines, especially Scotch pine, may not respond to the addition of fertilizer. **Therefore, use of fertilizer above the required rate is wasteful and may harm the environment.**

Excessive use of fertilizer, especially soluble forms of nitrogen such as urea or ammonium nitrate, can injure roots, produce foliage burn, reduce growth, and even cause death of the tree crowns. Some growers with many years of experience find that field observations of tree plantations help them to determine if fertilizer is needed. **But, fertilizers should always be applied according to soil test recommendations.**

Soil testing is essential. It should be done prior to planting the first seedling.

Testing the soil for nutrient availability is generally done for diagnostic purposes after plants are in a poor state of health. Soil tests should be done prior to planting to determine any nutrient deficiencies and soil pH so supplements can be added and worked into the root zone prior to planting. This is especially important for lime and phosphorous. Fall is an excellent time for testing soil since it allows adequate time before planting for the lime to actually change the soil pH.

Sampling requirements. There are two important requirements for sampling. First, a uniform slice be taken to the desired depth (usually the plow layer) and second, the same depth and volume of soil be taken from each spot sampled. A soil probe or auger is best; if not available use a garden spade or shovel. The technique for using a spade is to dig a hole to the sampling depth, cut a ½" thick slice of soil from the face of the hole, and trim both vertical sides of the slice to obtain a strip of soil about 1 inch wide from top to bottom.

Trees. Two samples should be sent to the laboratory: (1) a surface soil sample from the 0-8 inch depth, and (2) a subsoil sample from the 8-16 inch depth. The two samples are needed because these crops obtain many of their nutrients from the subsoil. The samples should be sent in separate mailing bags, with separate, completed information sheets. To keep these two samples together for analyses and recommendations, record both bag numbers on each information sheet.

Obtain a representative sample. Each soil sample should be a composite consisting of the soil from samples taken randomly at several places in the area. The purpose of this sampling procedure is to minimize the effects of local non-uniformity. Take samples that are representative of the plot. Stay away from fence rows, animal grazing areas, old straw or hay stacks, or recently applied commercial fertilizers and the like. If crop land, note if any herbicides had been used, how and when applied and rate. Sub-samples at about 10 locations over the area should be taken for each composite sample. Small or unusual areas should be avoided when the intent is to estimate the mean fertility level of the area. The soil sub-sample should be mixed well in a plastic bag or plastic bucket. Metal containers, especially galvanized metal, will contaminate the sample.

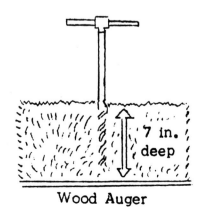

Wood Auger

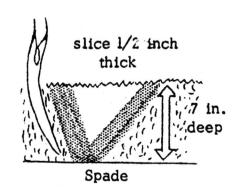

Spade

It is very helpful to prepare a map of the area sampled and location from which samples were taken. This serves as future reference and later sampling after corrective fertilizer or lime applications have been made.

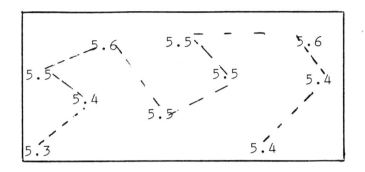

Establish a regular sampling time. For most crops, the soil should be sampled every two to three years. For soils under intensive use, as in high-value cash crops or where nutritional problems persist, the soil should be tested prior to planting each crop. Soil samples may be taken at any time during the year; however, avoid extremely wet soil conditions unless absolutely necessary. It is suggested that successive samples from any given field be taken at about the same time of year.

Prepare a sample for submission to the laboratory. Do not send wet samples to the laboratory. They may leak in the mail, and will be delayed in the lab until they are dry. If it should become necessary to sample wet soil, spread the sample in a thin layer on a clean sheet of waxed paper, and allow to dry out at room temperature before sending it on to the laboratory. Do not use heat to hasten drying. In a wet sample, rapid biological transformations of the amounts and forms of soil nutrients (particularly forms of inorganic nitrogen) can occur. Air drying is an effective means of preserving the field chemical characteristics of the soil sample.

An idea I have always followed is to keep a "retain sample" exactly like the one I submit to the lab. If further testing, or a secondary test need be done, another (almost identical) sample is available. I keep this in a sealed plastic container or canning jar, tightly sealed for not more than two years. You should find out exactly what your lab is going to test for. If you are involved with a nursery operation, it is necessary to test for micronutrients, organic content, etc. Nurseries should test yearly and it is best to use the same lab in order to compare prior results, etc.

Taking appropriate action after soil testing is the most important step in your entire tree-growing operation.

WEATHER AND CLIMATE

Weather is the day-to-day temperature, barometric pressure sunlight, precipitation, and related atmospheric condition. Climate is
the longer range (yearly and longer) pattern of these weather conditions.

Of all the factors influencing growth/survival of plants, weather and climate are the most influential, and the one major condition
that we cannot control or change!

For this reason it is essential that we learn as much as possible about the needs of the plants we want to grow in our respective
areas of the country. Specifically, you need to determine their
tolerance to temperature range, rainfall, sunlight, time of budbreak,
and so on.

Much weather information is available through your nearest weather bureau, library, and/or in printed form from the National Ocean-
ographic & Atmospheric Administration Weather Records Office in
Asheville, N.C. You may get helpful information in your nearest
metropolitan area weather bureau that may not be readily obtained
elsewhere, such as snow and temperature patterns over a relatively
small area.

Some weather data is generalized and may not account for considerable changes that could occur in the micro-climate of your tree
farm. The differences in plant development can be substantial due
to variations in the weather. It is not by accident that Tennessee
and Oregon are major ornamental plant-producing States.

Temperature range has been the basic guide to a plant's hardiness. We know, however, other factors may be more permissive or
limiting. Because temperature patterns have been changing in the
last three decades, the USDA had a new zone hardiness map developed.
This is similar, yet significantly different, from the Arnold Arbor-
etum guide used for so many years. In "Growing Conifer Seedlings,
Transplants, and Trees in an Outdoor Nursery - Book One" we presented a map (U.S.A.) developed by John Sabuco based on "Flora Adaptability to Winter". This interesting and useful map shows the
influence of temperature range in determining what plant types might
do satisfactorily in a specific region.

It must be remembered, also, that botanists and plant geneti-
cists have been working diligently over many years to develop varieties of a specie that can survive poorer climate than was previously
its natural range. This new USDA map follows.

Weather factors can greatly impact on the success of a tree or
nursery business; e.g., should precipitation be lacking, irrigation
must be provided; equipment and labor costs could greatly reduce
profitability. Some plant types won't survive if precipitation is
too meager or too excessive. We have recently observed that Fraser
fir is more sensitive to wet sites than previously believed. They
also succumb in extended periods of drought.

Planting site and soil type and condition have a great influence on the prosperity of a plant under weather influences.

Most farmers of yesteryear kept a diary of weather and climatic conditions. This is a good idea even today. Weather can vary greatly over just a short distance and a weather log of your farm will reveal the deviation from your nearest weather bureau data. You may be amazed at the degree and frequency of variation. Many northern growers have experienced frost injury to certain types of trees in varying site conditions. These observations should serve as a guide as to what to plant, and where, in the future.

It is better to live in harmony with nature than to try to out-guess it. When possible, know the tolerance of your plant types before you plant.

Observation of terrain and site conditions (preferably in early Spring) will help you to select the right specie for the right location. Air and water drainage are two of numerous factors that must be considered to avoid frost injury to crop and disease due to site stress. Many weather-related events may alter your decisions. (See photos on snow and frost injuries).

USDA Plant Hardiness Zone Map

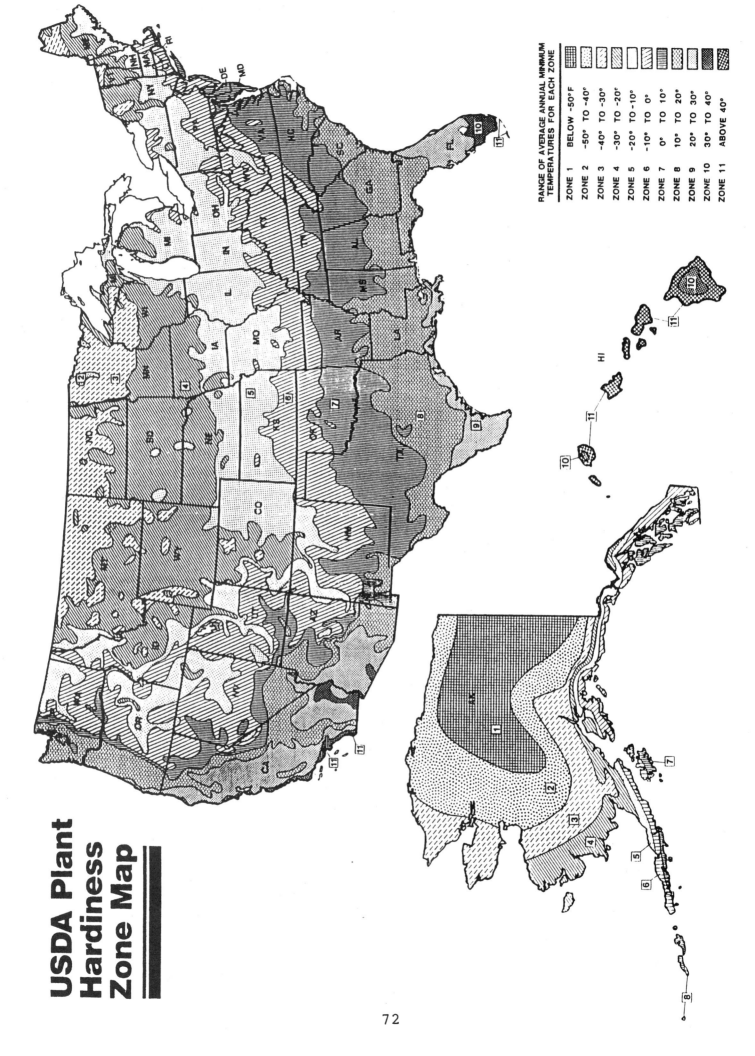

RANGE OF AVERAGE ANNUAL MINIMUM
TEMPERATURES FOR EACH ZONE

ZONE 1	BELOW -50°F
ZONE 2	-50° TO -40°
ZONE 3	-40° TO -30°
ZONE 4	-30° TO -20°
ZONE 5	-20° TO -10°
ZONE 6	-10° TO 0°
ZONE 7	0° TO 10°
ZONE 8	10° TO 20°
ZONE 9	20° TO 30°
ZONE 10	30° TO 40°
ZONE 11	ABOVE 40°

Christmas Tree Terminology

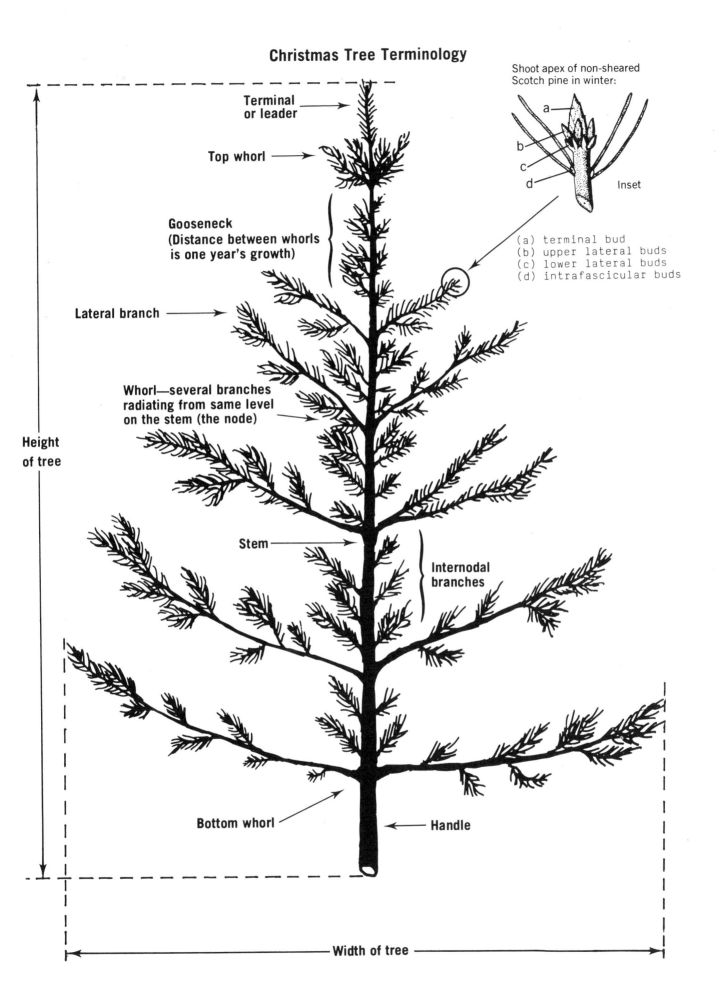

Terminal or leader

Top whorl

Gooseneck
(Distance between whorls
is one year's growth)

Lateral branch

Whorl—several branches
radiating from same level
on the stem (the node)

Stem

Internodal
branches

Height
of tree

Bottom whorl

Handle

Width of tree

Shoot apex of non-sheared
Scotch pine in winter:

a
b
c
d
Inset

(a) terminal bud
(b) upper lateral buds
(c) lower lateral buds
(d) intrafascicular buds

73

SHEARING AND SHAPING - These two terms are sometimes used interchangeably, but frequently, a tree can be "shaped" without being "sheared". At any rate, the sum and substance of this chapter is that people want a nicely shaped and "full" looking tree. Usually, not more than 10% of the pines nor 20% of the spruces and firs will grow that way naturally (partly due to seed source) - you will have to do the shaping.

Every activity in our modern everyday life has its own specific "dress code" and shearing Christmas trees is no exception!

Wear good quality, over the ankle work shoes or farm boots. (Slippers, thongs, bare feet, etc. won't do.) Slacks or jeans are definitely in order. Sharp needles, briars, thornapple, etc. will illustrate the reason. A belt that can hold a hand pruner sheath and a hook for holding a pair of shears is almost mandatory. If a knife is used for shearing, a sheath for it and a sharpening iron may be added to the belt. (I use shears and a knife) - the shears being used for some top work. Leg protectors are frequently used by those using a knife. A work glove is usually worn on the hand holding the knife.

SHEARING TOOLS - Hand pruners (carried with you at all times) should be comfortable to your hand and of good cutting quality. They may be the anvil type or by-pass type. Which type depends on the work you need to perform. We use anvil types because we are frequently cutting heavier branches (Pine varieties), not to mention brush. We feel they are a little more heavy duty. Branch cutting will necessitate a pair of loppers since soreness and injury can result if the task exceeds the capability of the hand pruner.

Hedge shears of good quality (comfortable, lightweight, retain sharpness, easy to clean, adjustable) are essential. Keep at least one (1) extra pair in reserve. Long-handled hedge shears are desirable when trees 6-1/2 feet and over are being worked. A pole pruner may also be needed. A pole pruner becomes a necessity if your trees reach the 8 ft. mark. At 8 ft. and over the tops and, specifically the leader, become difficult to reach. Sometimes, however, the main trunk can be bent over sufficiently to reach the top whorl leader for pruning. Pole pruners come in various lengths so a 5 ft. length may be adequate. Frequently the pole pruning is done as a separate step, hence, the handling of too many tools is avoided.

Shearing knives come in all sizes and quality. The steel in the blade must be hard enough to hold a sharp edge. Sharpening not more than once every half hour of use should be adequate. Length of the knife depends on your own strength and preference. We find a 30" (handle and blade) to be efficient and comfortable to use. A full downstroke will result in the knife going into the ground rather than into a leg. Procedure and techniques are key and should be demonstrated.

We will attempt to give you the basics in the next several pages, but quite often a grower will seek advice and, actual demonstration, from an experienced grower.

Treehaven Evergreen Nursery conducts 1/2-day "Hands On" sessions during July and August to show you procedures and methods. How to shear with a knife, the use and care of hand tools, and the use of electrical shears are part of these sessions. Please contact us if you have further interest.

If trees are of age/size to shear, the fields can benefit significantly from mowing even if a herbiciding program has been initiated. We know from experience that, in a field without any herbicide program and where no mowing has been done, the time (cost) to shear and shape is double what it would be in a mowed field where vegetation and other interference has been removed. It is especially important on younger trees since you do not have to take time chopping grass and weed in order to find the tree.

Several comments are in order before we discuss specific tree types. First, we do not shear a tree that does not need shearing! Do not work trees that are "over the hill". For most growers it means taking the time that could be spent more beneficially on other trees or on other projects. "Working" trees that require excessive effort over a period of years has proven to be foolish in most cases. The actual return on pines and spruce may not equal the value of time and effort required. Badly injured trees (due to mowing, etc.), disfigured trees (brush growing into them), are better cut out and removed from the plantation.

SHEARING OF PINES

New growth on pines comes about from budding on the tips of the branches. That is, the development of the tree comes from shearing, for successive years, each branch which will produce from one to as many as five or more new buds. The leader usually develops five or more (four become laterals and the central bud becomes the new leader). The number of buds on the lateral branches diminish in number from top to bottom of the tree. Most heavy growth on pines occurs on the upper half of the tree.

Spruces and firs not only bud at the tips but, also, along the branch itself. Last year's new buds send out new growth which also buds again in the same manner. Sometimes new buds form all the way back to the trunk. Occasionally, this happens on pine, but rarely. Lime and fertilizer benefit the bud development. Different seed sources within the same specie may behave differently. Trees from some seed sources require less work than others. That is true for all types of trees. Work load for shearing/shaping influences some growers' choices of seed sources of their planting stock.

We do nothing the first year. During the second growing season, usually the third week in July, we will walk the pine rows of the "two-year olds" (between two rows) and prune back any leader over 10" long. This is done with a hand pruner, with the cut on the leader at a 45° angle. Studies have shown that this angle stimulates one of the new buds to become predominant, that is, to become the central leader for the next year's growth. Double leaders should be removed. Any damages or disfigured seedlings should probably be flagged for replacement. If it is obvious that a whorl or partial whorl is closer than 8" to the ground, remove those bottom branches. This is known as "basal pruning". It is difficult to discipline yourself to remove that early growth but it helps greatly by improving the quality of the tree for harvest a few years hence.

The third growing season you will probably have undertaken some herbicide control so that the tree will begin to stand out. Repeat the same procedure as for the two-year olds. Now it is necessary to get the bottom whorls (basal pruning) under control and to make sure that a good "handle" is assured. If those bottom limbs get any larger they may need to be removed with a lopper instead of a hand pruner, thus making this cultural necessity a task. Some growers leave a 10" handle because they cut the tree higher off the ground. We cut within one inch of the ground, thereby eliminating the task of either re-cutting the stump then or later. (High stumps are deadly on mowing equipment, etc.)

Bottom branches too close to the ground get mower injury or sometimes are injured by herbicides. We like to have a complete bottom whorl. That means all four "quarters" of the tree are developing fully without gaps. The seedlings, at an early age, seldom have a complete first whorl, so you might as well remove those branches as early as possible - before you even plant them!

The young pine tree still looks pretty ragged the third year but that will begin to change in the following year. Usually through the third year we still use shears exclusively. There is usually not enough fullness to get full benefit from a knife at three years in the field. However, some people prefer not to use a knife at all.

Two people can handle the shaping job for up to 20,000 pines, during July, when the pines must be sheared. We have sheared pines into August because of time and weather factors but do not advise this. We have observed, over the years, that different seed sources exhibit different growth, healing and new budding characteristics, some early, some later in the growing period. They tend to break bud in the spring at distinct intervals. Since we have ten separate seed sources (and twenty-five in a provenance study) in or near production at our own Hill Top Acres main farm, these differences are noticeable when observed side by side. The trees hardening-off early are sheared first. Those still in the soft tassel or soft (limber) stage are sheared successively depending on the stage of development of the new growth.

Late/very late shearing will induce a prolific bud formation late that year and more evident the following spring. The growth the following spring will appear stunted, but the bud formations for the following year will be prolific (see photo series). Once the growth has "hardened-off", this same year's growth will still develop buds in the profusion previously described. The leader may have bud formation for most of its length. If you go back into the previous year's growth, you will probably get a stub - no growth. This illustrates why a 6 ft. pine tree is considered to be "over the hill" if it hasn't had prior shearing. Simply, you cannot develop adequate branching in one year's time to turn it into a quality tree. Three years are usually needed to achieve a reasonably good quality tree once the tree has been "brutalized" (our own description). Whether a "wildling" or just a neglected pine tree, the bushing-up process can begin even after five years in the field. (Some slower growing French strains of Scotch develop naturally into very nice trees; we still give them a helping hand, however, since they usually don't quite develop the heavy density our customers like).

The fourth through eighth years require a general shearing yearly. Some growers have a market for smaller trees (table top): apartment dwellers, people living in trailer courts, etc. The high quality, of course, needs to be established early so that the smaller tree will have the "prize" look and command the "premium" price.

When the tree reaches the five to six foot height (head high) you should be thinking in terms of finishing the tree for market the next year. The year the tree is to be sold we make sure the tree has the proper shape and any visible defects are corrected or removed. The final summer of shearing is done prudently so as not to remove excessive growth and to have the tree look as natural as possible. We avoid excessive shearing that makes the tree look artificial. Remember, most trees are going to be decorated. Ornaments are usually designed to hang from a branch, not lay against it.

As you proceed into Christmas Tree marketing you will develop your trees in accordance with your customers' wishes. Not everyone's preferences are the same so the customer's desires will guide you. (See section on grades and standards and the taper gauge that has been included for your use.)

Another reason we avoid excessive shearing the year we plan to harvest the tree is that in the event of heavy needle drop (shedding of interior needles) in the fall, the tree will still be of good marketable quality. (Current year's needles and, usually, second year's needles don't shed.)

The tight shearing over several years may result in loose (browned) needles building up in the interior of the tree. This is undesirable because these loose (partially loose) needles tend to shed when they are taken into a home. In the upper Midwest, especially, machines called "shakers" literally shake out the needles either prior to baling or when the tree is opened up on the retail lot. This shaking practice, by machine, has not been needed in our operation. However, on occasion, a tree can be held in an upright position, hitting the butt against the ground, causing most of the loose needles, chaff, etc. to fall out. If a serious problem does develop, you may consider purchasing a mechanical shaker.

Austrian and Red Pine are sometimes tended to prior to shearing Scotch. Because these two specie are not prolific budders, the branch density needs to be established early in the growing cycle. Even if the new growth is only five or six inches, it is best to nip back the tips. Remember, all the new growth will elongate or "stretch" needles on a new stem in contrast to the space between needles on a nature hardened branch. By nipping back the soft growth early, the new bud formation occurs. Studies have shown, too, that the early shearing/shaping procedure provides more buds and healthier buds on the ends of the new growth. This early procedure is accomplished by some growers without even using a pair of shears. It is done by pinching off the top of the soft "candle" with the thumb and the forefinger. (The word candle refers to the early soft branches.)

Later, or real late, shearing (August) of these two specie becomes a difficult and laborious effort. The branches become thick and hard, and even with sharp shears, this makes for a difficult job. Very little investigation has been done as to improving seed sources for Austrian Pine, but many sources are available. Treehaven Evergreen Nursery has begun a seed source study to find more suitable, if not more manageable, varieties of Austrian Pine. Not so stiff and not so heavy branching would be desirable. Better early height growth and better lateral bud development are needed.

Red Pine might even be shaped before Austrian since studies have shown that more fascicle buds will develop if the shaping is done in June rather than in July or later.

Eastern White Pine; Southwestern White Pine (Mexican Border Pine) and Western White Pine (Monticola) prompt some additional comments (all are in the White Pine family). Pruning should begin at an early stage because the bud formation is usually not as prolific as with Scotch Pine, (but more so than Red or Austrian Pine).

The long-needle length tends to hide gaps and low density, but this deficiency may show up in the fall if needle drop is especially bad. The denser the tree is to begin with, the less effect on quality from needle drop. The major concern is that this specie does not respond well to bud development if new growth has hardened. In fact, the fascicle buds may not take form at all, or, it may take a couple of years for new growth to appear. This long-response time is generally unsatisfactory.

In brief, Pine shearing should be conducted on the younger trees before the older. Red, Austrian and White Pines should be done before the Scotch Pine. Older Scotch, especially if sheared real early, can produce secondary growth, and this requires correction. On mature trees ready for market, this adversely affects their shape and general appearance. One general guideline for all pine specie and varieties is to begin when needle length on new growth is 1/2 to 3/4 as long as the old needles. If you have many trees to shear, begin at 1/2 needle growth stage.

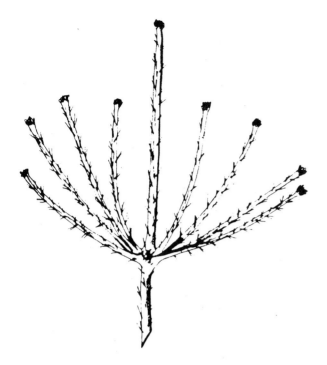

Hopefully, the terminal whorl will consist of a single terminal shoot and six to ten lateral branches.

- Terminal whorls with two or more leaders—The solution is to retain a vigorous leader in line with the main stem of the tree, and cut out the others. If the selected leader is not erect, it may be straightened by tying it to a stub of a cut-away leader.

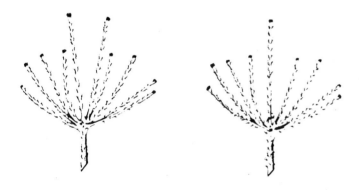

- Terminal whorls with multiple leaders and sub-dominant lateral branches—As in the case of two or more leaders, the most central and most vigorous leader should be selected and the others cut out. Subdominant laterals are likely to turn up and compete with the main leader. For this reason they usually should be cut out. Sometimes they may be kept to serve as lateral branches, in which case it would be necessary to bend them down to a normal branch angle.

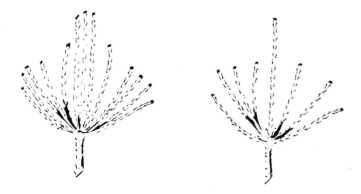

- Terminal whorls without a leader—The problem is solved by training a lateral branch to grow as a terminal leader. Two of the top-most laterals which are opposite, should be tied together near their base, and then the weaker should be cut above the tie.

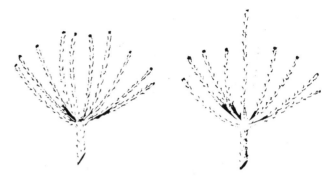

- Terminal whorls with secondary growth—This is a condition caused when a newly-formed terminal bud cluster breaks dormancy and produces a second extension of the main leader in a single season. Second growth arising in this manner is invariably short, weak and rarely forms a satisfactory terminal whorl. The recommended treatment is to prune it off as shown.

- Terminal whorls with too many lateral branches—The condition of an excessive number of lateral branches is commonly the result of shearing the previous year. Scotch pine is very responsive to shearing—often setting 20 or more buds in the terminal cluster. This number of lateral branches in the whorl is far too many. Encountering this situation, the grower should select 8 or 10 that are to be kept, and cut out the remainder. They should be pruned as flush with the main stem as possible.

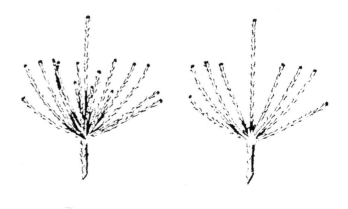

80

A double trunk tree. One part must be cut out if this is ever to become a saleable tree

"Wild" tops of Douglas fir illustrate need for yearly shearing/shaping

SHAPING SPRUCE AND FIR

We tend to think of the spruces and firs in terms of shaping since (unlike the pines) the major part of the densing of the tree is occurring from budding along the interior branches. We prune or shear the outriding tips; shearing severely only to bring the tree into proper shape and taper. The leader is frequently hand pruned.

Shearing/Shaping of spruces can be done year-round. These, like Douglas Firs and other firs, appeal to many growers because their work load can be spread out over much of the year. The summertime after the current year's growth hardens off (gets stiff and hard) is the preferred time. The next best time would be fall, spring and winter in that order.

On the leader, a single, strong bud should be left to form the new leader. All other buds an inch below that bud should be removed by pressing them off using your thumb. By removing all other buds in the immediate vicinity, the chance of double or multiple leaders is greatly reduced.

At the next opportunity look very carefully at a main lateral (or leader) branch of one of your spruces or firs. If you are examining a leader not previously sheared, measure it and find the midway point on its length. Then count all the buds (all around the stem) above the midway point. Then count all the buds below the midpoint. You will find two to three times as many buds on the upper half of the stem as on the lower half. This same approximate ratio holds true for the lateral branches, although, there is not as much budding.

Now that you are aware of this bud relationship, you can mentally set your shearing strategy for any given tree or field of trees. Some trees will be satisfactory with the maximum growth and may not be touched at all. Spruces and firs four, five, six and seven years in the field (from seedling) may not require any shearing other than remedial or touching up at the tips and on the leader. If a tree starts to get thin and leggy, or wild-looking, more severe shearing will be called for. What happens, in effect, is that more inter branches bud and fill out. Of course they will multiply and do the same the next year. Likewise, if the leader is excessively long (perhaps over 12") and the top of the tree is thin, more severe pruning of the leader may be necessary.

Now I want to make some specific suggestions for the firs since their growth and response can vary considerably from one another. No one can answer the question for sure as to how many trees you might shear per hour. Many factors are involved, not the least of which is the size of the tree. Using a knife on pines, is three times faster than shears. Land fertility, seed source of the planting stock and your own work speed are key factors. You will find that working on a sunny day with 85° and 60% humidity is far more draining than a 70° day with 30% humidity. At any rate, a survey of tree growers in Connecticut revealed this:

Tree Height	Number of Trees Sheared Per Hour		
	Least	Median	Most
Less than 3 ft.	20	90	500
3 ft. to 5 ft.	15	60	350
Over 5 ft.	10	50	200

It is important to keep a "shearing" log. This record should show: date, weather, person, hours in field and what field, age, size and specie; number of rows or trees worked, plus any comments. The comments are important because if considerable basal pruning was required, then this greatly reduced the number of trees sheared, and should be noted on the log sheet. This data provides a basis for knowing what your per-tree shearing cost is, and provides a basis for projecting cost as well as demand of your time.

SHEARING AND SHAPING DOUGLAS FIR

Basal pruning is necessary on Douglas Fir as on pines and spruces. Again, early attention to the handle of the tree saves much work later. Douglas Fir respond to shearing better than any other fir specie native to the west. Growth and development of the tree will reveal how good a planting site you have. All the cultural factors are important to raising high quality Douglas Fir in a reasonable time period. Site selection, fertility, healthy uniform planting stock and vegetation control are critical factors. Much more critical than for pine or spruce.

Side shearing may begin a year or two before leader pruning. For developing the popular 6-1/2 ft. tall tree, a good rule-of-thumb is to defer leader pruning until the total tree height first exceeds about 4-1/2 ft. to 5 ft. Then as a part of the shearing operation, cut the leader back sufficiently to reduce the tree height to about 4-1/2 ft. to 5 ft. Trees with exceptionally numerous leader buds can be pruned back a like amount shorter than 4-1/2 ft. to 5 ft. After the first year's leader pruning, an annually pruned leader (length of about 12") should be maintained each year until harvest.

Timing of shearing of market-size trees is important because the cut stems need adequate time to heal over, yet too early shearing may permit excessive Lammas growth (secondary growth in late summer). Mid August is a good time to start.

The illustration that follows relates one procedure for preparing Douglas Fir for market in the Pacific Northwest. This same cultural practice can be followed except that our growing season may be more like nine or ten years from a three year seedling. A large 2-2 transplant would more closely approximate the time span indicated. Once established, however, the growth rate and subsequent development will be essentially the same.

83

Development of a 7-foot Sheared Douglas-Fir in 6 Growing Seasons by the 5' method of Progressive Leader Pruning

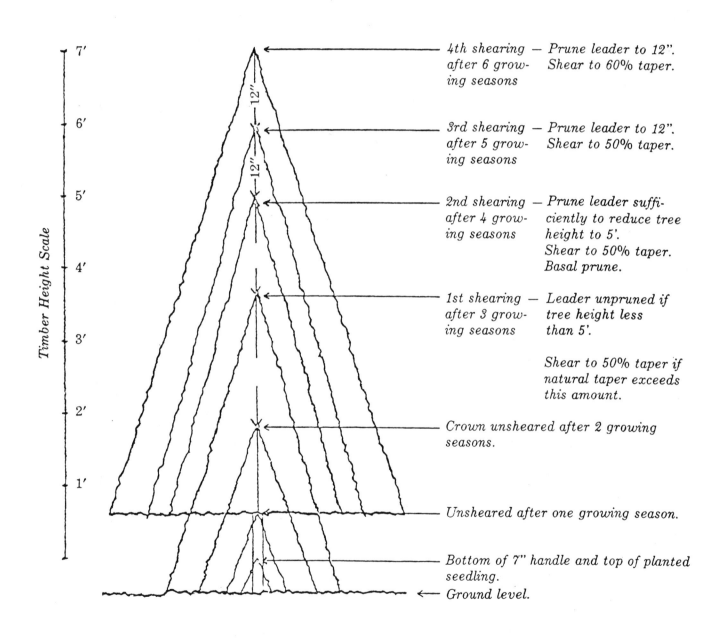

Timber Height Scale

4th shearing — Prune leader to 12". after 6 grow-ing seasons Shear to 60% taper.

3rd shearing — Prune leader to 12". after 5 grow-ing seasons Shear to 50% taper.

2nd shearing — Prune leader suffi-after 4 grow-ciently to reduce tree ing seasons height to 5'. Shear to 50% taper. Basal prune.

1st shearing — Leader unpruned if after 3 grow-tree height less ing seasons than 5'.

Shear to 50% taper if natural taper exceeds this amount.

Crown unsheared after 2 growing seasons.

Unsheared after one growing season.

Bottom of 7" handle and top of planted seedling.

Ground level.

A sheared tree using Saje-Shear. Note quality of west coast Douglas fir

Shearing Douglas fir with Beneke rotary blade

This will never develop into a quality tree

Deer browsed white cedar

SHEARING AND SHAPING BALSAM FIR

For both Balsam and Fraser Fir, the main leader is topped by a center bud that will grow straight up. This bud is surrounded by up to six or more buds that will grow horizontal to form a whorl of branches. On the stem between this year's buds and last year's whorl of branches are scattered smaller buds. Part of these internodal buds grow the same time as the top buds, but grow slower and make smaller branches. The leader buds on branches differ from the main stem leader buds in being smaller with only two lateral buds in a whorl behind the lead bud which keeps branches growing flat. Some varieties of Balsam Fir frequently have a third whorl bud that grows on the lower side of the branch. This is sometimes referred to as a "Double Balsam" effect.

This specie provides a good example of how shock affects behavior of new growth: basal pruning, removal of multiple leaders, trimming of lateral branches, trunk injury, weed/grass interference, general shearing and even leader pruning.

Like Douglas Fir, the top portion of the tree may be thin due to a long leader and thin bud formation. It may be necessary to remove the bare stem and tie up one of the laterals to form a new leader.

Cutting off tip buds stimulate greater growth to lower buds on the stem and to the rest of the tree. The tree becomes so excited when the leader stem is cut that it not only stimulates some buds that would have been left dormant into new growth but, also stimulates some advantageous buds (forms interfascicular buds) to break out of the bark and grow. Advantageous buds before growth cannot be seen except by microscopic inspection of the bark and do not grow under normal conditions.

Anytime the top whorl of buds is cut off the leader, the tips of each branch in the top whorl must be cut off. If not, each branch in this top whorl will be stimulated to turn up and form a new leader.

When pruning the leader, cut at a 45° angle, as with pines, and allow about 1/4" between tip and the first bud. Some growers leave a bud on the north or east side of the leader stem so that the sun will help to straighten it up. Again, as with Douglas Fir, pinch off any competing buds to avoid double or multiple leaders.

We thank Bill Ballagh, Lowville, NY, for some of the comments and suggestions presented here.

SHEARING AND SHAPING FRASER FIR

The preceding comments about Balsam Fir apply basically to Fraser Fir. Fraser has some unique characteristics that should be recognized.

Fraser Fir responds to fertilizer, in fact, the more fertile the soil the better. If your soil is poor, then an ongoing fertilization program is in order. This matter of fertility is mentioned again here because it is the key to growth.

In a leader pruning study at North Carolina University, three variables were compared:

A. Different months of the year for leader pruning.
B. Degrees of cutting back the leader. Removing only the tip just above the highest internodal bud on the leader; removing 1/4 of the leader; removing 1/2 of the leader.
C. Fertilization.

The findings were:

1. The best time to prune, from the standpoint of future leader development, was the late succulent season. The resulting new leaders tended to be straighter, taller, more profusely budded and freer of multiples. The succulent stage occurs in early summer when leader elongation is barely complete and the new growth is still succulent and brittle. Poorest results occurred when the leader was cut in early spring just before the buds burst.
2. Effect of degree of leader pruning on next year's leader development revealed this:
   a. All degrees of leader pruning reduced the length of next year's leader. The shorter a leader was cut, the shorter next year's leader grew.
   b. The shorter a leader was cut, the greater the chances that next year's leader would be dog-legged, multiple or lacking in terminal buds.
3. The effect of fertilizing revealed that nitrogen, lime and sulphur stimulated growth under North Carolina conditions. Nitrogen gave the strongest results.

Because growing Fraser fir is new to most New York State growers and to most growers in the Northeast, the traditional shearing to a line with a basic balsam fir technique is generally followed.

The procedures set forth by Mr. Darwin Pound, a grower of Fraser Fir for 20 years, from St. Louisville, Ohio, merit consideration. Mr. Pound says this:

"We start shearing Fraser Fir the third growing season and with this size tree we try to walk right past them if at all possible. Mother Nature can grow a Fraser Fir better than we can if the center stem stays within limits. This first year of shearing we just cut the top center stem if it is over fourteen inches and one-half the branches on the top whorl as described in Shearing Method Number Three. The fourth year and each year thereafter we use the following one of three methods.

Method Number One - We walk past the tree if top center stem and side branches are within our limits.

Method Number Two - We shear only the center stems on each of the side branches of the second whorl down plus the center stem of the second, third, and fourth whorl down the tree to maintain the right taper. We are allowed to do this minimum of shearing as long as the top center stem is within bounds.

Method Number Three - Shear the second whorl as described above plus cut the top center stem back to sixteen, fourteen, twelve, ten or eight inches according to the density of the overall tree. The thin tree we cut back to eight inches and the thick tree we cut fourteen to sixteen inches long plus we can shear one-half of the stems on the top whorl of the tree.

In order to maintain a balance to the tree, when you have to cut the top center stem you have to cut some of the top whorl. When you cut some of the top whorl, you have to cut the top center stem. We say we cut one-half of the top whorl but when you have four stems, we cut four - when you have five, we cut three - when you have six, we cut three - when we have seven, we cut three or four. The object of cutting only one-half of the top whorl is that it fills the tree in faster and makes the tree thicker. The unsheared side branch will grow six or seven or eight inches. The sheared branch usually grows only two, three or four inches. The following years growth will thicken the tree with this sequence or method of shearing. Also we cut the center stem of each side whorl on down the tree if necessary to maintain the proper taper.

The center stem of this whorl (picture 1) is marked with a yellow twist tie. Now with this center stem being one of five stems at the end of this branch. It is important when cutting this center stem that you do not cut the branch immediately under the marked stem because this smaller stem will continue to grow normally the following year and maintain the desired shape of the tree. If when cutting the center stem marked with yellow twist tie you cut both of these stems, the tree will develop a flat spot on that side.

These Fraser Fir (picture 2) were planted in 1974 and have never been sheared. The tree on the left grew the last four years as twenty-one, sixteen, twenty-three, and twenty inches. The next tree on the right grew twenty-one, sixteen, and eleven inches. The next tree on the right grew twenty-three and one-half, fourteen, and ten inches. I believe we all can agree that these trees could not be sold.

Although my standard shearing method for Fraser Fir is to walk past the tree if at all possible, I think we can say we walked past these trees a few too may times. The top center stem grew beyond the limits set forth in Method Number Three.

It was necessary to shear this tree (picture 3) with eight cuts - the top center stem, three at the top whorl, and four cuts on the second whorl. The yellow twist ties mark each cut except at the top center stem.

Center stem of this whorl is marked with twist tie.

1.

Twist ties mark needed cuts.

2.

Fraser Fir planted in 1974 and never sheared.

3.

Before first shearing   Two years later

Photos courtesy of The Kirk Co., Tacoma, Washington

PLANT DISEASES & INSECTS

Characteristics

A plant disease is any condition in which a plant is different in some way from a normal (healthy) plant in either structure or function. A diseased plant may be shorter or have more branches or fewer leaves than normal, making it different in structure. It may wilt and die prematurely or it may not produce flowers or fruit, making it different in function.

A plant disease has four main features: Disease is a **process**; it does not occur instantly as does an injury. It is **physiological**, affecting all or some of the functions of the plant. It is **abnormal** to the plant. It is **harmful** in some way, even though the harm may not always be immediately detectable.

Three ingredients must be present for a disease to develop:

- a susceptible host plant.

- a disease producing agent (the pathogen), which may be living or nonliving.

- an environment favorable to disease development.

Causes of Plant Diseases

The definition of plant diseases is very broad and encompasses all possible causal agents, including insects; as long as the four criteria cited above are satisfied. For example, insects that produce galls or plant parts are true causal agents of disease. Insects, however, are generally omitted from the area of plant disease and covered in the field of entomology.

Plant diseases are divided into two broad groups based on their cause.

Nonparasitic diseases are caused by factors such as nutrient deficiency, extreme cold or heat, toxic chemicals (air pollutants, weed killers, too much fertilizer), mechanical damage, lack of water, adverse genetic changes, and many others. These diseases cannot be passed from one plant to another. Their control depends solely on correcting the condition (usually something in the environment) that causes the disease.

Parasitic diseases are caused by living organisms that live and feed on plants. The most common causes of parasitic diseases are fungi, bacteria, viruses, and nematodes. A few seed-producing plants, such as the mistletoes, also can cause plant diseases.

Fungi are plants that lack the green coloring (chlorophyll) found in seed-producing plants, so they cannot make their own food. There are more than 100,000 kinds of fungi of many types and sizes. Not all are harmful and many are helpful to man. Most are microscopic, but some, like the mushrooms, are quite large.

Most fungi reproduce by spores, which vary greatly in size and shape. Some fungi produce more than one kind of spore, and a few fungi have no known spore stage.

Bacteria are very small one-celled plants that reproduce simply by dividing in half. Each half becomes a fully developed bacterium. This type of reproduction may lead to rapid buildup of a population under ideal conditions. Some bacteria, for example, can divide every 30 minutes. In 24 hours, a single cell could produce 281,474,956,710,656 offspring.

Viruses are so small they cannot be seen with the ordinary microscope. They are generally found and studied by their effects on selected "indicator" plants. Many viruses that cause plant disease are carried from one plant to another by insects, usually aphids or leafhoppers. Viruses cause serious problems in plants that are propagated by bulbs, roots, and cuttings because the virus is easily carried along in the propagating material. Some viruses can be easily transmitted by rubbing the leaves of healthy plants with juice from diseased plants. A few viruses are transmitted in pollen. The big vein of lettuce virus is transmitted by a soil-borne fungus, and a few viruses are transmitted by nematodes.

Nematodes (or nemas) are small, usually microscopic, worms that reproduce by eggs. Their rate of reproduction depends largely on soil temperature, so nematodes are usually more of a problem in warmer areas. Most nematodes feed on the roots and lower stems of plants, but a few attack the leaves and flowers. They usually do not kill plants, but they do reduce growth and affect plant health.

All nematodes on plants have a hollow spear that they use for puncturing plant cells and feeding on the cell's contents. Nematodes may develop and feed inside or outside a plant. A complete life cycle involves an egg, four larval stages, and an adult. The larvae usually look like the adults but are smaller. The females of some, such as root knot and cyst nematodes, become fixed in the plant tissue and their bodies become swollen and rounded. The root knot nema deposits its eggs in a mass outside its body. The cyst nema keeps part of its eggs inside its body, where they may survive for many years.

Development of Plant Diseases

Parasitic diseases depend on the life cycle of the parasite, which is greatly influenced by environmental conditions, especially temperature and moisture. These conditions not only influence the activities of the disease organism, but they effect the ease with which a plant becomes diseased and the way the disease develops.

91

The life cycle of a pathogen begins with the arrival of some portion (fungus, spore, nematode egg, bacterial cell, virus particle) at a part of the plant where infection can occur. This step is called **inoculation**. If environmental conditions are favorable, the parasite will begin to develop. This stage is called **incubation**. If the parasite can get into the plant, the stage called **infection** starts. The plant is diseased when it responds to the invasion of the pathogen in some way.

A diseased plant, like a sick person, generally shows some symptoms, in fact, a disease often gets its name from the plant's symptoms. The three general types of symptoms are:

- overdevelopment of tissue (galls, swellings, leaf curls).

- underdevelopment of tissue (stunting, lack of chlorophyll, incomplete development of organs).

- death of tissue (blights, leaf spots, wilting, cankers).

Identifying Plant Diseases

Because several different diseases may cause the same symptoms, you can't always identify a plant disease by looking at symptoms alone. Looking at the signs, the structures of the pest, is a better way of identifying a disease. Signs include such things as fungus spores, nematodes or their eggs, and bacterial ooze. Usually you need a microscope or magnifying lens to see the signs. You need more training to find and identify signs than you need to observe symptoms.

Principles of Control

To control plant diseases, you must first consider the three factors involved in the disease: the host plant, the pathogen, and the environment. Then you must consider the cost.

Not all control measures work for all kinds of pathogens. Some hosts will not tolerate some controls, and the environment limits the kind of control measure that can be used and the time it can be used. One categorization of plant disease control methods includes:

- avoidance of the pathogen.

- exclusion of the pathogen.

- eradication of the pathogen (and its vectors).

- protection of the host from the pathogen.

Avoidance and protection are both aimed at keeping the pathogen away from the plant. Exclusion and eradication are directed at the pathogen itself, either by killing it or by preventing it from reaching a host.

Examples of Control

Avoidance: by choosing planting sites and dates of planting, by using resistant varieties, and by employing sanitation, crop rotation, and primordium tip-culture techniques.

Exclusion: by following quarantine regulations supported by adequate inspections to prevent the introduction of pathogens on or in plants or equipment into areas where they do not already exist, and by certifying seed and nursery stock.

Eradication: by roguing (removing) infected plants or plant parts, by treating soil or plant parts with heat, by fallowing fluid, and by using pesticides, for example, in controlling nematodes.

Protection: by using chemical applications, by using proper storage of curing methods for plants and plant products and proper nutritional programs to ensure maximum plant vigor; by employing biological methods such as the use of hyper-parasites, antagonistic microorganisms, or cross-protection techniques for viruses.

Avoidance and exclusion are by far the best methods for controlling plant diseases. Once a plant is infected, it is usually too late to prevent its death or serious reductions in crop yields. Where only part of a crop is diseased, chemical control may prevent further spread. Always weigh the cost carefully before making treatment decisions.

INSECTS

A large number of different insects affect crop plants in a variety of ways. They may cause damage by chewing off foliage; by tunneling or boring into stems, stalks, and branches; by pruning off and tunneling into roots; by sucking the sap from leaves, stems, roots, fruits, and flowers; and by transmitting plant diseases.

These activities result in killed, weakened, and disfigured plants which in turn cause reduced yields, lowered quality, and unmarketable, unsightly plants or their products. Even after harvest, insects continue their damage in stored or processed commodities.

Insects are very adaptable animals with high reproductive capacities. Since they are arthropods, they have external skeletons like suits of armor and three pairs of jointed legs. Many species of insects can fly, and some of these are capable of migrating long distances.

Insects grow through a process of change called **metamorphosis**. Some, like grasshoppers and plant bugs, develop gradually. Their eggs hatch into nymphs that shed their skins, or **molt**, between growth stages, called **instars**, before becoming adults. Others, like beetles, armyworms, and cutworms, change more completely. Their eggs hatch to produce **larvae**, which grow through instars to a **pupal** stage, in which the adult is formed. Plants can be damaged by the immature stages of some insects, by the adults of others, and by both in still others.

Effective insect control is often based on knowledge of the pests' growth habits.

Insects are subjected to limiting factors, or hazards, during their lives. These forces may hold the numbers of a crop pest below the economic level. When the effects of these limiting factors are reduced through natural events, farming methods or other human activities, the numbers of these pests will rise to levels at which damage may occur. The challenge lies in our ability to manage crops in such a way that the injury caused by insects is held to a minimum and to recognize when more direct action, such as pesticide applications, is necessary.

Principles of Control

Controlling insect pests or the damage they do can be considered from two standpoints. One is a short term, direct sort of action; the other is a long range damage prevention program. Either type may be needed, depending on the circumstances. As needed information becomes available, we should arrive toward total crop management systems that approach the ideal of damage prevention. Whether it is short or long term, however, an effective crop insect control program should follow some logical sequence.

Steps in Crop Insect Control

Detection. Too often, controls are attempted only after the damage has been done. It is important to develop and maintain a survey or detection plan to provide early warning about pest populations. Some of this warning is made available by the Cooperative Economic Insect Survey operation in most states. Pest management projects, scouting programs, and individual grower vigilance are other techniques.

Identification and Diagnosis. Most growers learn to recognize the most important insect pests associated with their crops, but, as mentioned previously, unfamiliar or new pests may appear occasionally. Identification aids, publications, and pictures can be helpful, but the best course of action is to call on competent consultants (see "Pest Control Principles").

Sometimes insect infestations show up as damaged plants without any signs of the responsible insect itself. In these cases, a diagnosis must be made to determine whether the symptoms are due to insects or to some other cause.

Economic Evaluation. Determining the economic significance of an infestation (in terms of yield and crop quality) is essential. It can be done by considering the numbers and stage of development of the pest, the stage of growth and economic potential of the crop, the numbers of parasites and predators, the weather conditions, and all the

Cultural Control. These methods relate to crop rotations, tillage practices, planting dates, field locations, drainage, fertility, and all other crop culture procedures that might adversely affect insect pests, either directly or indirectly.

Using insect-resistant or tolerant genetic lines of crops might also be considered a cultural control method although it usually is considered a biological method.

Biological Control. Predators, parasites, or diseased organisms can be released into a pest population to help stabilize it. The release of sterile males and the use of pheromones, insect growth regulators, and sterilants are other control methods that can be considered biological methods, even though they sometimes involve the use of chemicals.

Mechanical-Physical Control. The use of traps, barriers, light, sound, heat, cold, nuclear radiation, and electrocution are some physical control methods. Such methods have limited application in crop insect control, except where storage pests are involved.

Legal Control. Quarantines, inspections, embargoes, compulsory crop or product destruction, and similar actions taken under the provisions of federal, state, or local laws and regulations are examples of legal control measures.

Chemical Control. Chemicals can be used to kill, repel, attract, or sterilize insects or to interfere with their normal behavior. The most widely known chemicals used in crop insect control are insecticides. Little use is made of sterilants, repellents, or attractants at this time.

Integrated Control. This method involves the use of a combination of practices that fit into an effective program of pest reduction. An integrated program usually involves the selection of planting and harvest dates and resistant varieties, the use of pest-specific insecticides, and the encouragement or distribution of biological control agents. It usually includes elements of pest management, so insecticides are applied only when numbers of pests observed reach economic thresholds.

Increasing environmental concerns about pesticides and their use, plus ongoing developments and products for natural pest control might prompt you to retain an integrated pest management specialist. Other books written by us contain much more information on this subject.

The foregoing discussion should help you understand disease and insects and to present ways of dealing with them other than just with a spray tank and pesticides. In our nursery, we select seed sources to provide the most desirable physical traits and that present the least cultural problems. We try to avoid varieties that are prone to insects and diseases which, we know, are prevalent in the Northeast U.S. Healthy trees resist insects and diseases. Proper planting site means planting the seedling in a place where it can grow best without disadvantage due to its environment. Avoidance and/or preventiion is the best policy to follow in regard to diseases and insects.

other many factors that might affect the impact of the pest insect on the crop. In many cases, **economic thresholds** have been determined. In such instances, fields should be surveyed properly by the grower or the scout to accurately gauge the insect population. This determination is one of the important pieces of information necessary for making decisions involving economic thresholds.

Knowledge about Life Habits of Pests. When an insect pest is new to an area, it may be necessary to conduct research or to make observations to learn about its habits so control methods can be developed. This process may range all the way from making a few observations to a long range, complex research project.

Development and Improvement of Control Methods. Obtaining accurate information about the habits and economic importance of a pest will lead to the development and selection of the best combination of practices to minimize damage. Continued experience will lead to a refining of the techniques that work best for specific locations and situations. This process also may be very simple or highly complicated and may extend over many years.

Prescriptions or Recommendations. Ultimately, a decision must be made based on all available information. It may be a recommendation by a professional advisor or consultant to a farmer, a legal order or prescription by a government official, or simply, a decision made by a grower after making certain field observations. The decision may involve a long-range crop management plan or it may simply involve the selection of a certain rate of a pesticide.

Implementation. The success or failure of a plant control or management program depends on its execution. Crop rotations must be followed. Certain tillage practices must be carried out on time. The proper variety must be planted. The right pesticide must be applied at the right time at the right rate in the right place. If any part of a total management program is neglected, the whole job may fail.

Evaluation, Recording, and Improvement. Most human effort can be improved. To bring about changes in a pest management program, it is necessary to measure the effectiveness of individual practices. This can be done, for example, by making careful observations and taking notes, by leaving check strips, or by determining yields or quality improvement.

It is also important to keep accurate records of dates, weather conditions , and similar information related to pest control practices, especially pesticide application. Such records will be valuable not only for possible legal purposes but for use as an action guide should the same problem recur.

Methods of Crop Insect Control

A great deal of natural control goes on in most pest populations. This natural control results from the hazards, or limiting factors referred to above. The controls described below include only artificial or man-manipulated measures.

96

Some disease problems can be "nipped in the bud", so to speak, with some preventative medicine. Here are a few suggestions:

Pine stumps (portion remaining in the ground) are a prime source of Pales Weevil. At the time of cutting during the harvest season, or sometime in very early spring (March) treat all fresh stumps with a wood preservative. This prevents entry of weevil for breeding purposes. We used to use "Penta", Pentachlorophenol, in kerosene and drench the stumps using a detergent bottle with a pull-up spout. Penta has been banned. The stumps can also be painted or sprayed; old crankcase oil can be used if you paint the stumps. Thin with kerosene or diesel fuel, if necessary. If stumps (trees) are infected, then Lindane is the best answer. Consult literature for timing, dosage, etc. It is much easier to treat stumps than to fight the disease.

Because chewing insects invade the pines on a fairly regular basis, we use a dormant spray in late March or early April. Dormant oil or lime-sulfur are effective. We prefer lime-sulfur because, we believe, it is more effective. We do not spray all tree areas every year. When we see signs of increased insect outbreaks, treatment before or immediately after spring planting frequently brings it under control. Dormant oil is less hazardous to use so most people use this. Dormant sprays kill emerging chewing insects and discourage entry into needles or stems.

We have a 3-gallon spray tank charged at all times (small quantity) from late spring until fall. This is used for "spot spraying" only: (Sawfly, Tortoise Scale). We use Sevin because it contains a "sticker", hence, stays on foliage/branches for a sufficient period of time to kill the pest. Malathion is also a broad spectrum insecticide that is effective in combating many diseases.

Indiscriminate use of chemicals can be worse than not using them at all. We try to avoid upsetting the balance of nature; therefore, only warranted and careful use of chemicals should be your guideline. The section on Toxicity will provide some insight into environmental concerns and why you must be aware of potential hazards in the use of pesticides.

When the time comes that you identify an insect or disease in your plantation, you first must decide the consequences of that finding. Consult literature promptly. For example, every three to four years we seem to get a serious outbreak of Sawfly (see photo). These "caterpillars" can devour a field of 500 trees in three or four days. (They eat second-year needles only, not new growth). They move from one tree to the next. Some years, however, they attack one, two or just a few trees and seem to die out. (Birds and other predators probably eat them). Most disease situations are slow to evolve, as stated earlier, but insect outbreak can occur quickly and require regular monitoring.

Chemicals approved to combat problems are changing regularly. Harmful materials are being banned regularly due to toxic effects and environmental contamination. The section on Toxicity and Environment will bring these concerns into focus. Many products have been banned entirely or have become restricted: DDT, Chlorodane, 2,4D, - 2,4,5T, Pentachlorophenol and Endrin are a few. Each state is different so you should consult Cooperative Extension to get the most up-to-date bulletin on the subject.

In New York State "Cornell Recommendations ... For Pest Control For Commercial Production and Maintenance of Trees and Shrubs" gives a listing of those banned and/or restricted. Contact Cooperative Extension for your copy. This biennial publication from Cornell University is a must for many reasons.

In addition to Cornell Recommendations ..., consult bibliography in back of book for sources of insect and disease information. In New York State a series of leaflets are available providing current information and control measures for many insects; again, contact your Cooperative Extension office. The Northcentral Experiment Station also has leaflets on specific insects/diseases. (Their "How to..." Series). Their address is 1992 Folwell Ave., St. Paul, MN 55108.

More discussion and reference material will be found in the "Addendum to Basics of Growing Christmas Trees".

LARVAE ENLARGED ABOUT 3X

POISONING HAZARD TO HONEY BEES OF INSECTICIDES AND MITICIDES ON BLOOMING CROPS

Use Rating	Residual Toxicity	Material
Highly toxic to honey bees at any time. Severe losses may be expected if present at time of treatment or within a day or two thereafter.	High, 1 day to 2 weeks	acephate (Orthene), aminocarb (Matacil), bendiocarb (Ficam), carbaryl (Sevin 80 S, Sevin 50 WP), chlorpyrifos (Dursban, Lorsban), Diazinon, dimethoate (Cygon, De-Fend), fensulfothion (Dasanit), fenvalerate (Pydrin), fenthion (Baytex), Guthion, isofenphos (Oftanol, Amaze), lindane, malathion, methidathion (Supracide), methomyl (Lannate, Nudrin), Penncap M, permethrin (Ambush, Pounce, Pramex), phosmet (Imidan), resmethrin.
Moderately toxic. Can be applied in either evening or early morning when honey bees are not foraging, but not directly on bees in the field or on colonies.	Moderate, 3 hours to 1 day	carbaryl (Sevin 4 oil, Sevimol), demeton (Systox), disulfoton (Di-Syston), endosulfan (Thiodan), ethoprop (Mocap), oxamyl (Vydate), oxydemetonmethyl (Metasystox-R), phorate (Thimet), phosalone (Zolone), temephos (Abate), thiocarb (Larvin).
Relatively nontoxic. Can be used around bees with a minimum of injury.	Low, 1 hour to 1 day	amitraz (Baam, Mitac), Bacillus thuringiensis (Dipel, Thuricide, Bactur), carbaryl (Sevin SL, Sevin XLR), cyhexatin (Plictran), dicofol (Kelthane), dienochlor (Pentac), diflubenzuron (Dimilin), ethion, hexakis (Vendex), methoxychlor (Marlate), oil (dormant superior types), pyrethrum - natural, rotenone, sulfur tetra-difon (Tedion), trichlorfon (Dylox), plus most fungicides and herbicides.

VEGETATION CONTROL

The purpose for controlling grass, weeds, brush surrounding vegetation is to provide a more favorable environment for your seedlings and trees.

Unwanted vegetation deprives crops of water, light and soil nutrients. Weeds often serve as hosts for crop diseases and they may produce a haven for insects, sometimes to over-winter.

The benefits of a weed-free vegetable or flower garden are known to everyone. These same benefits to the Christmas Tree grower mean higher quality and fewer years growing time.

In a large acreage situation the ways and means that are needed to give good ground control vary considerably depending on the nature of the ground cover, terrain, field conditions, size of the area, size/age of the seedlings/trees and other factors. The grower's resources frequently have a bearing on the ultimate measures and procedures used. (Money, time, labor, equipment available, "know-how", etc.)

One to two years can be erased from a growing cycle. A tree's quality relates directly to its value. The better the quality, the more it is worth. It may be a matter of just "upgrading" your trees to be more competitive with a nearby competitor, or simply to develop a reputation of having "the best trees around".

In some areas of the country a "bare ground" policy can be employed, i.e. the plantation areas are kept completely weed-and-grass-free. This ultimate control is done chemically and is a continuous cultural procedure. Most growers will not do it because of soil conditions (drainage), slope and erosion conditions, time and cost commitment, problems with mud and equipment at harvest time, fear of water contamination, etc. Slope and poor "perk" of the soil (heavy soil) are the principal deterrents.

Vegetation control immediately around your trees is desirable in most cases. (See Chapter on Insects and Diseases). This is especially true of Douglas Fir and all the true firs, they are especially light sensitive.

Smaller sizes of some true fir seedlings can benefit from the partial shade of ground cover the first year provided it is not tight grass and tall weeds over 12" or so.

Several other major advantages of vegetation control is to provide a pleasant appearance to your tree areas. This is especially important if you plan to wholesale trees. Tree areas "show" much better if mowed.

Rodent injury in a mowed field is generally much lower than where little or no practices are employed. The isle and field areas become more exposed to fox, hawks, and other predators that feed on field mice.

A mowed retail area (U-Cut) is much better appearing and has less annoyances than where vegetation is not controlled. Weeds and grasses that grow into the trees are unsightly and undesirable to the buyer. The intense competition of grasses and weeds is also injurious to limb and bud formation in lower whorls of branches. (See Photo).

Where Morning Glory is prevalent, vegetation control around a tree may become essential. Vines like these are unsightly and can be injurious or even kill a tree. Vines can literally strangle a tree. We mow on a continuous basis for all the aforementioned reasons and also to control brush that encroaches from the perimeter of our fields. You may want to use some herbicide control in addition to mowing of brushy areas. This is especially recommended where initial ground preparation is being undertaken. Any area with brush and trees in abundance will require working these out of the ground before any planting is undertaken. Generally it is easier and in the long run, less costly, to adequately prepare the ground beforehand than to try to do it on a continuous basis after planting. A brush control herbicide such as Weedone 170, or Weedone BK-32 sprayed on fresh mowed stumps and whips will provide longer lasting control. Most brush is not killed by mowing. It is only controlled and the problem is an ongoing one.

Some vegetation besides brush can become a major problem. Milkweed and Goldenrod are two that can cause future insect problems and tree injury. Both can adversely affect the value/quality of a tree. The tall strong stems of Goldenrod grow into the tree and injure branches and buds by rubbing and even breaking small branches in the tree. Milkweed infestation results in the silk (seed) being dispersed in October/November and being blown into trees. This can become unsightly and even result in loss of harvest. Fields having severe infestations should be plowed under and then disked to give a smooth surface. A ground cover can then be planted. This may not eliminate either one entirely as the seed/roots can regenerate. Selective spraying in the late summer with a 2% solution of Roundup has been effective. A summer mowing just prior to the pods maturing is necessary. Goldenrod between rows is readily controlled by mowing also!

Excessively heavy ground cover might necessitate reworking of the ground with a less competitive ground cover.

Some areas require extensive preparation. Read the section on "Site Preparation".

"Wind Rows" to create sheltered areas are not always the best procedure to follow. Most tree specie do not tolerate shade well. As a wind row matures (Red Pine, etc.) the shade and shelter increases. Wildlife and brush also make their presence known. These windbreaks can also cause excessive snow accumulations in severe winters resulting in moderate to total damage to some trees. (See Photo.)

Also, wind rows hamper wind drainage that is vital to eliminate or reduce possible frost damage in late spring/early fall. In short, treed, wooded and windbreak situations can negatively affect Christmas Tree Growing areas. Grand Fir and

101

several other true firs have varying tolerance for shade but most pines, spruces and Douglas Fir do not. For example, a spruce will shed its needles readily, after being cut, on the side of the tree that was shaded. Excessively shaded areas also seem to encourage more disease problems as well as predator problems. (Creates a haven for other life forms).

Perimeters of tree areas tend to get neglected, especially if large trees or forested areas are adjacent. Wild raspberry, Goldenrod, brush, etc. need to be mowed and, in some instances, controlled chemically. A 2% solution of Roundup in the late summer controls wild raspberry, multiflora rose, other viney vegetation and brush. It is also effective on poison ivy. Spring or summer control of poison ivy can be best accomplished with Amitrol T. Using this chemical may be desirable since it does not remove all the vegetation, (selective).

Mechanical control by mowing is a job to be repeated, perhaps, two to four times in the course of a season. This is why chemical weed control, at least in part, is practiced by most growers. Black plastic and, better yet, a roof shingle can be helpful in controlling grass and weeds immediately around a new seedling. (See illustration). This may prove prohibitive on a large scale, however. Mowing both directions ("Check-Row") is practical by some growers. (See Photo). We do this in some areas, but not in all. Basal herbiciding controls vegetation adequately.

The mechanical equipment you use (purchase) must be adequate to do the job effectively and with time/cost considerations in mind. We recently purchased new mowing equipment because it would enable us to reduce our mowing costs by 60%. One pass between a row of trees, better mowing speed, better maneuverability, better traction on soils and slopes, fuel efficiency (diesel) and last, but not least, the overall time involved were the benefits. (Accelerated depreciation and investment credit were also motivating factors). (See Photo). Since we hire men to do much of our mowing work, efficient mowers became a great cost reduction measure.

Small areas might require other mechanical equipment. Sickle bar mowers and walk-behind rotary mowers are very effective.

Besides eliminating competition, herbicide use around trees reduces the likelihood of predator damage/injury.

Some weed types even have an adverse effect (through leaching) on neighboring plants. This has been found true with fescue turf around pines. Some weeds such as ragweed cause personal irritation and distress. Poison ivy and havens for bees are combated by mowing also.

The use of a mulch has proven to be effective in shading and smothering undesirable foliage around the plants. This mulch may be wood or a similar biodegradable material. A mixture of lime and fertilizer banded around the plant may become necessary, however, since decomposing materials such as these draw nitrogen from the soil with a tendency to have an acid effect on the soil.

Thin and bare lower branches due
to weed and grass interference.

Brush, double stems, and errant
branches removed for proper development.

Shielded herbicide applicator in field of two-year old Virginia pine. Photo
by T.S. Davis, Forester and J.T. Reid, Engineer. University of Georgia, Athens.

Hand weeding is employed for weed and grass control in seedling or transplant beds but not in plantation practice.

Before we get to specific chemical control measures, a few words about weeds and grasses will be helpful. Their growth characteristics provide insight for their control.

These (undesirable) plants can be classified as annuals (one year cycle), biennial (two year cycle), perennials (same plant grows from year to year) and woody plants (trees, brush, vines, etc.).

Annuals and biennials reproduce from seed while perennials may reproduce from seed but, also, by roots, rhizones, stolons, and tubers. This is also true for (what we refer to as) brush and woody plants. Vines reproduce from basal sprouts and root suckers as well as seed.

Examples of the above weeds are:

- Annuals - Crabgrass, Pigweed, Purslane, Lamb's-Quarters.
- Winter Annuals - Annual Bluegrass, Common Chickweed, Groundsel, Shepard's-Purse.
- Biennial Weeds - Wild Carrot.
- Perennial Weeds - Perennial Grasses, Milkweed, Goldenrod, Dandelion.
- Brush and Woody Plants - Wild Raspberry, Sumac, all forms of bushy shrubs as well as trees. (Maple and Poplar readily invade plantations).

Since a whole book can be written just on weeds and grass plants, we suggest you refer to other literature for more indepth study.

One excellent source for weed identification is: "Weeds of the North Central States", Circular # 718, Univ. of Illinois, Ag. Exp. Station, Urbana, Illinois, Reprinted 1977. Some chemical companies have charts of grasses and weeds: Lesco Chemical Co., Stauffer Chemical Co., and Monsanto Co. can be contacted directly. (See listing of chemical suppliers in "Addendum to Basics of Growing Christmas Trees").

CHEMICAL VEGETATION CONTROL - HERBICIDES

The more you learn about weeds and other plants, the better you can understand the function of various chemical compounds. Likewise, it is essential that you know how a particular herbicide works in order to evaluate its effectiveness.

For example, Roundup is used as a folar spray, i.e., it is absorbed by the plant through its actively growing tissue and translocated to the roots, stopping the photosynthesis process. Although it has killed all existing foliage in a particular spot, it has not killed weed seed or anything under the ground. What happens is that the seed that was prevented from germinating before now has a chance to do so; also, surrounding vegetation may invade that spot because there is nothing there to prevent it.

Similarly, a compound such as Simazine (Princep) may be used where annual weeds predominate and, at a time (early spring), when Roundup would not be effective. Kerb (Pronamide) is effective in cold weather but does poorly in warm weather because it volatizes (escapes into the atmosphere).

To understand these chemicals better, it will be helpful to know the forms they are available in and how they function. Insecticides, fungicides and other compounds are included in the section on Pesticides and Toxicity.

FACTORS AFFECTING HERBICIDE RESULTS

Since soils and circumstances vary greatly, it may be helpful to have more awareness of factors affecting herbicide activity.

Soil Factors - Organic matter in soils limits herbicide activity. Soils with high organic matter content require higher rates of herbicides for effective weed control than do soils with low content. Most herbicide labels include charts showing the rates to be used on soils with varying levels of organic matter.

Soil texture also affects herbicide activity. Soils with finely divided particles (silts and clays) provide more surface area than coarser soils (sands). High herbicide rates are generally used on clay or silt and low rates on sandy soils.

Soil acidity - The activity of some herbicides is influenced by soil acidity. Chemicals such as atrazine and metribuzin are more active in soils that are less acid (higher pH).

Environmental Factors - Soil moisture and rainfall affect herbicide activity and disappearance from soil and plants. Good soil moisture conditions allow the highest levels of herbicide activity. Dry conditions may cause the herbicide to evaporate, whereas wet conditions may keep the herbicide from contacting soil particles. Warm, moist soil may cause herbicides to disappear through microbial activity and chemical reactions. Rainfall causes soluble herbicides to leach downward into the soil profile, a process that may be desirable with relatively insoluble herbicides and undesirable with more soluble herbicides (due to possible crop injury). Heavy rainfall may result in poor weed control or possible crop injury, depending on the relative solubility of the herbicide.

Rainfall is needed to carry surface-applied preemergence herbicides down into the soil where weed seeds are germinating. Soil moisture is needed for weed seed germination so seeds can absorb lethal amounts of herbicide. Rain during or soon after postemergence applications may wash herbicides from leaf surfaces, resulting in poor weed control.

Humidity affects herbicide penetration and absorptioin. High relative humidity indicates favorable soil moisture conditions for rapid plant growth, a time when plants are very susceptible to herbicide effects.

Dew on the weeds or crop at the time of herbicide application or formed on the plant shortly after application may increase the activity of some herbicides but decrease the activity of others, depending on how quickly the chemical is absorbed by plants and how it kills plants.

Temperature affects the rate of plant growth and plant susceptibility to herbicide effects. In addition, some herbicides will evaporate quickly at high temperatures.

Light may break down some herbicides if they are left on the soil surface for extended periods.

Other Factors - Plant species and varieties - Perennial plants are generally more difficult to kill than annual plants. Repeated applications may be required to destroy infestations of perennial weeds. Translocated herbicides are more effective than contact herbicides because they move into all parts of the plant, whereas contact herbicides kill only aboveground plant parts.

One weed may respond differently to different herbicides, and slightly different weeds within the same species may respond differently to the same herbicide.

To minimize herbicide residues in the soil, employ these practices:

-   Apply the lowest practical rate of herbicide.

-   Apply the herbicide uniformly, avoiding double coverage. Equip sprayer nozzles with check valves and quick-closing cutoff valves for turns. Shut off the applicator when turning.

-   Select crop sequences that are tolerant to the herbicide used on the previous crop.

-   Rotate herbicides when the same crop is grown continuously and rotate herbicides on all crops grown in a rotation.

Spraying equipment and accessories are available in many forms and capacities. The size of the job or overall workload will dictate what piece or pieces of equipment are most efficient and cost effective. Back-pack, canister (1,2,3 gal. sizes) and/or "solo"-type units are a minimum requirement for insecticide or herbicide work. Larger equipment may be needed depending on the size of your operation and/or "size" of the problems you have to solve.

Using your equipment to deliver the proper amount of chemical in the correct manner is essential. Improper use of chemicals and equipment can cause mortality to trees or total failure of the operation.

A few of many chemicals you may need in growing Christmas trees

Spray rig for field & nursery use

Field mowed earlier, and then herbicided in "rows" for spring planting

Killing milkweed with Roundup in late summer before pods mature

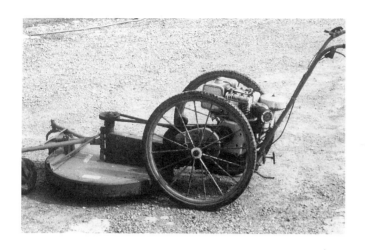

Walk-behind Roof Mower

Front-mounted mower on Honda ATV

A John Deere 750 diesel tractor with rear rotary mower can do a lot of work in a short period of time

A portion of a roof shingle or plastic (posted sign) square makes for good ground cover control

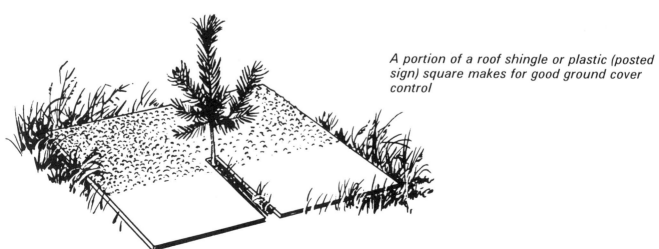

APPLICATION EQUIPMENT

The rapidly expanding use of pesticides places increasing emphasis on the need for understanding the proper care and calibration of spray equipment. Precise control of the amount of chemical applied is essential to obtaining efficient control of the pest involved and to avoiding damage to desirable plants and animals in the area. Applying too little chemical wastes time and materials; applying an overdose adds to the cost and may leave dangerous residues.

Care and calibration go hand-in-hand. Before any sprayer can be reliably calibrated, it must be in good mechanical condition, in fact, inspecting the equipment is the first step in calibration. Sprayers are particularity susceptible to poor maintenance, which is costly in terms of excessive replacement of parts and poor control over application of the pesticides. Pesticides may be corrosive, so thorough cleaning after each use is essential.

The preliminary inspection should detect any loose bolts or connections. Check hoses and transmission lines for general condition and evidence of leaks. Inspect strainers and screens and clean them if necessary. Replace any parts that are worn or damaged.

THE TANK

The sprayer tank should be of a material that cannot be corroded by the solutions handled. Fiberglass and stainless steel tanks are very corrosion resistant and satisfactory for most chemicals. Plastic coated tanks are also corrosion resistant, but they are less durable than the fiberglass or stainless steel ones. Cracks or chips in the coating will expose the base metal to corrosion. Metal tanks can be used for non-corrosive solutions if precautions are taken to prevent rust and scale. Whatever the material, the tank should have a large opening to allow for thorough inspection and cleaning.

THE PUMP

Roller and piston pumps are the types most commonly used on agricultural sprayers. Gear, vane, or diaphram pumps may be used for special applications.

The pump must supply the solution to the distribution system under pressure and at a reasonably even flow. Its capacity must be sufficient to supply the nozzles and agitator, plus a slight excess to operate the relief valve. It is wise to select the pump slightly oversize to allow for some loss of efficiency due to wear.

Whether basal spraying herbicides or spraying for insect pests, the nozzle used may govern effectiveness. It may enable the operator to develop a technique using one nozzle that may not be effective with another. Illustrations of basic spray patterns are shown below. Some spray equipment suppliers offer more sophisticated nozzles. Spraying Systems Co., for example, has various angle patterns and nozzles covering a wide range of orifice size.

NOZZLES

Nozzles should be selected to give the proper particle size, spray pattern, and application rate within the recommended range of pressures. Each nozzle is rated as to application rate at a specified pressure and ground speed. These two factors can be varied, within limits, to change the application rate. Too high pressure on a given nozzle will result in a small particle size and a distorted spray pattern. Excessive drift is a symptom of this condition. Pressure that is too low results in large droplets and an incomplete spray pattern and uneven coverage.

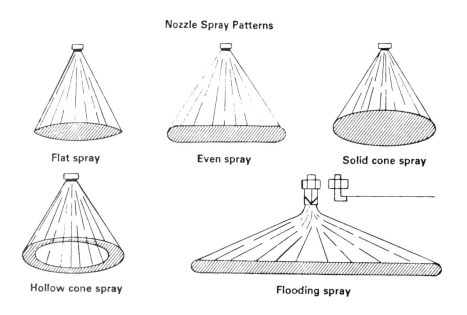

Nozzle Spray Patterns

Flat spray   Even spray   Solid cone spray

Hollow cone spray   Flooding spray

The flat spray nozzle produces a rather coarse spray in a fan-shaped pattern. It produces even coverage when overlapped with other nozzles in boom sprayer applications. It is suitable for most field weed control and some insect control where penetration of the foliage is not necessary. A wide angle nozzle with this pattern can be operated close to the ground to minimize drift.

The even spray nozzle applies a more uniform coverage across its pattern than the flat spray nozzle. It is used for band applications in row crops where there is no overlap from adjacent nozzles.

Solid and hollow cone nozzles give a smaller droplet size than the flat or even spray ones and are used for insect and disease control where penetration of the foliage is desired and some drifting is not objectionable. The round pattern does not produce an even coverage when placed in line on a boom.

The flooding spray nozzle produces a wide pattern and is used close to the ground. It operates at low pressure and the danger from drift is very low.

Spray pattern angle, spacing on the boom, and height from the target area must all be considered to get the proper overlap for uniform coverage.

110

Rate of Application

Application rates of most chemicals are quite small, yet the spray equipment must apply the chemical uniformly over the area to be covered. The chemical is mixed with a carrier, usually water or oil, to facilitate uniform distribution. The amount of carrier varies with the chemical and the area to which it is applied. **Read the label on the chemical container for recommendations.** Calibrate the sprayer to apply the proper amount of carrier; then add the chemical to the carrier in the right proportion for the desired application rate. Sprayers that use air as a carrier, such as mist blowers and some bi-fluid systems, require calibration of the liquid system to supply the proper amount of concentrate to the air stream.

Hand sprayers should be calibrated before applying any materials. Calibration for herbicide application is simply making a trial on a known area and determining the application rate. The method below is easy, quick, and accurate if measurements are made carefully. The procedure is for knapsack (backpack) sprayers but will also work with most hand sprayers.

Simplified Sprayer Calibration

1. On an area that best represents the average topography for the area to be sprayed, measure and mark off the Calibration Distance that coincides with your band width, if band applying, or your nozzle spacing (width covered by single nozzle) if broadcast applying. See Table 1.

Calibration Distance = _____ Feet

2. Fill the sprayer with water only and record the number of seconds required to walk the Calibration Distance at a comfortable, steady speed while spraying and pumping to maintain a uniform pressure.

Time = _____ Seconds

3. While pumping to maintain the selected application pressure, collect the spray output from one nozzle for the same number of seconds needed to travel the Calibration Distance.

Collected Water = _____ Fluid Ounces

Example: With a 32" band, if it took 28 seconds to travel 127', collect the nozzle discharge for 28 seconds.

(Editor's Suggestion - Use a 1-quart size plastic food bag and put it over the nozzle. Use a twist tie to attach it to the nozzle end of the wand.)

THE NUMBER OF FLUID OUNCES COLLECTED EQUALS THE GALLONS PER ACRE (GPA) APPLIED.

Example: 16 ounces collected equals 16 GPA.

4.   If using a boom, repeat step 3 two more times, collecting water from a different nozzle each time. The <u>average</u> number of ounces collected for each of the three nozzles is equal to the gallons of water applied per acre for that boom, speed, and pressure.

5.   To determine the amount of chemical to add to the spray tank, divide the capacity of the tank by the number of gallons of water per acre (GPA) to determine the fraction of an acre that can be covered with a tankful of spray.

Example: 16 GPA $\overline{\big)\ \text{3.000 gal. tank}}^{\ \text{.188 acre covered per tank}}$

6.   Multiply the application rate of the product per acre times the fraction of the acre covered per tank and add that amount of chemical to the sprayer tank.

Example: 2 qts. per acre = 64 fl. oz. per acre x .188 acre per tank = 12 oz. per tank.

Example: 5 lb. per acre = 80 oz. per acre x .188 acre per tank = 15 oz. per tank.

Table 1.   Select the Calibration Distance to be used based on nozzle spacing if broadcast applying, or on band width if band applying.

Band Width or Nozzle Spacing	Calibration Distance	Band Width or Nozzle Spacing	Calibration Distance
10 inches	408 feet*	24 inches	170 feet
12 inches	340 feet	28 inches	146 feet
16 inches	255 feet	32 inches	127 feet
18 inches	227 feet	36 inches	113 feet
20 inches	204 feet	40 inches	102 feet

Uniform Application Check

Hand sprayers require skilled operators to achieve a uniform broadcast application. A simple and quick test is to spray an area on a paved surface with water in your normal spraying manner on a warm day. In a few minutes the drying pattern will indicate your distribution. Fast drying areas indicate low application rates while slow drying areas received high amounts of spray. Uniform drying without streaks indicates uniform application. Practice until uniform distribution is obtained.

* For calibration of a small walk-behind or hand-carried boom having a 10" nozzle spacing use a distance of 102 feet and multiply the time of walking by four (4).

112

Power driven spray equipment must also be calibrated. Again, the best method of determining application rate is to make a calibration test - a trial run over a small known area. The method described is a very easy straightforward procedure.

Simplified Boom Sprayer Calibration

1. On an area that best represents the average topography for the area to be sprayed, measure and mark off the Calibration Distance that coincides with your band width or nozzle spacing. See Table 1.

Calibration Distance = _____ Feet

2. Select a safe speed which can be maintained while spraying. Note and record the engine R.P.M.'s and the gear selection so the same speed is used during calibration and application.

_____R.P.M.'s   _____Gear

3. With the tractor traveling at this selected speed, time and record the seconds needed to travel the Calibration Distance.

_____Seconds

4. Fill the sprayer, engage the pump and adjust the pressure regulator to the desired boom pressure (between 15 and 50 PSI for herbicides). Collect all the water from one nozzle for the same number of seconds needed to travel the Calibration Distance.

Example: With 20" nozzle spacing, if it took 35 seconds to travel 204', collect the discharge of one nozzle for 35 seconds.

THE NUMBER OF FLUID OUNCES COLLECTED EQUALS THE GALLONS PER ACRE (GPA) OF OUTPUT OF THAT NOZZLE.

Example: 20 ounces collected equals 20 GPA.

5. Repeat Step 4 two more times, collecting water from a different nozzle each time. The average number of ounces collected from each of the three nozzles is equal to the gallons of water applied per acre for that boom. Remember to maintain the same pressure and travel speed when spraying.

6. To determine the the amount of chemical to add to the spray tank, divide the capacity of the tank by the number of gallons of water applied per acre (GPA) to determine the area, in acres, that can be covered with a tankful of spray.

Example: 20 GPA /200 Gal. Tank $\dfrac{\text{10 acres covered per tank}}{}$

7. Multiply the application rate of the product per acre times the acres covered per tank and add that amount of chemical to the sprayer tank.

113

Example: 2 qts. per acre x 10 acres per tank = 20 qts., or
         5 gals. per tank.

Table 1. Select the Calibration Distance to be used based on
         nozzle spacing if broadcast applying, or on band width
         if band applying.

Band Width or Nozzle Spacing	Calibration Distance
10 inches	408 feet *
12 inches	340 feet
16 inches	255 feet
18 inches	227 feet
20 inches	204 feet
24 inches	170 feet
28 inches	146 feet
32 inches	127 feet
36 inches	113 feet
40 inches	102 feet

* For calibration of a small walk-behind or hand-carried boom
having a 10" nozzle spacing use a distance of 102 feet and
multiply the time of walking by four (4).

   For additional information on this subject contact your
cooperative extension office. Another bulletin by Mr. Ahrens
may be helpful: "Modifying Knapsack Sprayers For Precise
Applications Of Herbicides", by John F. Ahrens, the Connecticut
Agricultural Experiment Station, Valley Laboratory, S. Windsor,
CT 06095.

   Another subject that needs more than a passing mention is
that of "Drift", i.e. a herbicide, insecticide or any other
chemical that misses its target. Atmospheric conditions are a
part of the equation, but the physical features of the equipment
have a large bearing. Read "The Drift Problem" in the companion
publication, "Addendum to Basics of Growing Christmas Trees".

The Herbicide Program

Let's discuss weed control problems in more detail and examine the nature of controls available to us. Larry J. Kuhns, Pennsylvania State University has this to say:

Too many growers look at weed control as fire fighting - when weeds appear, kill them. this is a difficult and dangerous system. It is much easier to prevent weed growth than to kill existing weeds because the preventative measures are safer and longer lasting.

Christmas Tree Growers must think in terms of a weed control program. This means planning how to control weeds before ever planting the crop. The program has three parts:

1) <u>Eliminate all weeds prior to planting.</u> It is especially important to kill all perennial weeds because they are not controlled by preemergence herbicides (the safest). Postemergence herbicides that can be applied freely prior to planting must be used with extreme caution after planting.

Near total vegetation control can be achieved on sandy soils (flat) such as in Michigan

Shield on a stick protects seedling from herbicide spray

2) <u>Prevent weed growth.</u> Preemergence herbicides work very well for controlling weeds from seed. Repeat applications of herbicides are necessary for season-long control.

3) <u>Eliminate weeds when they appear.</u> There will always be some weeds that escape your preventative measures. Careful spot-treating with a postemergence herbicide is especially important to keep perennial weeds such as quackgrass, goldenrod, and Canada thistle from getting established.

Before outlining specific recommendations, there are several <u>principles of weed control</u> that you should consider when designing your <u>program</u>.

1) One application of an herbicide at the recommended rate does not give season long control. Repeat applications are needed. If you are getting season long control with one application, you are probably applying at too high a rate and may be stunting the growth of your trees.

   This situation may change as we learn more about some recently introduced herbicides.

2) No single preemergence herbicide can control all weeds. Postemergence herbicides control most weeds, but their use is restricted in established plantings.

3) If one type of weed is controlled and another type in the same field is not, the uncontrolled one will take over. For example, if a herbicide controls broadleaved weeds but not grasses, grasses will fill the entire field. This problem can be prevented by using combinations of herbicides or by alternating them.

4) If you go to the time and expense of getting a field weed-free by cultivating or applying a postemergence herbicide, apply a preemergence herbicide to prevent immediate weed regrowth.

At this point, we are ready to combine the principles of weed control with the concept of a weed control program to come up with specific <u>recommendations</u>. ALL RECOMMENDATIONS ARE PRESENTED IN ACTIVE INGREDIENT PER ACRE (AIA). The manufacturer's label usually lists the number of pounds of active ingredient contained in each gallon of herbicide concentrate. The percentage of active material is listed for wettable powders and granular materials. The active ingredient is the amount of pure herbicide in the material you buy.

EXAMPLE. To compute the amount of Princep liquid, wettable powder, or granular product needed to provide three pounds of active ingredient, the following calculations are done:

4 lbs./gal. liquid formulation
3/4 x 1 gal. = 3 quarts of Princep 4 L

4% Granular formulation
3.0 divided by .04 = 75 lbs. of Princep 4 G

80% Wettable powder
3.0 divided by 0.8 = 3.75 lbs. of Princep 80 W

So three quarts of Princep 4 L, 75 lbs. of Princep 4 G, or 3.75 lbs. of Princep 80 W equals 3 lbs. AIA.

Weed control recommendations for nursery, landscape and Christmas tree plantings, 1984-1985, Cooperative Extension Service, Penn State University, Dept. of Horticulture, 103 Tyson Bldg., University Park, PA 16802.

Different herbicides are useful for different purposes. How they are applied, the rate of application (AIA), the frequency, the weather conditions, environmental conditions, type of soil, percentage of organic matter and other factors should all be taken into account in the use of herbicides. All these variables indicate why label directions and recommendations by the manufacturer must be followed precisely.

=====================================

The following is taken from printed information from J. H. Ahrens, Plant Physiologist, The Connecticut Exp. Station Valley Laboratory, South Windsor, CT 06095: "Experiences With Herbicides In Christmas Trees In The Eastern United States".

Herbicides for Site Preparation

Many growers take advantage of the season before planting to control perennial weeds and brush. this is essential in fields to be planted to seedbeds or transplant beds, and is also important for plantations. Roundup controls a broad spectrum of perennial weeds and brush. Garlon (triclopyr) controls many brush and broadleaf species including legumes, but does not control grasses. Several other herbicides and combinations also are useful for brush control the season before planting. However, persistent soil-applied herbicides such as Hyvar (bromacil) and Spike (tebuthiuron) could seriously injure conifers planted the following spring. The newer non-selective herbicides such as Arsenal (imazapyr) and Oust (sulfometuron) have not been tested widely enough to establish safe uses for site preparation.

Herbicides for Transplant Beds

The most effective weed control programs in transplant beds (seedlings 1-0 or older) involve the application of herbicides shortly after planting, before weeds emerge, and follow-up treatments two months or more later. Broad spectrum weed control often requires the use of herbicide combinations. Herbicides such as Goal or Princep (simazine) that are effective against broadleaves are combined with grass herbicides such as Devrinol, Dacthal (DCPA) or Enide (diphenamid). The grass herbicide, Surflan, can cause girdling and root inhibition to younger transplants of firs and is less used in transplant bed. Rates of Princep are kept very low (1-1.5 lb ai/A) to avoid injury. Goal is applied before bud break to avoid injury to spruces and true firs (Abies spp.).

Since early treatments rarely provide season-long control it usually is necessary to use other controls later on. Goal 1.6E at 1 qt/A effectively controls many seedling broadleaves and vetch and is safely applied after the first flush of spruces and

117

firs start to form buds, usually five to six weeks after bud
break. Pines and Douglas firs seem to tolerate Goal at any
growth stage. Poast or Fusilade plus added surfactant or crop
oil concentrate may be applied at any time to control emerged
grasses. Combinations of Goal plus Poast or Goal plus Fusilade
with added crop oil concentrate or surfactant have been very
effective at the same timings as for Goal alone (after first
flush of spruce or fir is completed). After applying the
postemergence combination it is then only necessary to hand weed
any broadleaves that remain a week or more after application.

Roundup at 1 to 1 1/2 pts/A (**without added surfactant**) is
effective against most emerged annual weeds and safe on spruces
and pines and Douglas firs only, after growth is hardening in
mid-season or later. Pines and Douglas firs in transplant beds
are injured by Roundup. Roundup at the above rates has been
safely combined with Princep on spruce and fir in mid-season but
combinations of Roundup and Goal have been very injurious.

Herbicides for Field-Grown Christmas Trees

Site conditions, conifer species, and the associated weed
complexes largely dictate the types of herbicides used. The
most effective programs may involve at least two applications a
season; the first in early spring and the second early in the
fall to control perennials and brush. Special weed problems may
also require spot or broadcast applications in mid-season.

Early season applications: On tilled sites and sites where
Roundup was applied in the fall to control perennial weeds it is
best to apply preemergence herbicides in late winter after frost
is out, in early spring before weed growth starts, or
immediately after planting. Failure to apply a preemergence
herbicide in the spring usually results in severe competition
from germinating annual and perennial weeds. Combinations of a
grass herbicide such as Surflan (oryzalin) at 3 to 4 lb ai/A or
Devrinol at 4 to 5 lbs ai/A plus a broadleaf herbicide such as
Princep or Goal are most common. In northern New England where
annual grasses are less of a problem than further south, Princep
alone at 2 or more lb ai/A has been a satisfactory postplanting
treatment. If seedling weeds are present at the time of
application it can be advantageous to add Goal at 1 qt/A to the
preemergence herbicides. Although early spring applications of
Princep at 2 lb ai/A often control many emerged winter annuals
before their growth starts, the addition of Goal improves
control of other weeds such as common dandelion and field pansy
that are resistant to Princep.

When planting into sodded sites (hay or pasture land) the
options vary with the species grown and the locals. Scotch and
Austrian pines tolerate Velpar which can provide broad spectrum
weed and brush control. In northern areas, especially on
heavier soils, where balsam and fraser fir are grown,
combinations of Astrex (atrazine) + Princep at 2 to 2-1/2 lb
ai/A of each are commonly used and effectively control many
perennial grasses and broadleaves when applied as early as
possible in the spring. Other options include Princep plus
Poast or Fusilade, applied when perennial grasses are 6 to 10
inches tall. For example, these treatments would find favor in

newly planted white pine and white spruce which are susceptible to Aatrex. Dosages of Poast or Fusilade required to control perennial grasses are at least double those required to control annual grasses. For Example, at least 1-1/3 qts/A of Poast is necessary for quackgrass suppression when combined with Princep at 3 lb ai/A.

Mid-season applications: Regardless of the spring application some perennial weeds, brush species, and even some annual weeds may not be controlled. Seasons of heavy rainfall leach herbicides and shorten their persistence. Grasses can be controlled at any time with Poast or Fusilade, applied over any conifer, provided adequate soil moisture and active grass growth occurs. If broadleaves are also a problem, many can be controlled with Goal at 1 to 2 qts/A. While not always giving root kill, Goal sprays in mid-season burn back many troublesome perennials such as vetch and brindweed, for example, as well as annuals such as pigweed, groundsel, purslane, ragweed and others. Woody weeds beyond the seedling stage are rarely controlled by Goal.

As in transplant beds, Roundup at 1 to 1-1/2 pts/A (without added surfactant) can be useful in mid-season on spruces and true firs for broad spectrum control of annuals and suppression of perennials. The dosages of Roundup tolerated by conifers in mid-season are about half the dosages tolerated by fully mature conifers in the fall. Directed (shielded) sprays of Roundup at 1-1/3 to 2 ounces per gallon of water also are effective on a broad range of weeds and can be safely used in any conifer plantings.

Most growers prefer band treatments of herbicide down the row and a mowed grass strip between rows. This system reduces herbicide costs and soil erosion. Unfortunately, perennial weeds often grow in the grass strips and send their rhizomes into the treated bands, resulting in perennial weed problems in the rows by mid-season. Vetch and bindweed are two such examples and if left alone will deform trees. Goal or Roundup applications can provide some control for these and certain other weeds in the row, but not in the grass strip. In current research, Garlon 4E at 1 pt/A also appears feasible as a semi-directed spray. Since Garlon is non-injurious to grasses a low broadcast spray could be used to kill broadleafed weeds including vetch and poison ivy in the grass strip as well as in the row. Hardened growth of true firs and spruces appear tolerant, but non-hardened or active growth is very susceptible to contact injury from Garlon. Garlon sprays on lower foliage of white pine and fraser fir caused very little injury in mid-August, but moderate to severe injury in June or mid-July. Damage to conifers can be minimized in larger trees where sprays with wide angle or off-center nozzles contact only the lower foot of conifer growth.

Late season application: Roundup and Garlon are effective in conifers late in the season for brush and/or perennial weed control. Neither provides residual control of weeds emerging from seeds later in the fall or in the spring.

The proper use of Roundup can be credited with the great strides that Christmas tree growers have made in recent years in controlling brush and perennial weeds. However, new information about Roundup selectivity in conifers continues to be developed. Timing, dosage, spray volumes, surfactants, and spray techniques, all effect selectivity and desired results.

Timing - Whereas herbaceous and most deciduous woody plants are susceptible to Roundup in late season, conifers are most tolerant after their growth has fully matured. Sprays before frost in early fall, can kill brush species and leave conifers little affected. Perennial grasses and brambles (Rubus spp.) are controlled by Roundup well after early frosts, but many woody plants shed leaves and are not controlled after frost. The most effective timing, therefore, is when conifer growth is hardened, brush and weeds have green leaves, and soil moisture is adequate to allow translocation into root zones.

Hardening varies somewhat with the conifer species and locale. Douglas fir and white pine mature later in the season than spruces, most true firs and Scotch pine. Fraser fir and some seed sources of concolor fir harden later than balsam fir. At an effective time for both weed and brush control in early fall spruces, most true firs and Scotch pine are tolerant of Roundup sprays, whereas white pine and Douglas fir in particular, are very susceptible, especially when their terminal leaders are sprayed. Since heavy rainfall within 2 to 6 hours after Roundup application reduces its effectiveness, it is wise to spray on days when rain is not expected. The presence of heavy dew on weeds may also reduce the effectiveness of Roundup.

Dosage - Selective rates of Roundup are 1-1/3 to 1-1/2 qts/A; even the most tolerant conifers (spruce) may show growth suppression at extreme rates (> 2 qts/A).

Spray volumes - Low spray volumes (5 - 10 gal/A) are more effective than high volumes (20-40 gal/A), but low volumes may also increase injury to conifers if proper spray techniques are not used.

Surfactants - The addition of a non-ionic surfactant (i.e., X-77, Frigate) at 0.5% by volume (2 qts/100 gal) can improve control with Roundup on some weeds but our research shows that such addition increases the potential injury in conifers. Adding surfactant can improve control with minor hazard to trees where the target is primarily annual or winter annual weeds, the conifers are fully dormant spruces or true firs, and semi-directed sprays of Roundup are applied at dosages not exceeding 1 to 1-1/2 pts/A.

Spray Techniques - Since white pine and Douglas fir are especially sensitive, Roundup can only be used in these species with shielded spray applications during the first 2 years of a planting. In older, taller trees Roundup can be safely used as directed or semi-directed sprays where only the base of the conifer is hit. Semi-directed sprays are applied with off-center (band) or wide angle flooding (broadcast) nozzles. In dormant spruces, true firs (Abies spp.) and Scotch pine, aerial or other over-the-top applications where the nozzles are high enough to provide an even spray over the whole plant, have been successful. In the case of fan-type or even-spray nozzles this means raising the boom so that it is held at least 20 inches above the tallest conifers. Nozzles held too close to terminal leaders can cause growth suppression even at proper acre rates.

Although Christmas trees frequently are grown in perennial grass sods, where Roundup is used only in bands, an optional technique uses weeds as a cover between rows. It involves broadcast spraying of Roundup in the fall and band spraying of preemergence herbicides in the spring. This kills the perennial grass as well as brush and other weeds, but allows weeds to reestablish from seed between the rows, providing a soil cover that can be periodically mowed.

When spraying Roundup in the fall some growers find it advantageous to add a low rate of Princep (1-1/2 lb ai/A) to control winter annual weeds until spring. However in most cases, preemergence herbicides applied with Roundup in the fall will not provide satisfactory control of annual weeds for all of the following season, and high rates of preemergence herbicides also can reduce activity of Roundup in tank mixes.

In many experiments over several years we have found that Garlon can be an effective late season herbicide for Christmas trees. Garlon 4E at 1 to 2 qts/A is effective primarily in controlling brush, branches, and certain broadleaved perennials, but not grasses. Conifer tolerance to these dosages is similar to that of Roundup and the same timing and techniques of application apply. Semi-directed broadcast sprays of Garlon can be especially useful in banded tree culture where grass center strips are desirable. It is important to avoid mowing for 2 to 3 weeks prior to and at least one week following Garlon treatment so that broadleaf weeds have adequate foliage to absorb the herbicide and move it to root zones. Tank-mixes of Garlon and Roundup can injure conifers more than either herbicide alone, but reduced rates (1 pt of each/A can provide improved control of weeds such as vetch over Roundup alone.

Asulox (asulam) can be useful in late season primarily to control bracken fern. At 2 to 4 qts/A in August, Asulox has been safe on balsam fir and white pine in New England, but spruces at any stage and actively growing firs are injured.

Kerb 50W (pronamide) is a late season or very early season (Nov. to March) herbicide used in some areas primarily to control perennial grasses and annual mustards. At 1-2 lb ai/A, applied from late fall to very early spring, preferably just before rain or snow, Kerb is especially useful in conifers that are susceptible to Roundup (Douglas fir, white pine). To provide season-long control of annual weeds, however, Kerb must be combined or followed with spring applications of other preemergence herbicides such as Princep or Princep plus Surflan.

More information about weeds and herbicides is given in the book "Addendum to Basics of Growing Christmas Trees".

PARTIAL LIST OF HERBICIDES USED BY CHRISTMAS TREE GROWERS (ALPHABETICALLY)

Trade Names	Common Name	Type	Description (Use/function)
Asulox	asulam	phenylcarbanilate	Postemergent control-mostly grasses-Scotch pine, Doug. fir, Noble and Grand firs
Aatrex, Atrazine	atrazine	triazine	Broad spectrum control-medium to long residual Several firs & pines
Banvel	dicamba	benzoic acid	Both foliar & soil activity. Use on broadleaf weeds; non-crop lands
Devrinol	napropamide	- - -	Preemergence weed seed; used in seed-beds/field; short-term activity
Goal	oxyfluorfen	diphenyl ether	Pre+post emergence; a medium residual broad spectrum herbicide
Kerb	pronamide	acid amine	Pre+post emergence; a medium to long residual, cold weather, restricted use, firs, pines, Doug. fir
Lasso	alachlor	acid amine	Postemergent
Oust	sulfometuron methyl	- - -	Pre+post emergence; field use on Red & Virginia pines
Pennant	metolachlor	acid amine	Preemergent; field use on pine, spruce, & all firs
Ronstar	oxadiazon	unclassified	Broad spectrum; preemergent on grass and broadleaf in fields of pine/spruce
Roundup (Rodeo, others)	glyphosate	aliphatic	Postemergent; broad spectrum, foliar applied; very useful selectively after trees go into dormancy; wide use
Simazine, Princep others)	simazine	triazine	Preemergent; broadleaf & grass control; medium to long residual; use on established trees only: pine, spruce, fir & Doug. fir
Stomp	pendimethalin	triazine	Preemergent. Doug. fir, balsam & Grand firs, white & Colorado spruce
Surflan	oryzalin	dinitroanaline	Preemergent with medium residual both grasses & broadleaf

122

Trade Names	Common Name	Type	Description (Use/function)
Tordon (Amdon, Grazon)	Picloram	picolinic acid	Broadleaf control (soil & foliar) range and non-crop application
2,4-D	2,4-D, various trade names	phenoxy	Foliar applied; broadleaf control in grass and rangeland
Treflan	trifluralin	dinitroanaline	Preemergence. Medium to long residual; Balsam & Doug. fir, pine, nursery hardwoods
Velpar	hexazinone	unclassified	Preemergence. Medium to long residual; Balsam & Doug. fir, pine, & non-crop use

Notes:

"Nursery - Book One" contains extensive information about the function, type and use of more herbicides for both nursery and field use; a valuable reference.

"Addendum to Basics---" discusses the equipment, its calibration, weed identification, shelf-life of pesticides, and other essential subject material.

See listing of chemical product manufacturers in Appendix A

CALCULATIONS

Amount of Herbicides for small areas

1) When converting rate per acre to 1,000 square feet or 100 square feet, the amount used must be very exact. Overdosing by double the rate may severely injure the crop and result in a carryover in the soil the following year. Half the rate may result in poor weed control.

2) Water is the carrier to distribute the herbicide <u>exactly</u> over the area. You need to know if it will take 1 pint/100 square feet (50 gallons per acre) or 1 quart/100 square feet (100 gallons per acre) to cover the area with your sprayer.

3) Next, you need to know how fast to walk to spray the entire volume of water <u>evenly</u> over the given area.

4) Perhaps, it might be easier to hand weed and cultivate or use black plastic mulch.

GUIDE TO USING WETTABLE POWDER HERBICIDES

1 level tsp./100 sq. ft. = approx. 2 lbs./acre of product

Example: Rate per acre - 3 lbs. of AAtrex 80W/3000 sq. ft.
Need 45 tsps. or 15 Tblsps. or 1 cup minus 1 Tblsp.
(1 Cup = 16 Tblsps.)
1 level tsp. will weigh approx. 2 grams (1 oz. = 28.4 grams

Different powders have different volumes, therefore, the formula will be less than the rate per acre given above.
Example:

Enide 90W @ 1 tsp./100 sq. ft.	=	1.5 lbs./acre
Princep 80W @ 1 tsp./100 sq. ft.	=	1.9 lbs./acre
Dacthal 75W @ 1 tsp./100 sq. ft.	=	2.0 lbs./acre
Devrinol 50W @ 1 tsp./100 sq. ft.	=	1.8 lbs./acre

Herbicide	Rate/Acre	Rate/100 sq. ft.	Rate/1000 sq. ft.
Enide 90W	4.4 lbs.	1 Tblsp.	10 Tblsps.
Enide 90W	2.2 lbs.	1-1/2 tsps.	5 Tblsps.
Princep 80W	2.5 lbs.	1-1/3 tsps.	4 Tblsps.+ 1 tsp.
Devrinol 50W	8.0 lbs.	4-1/2 tsps.	15 Tblsps.
Devrinol 50W	4.0 lbs.	2-1/4 tsps.	7-1/2 Tblsps.
Dacthal 75W	12.0 lbs.	2 Tblsps.	20 Tblsps. or 1 Cup + 4 Tblsps.

HERBICIDE IN LIQUID FORM

1 pint per acre	=	1/5 tsp. per 100 sq. ft.
1 quart per acre	=	2/5 tsp. per 100 sq. ft.
2 quarts per acre	=	9/10 tsp. per 100 sq. ft.

Spacing	Area Treated(acres) Per Acre Planted		Spacing	Area Treated(acres) Per Acre Planted
Spots	2'x2'	2' Dia.	Bands	
5 x 5	.160	.125	5 x 5	0.40 acres
6 x 6	.111	.087	6 x 6	0.33 acres
7 x 7	.082	.064	7 x 7	0.28 acres
8 x 8	.062	.049	8 x 8	0.25 acres

Acute Toxicity Table*

categories	Signal Word Required on The Label	mg/kg Oral LD 50	Dermal LD 50	mg/l Inhalation LC 50	Probable Oral Lethal Dose for 150 lb man
I Highly Toxic	**DANGER—** (skull and crossbones) **POISON**	0-50	0-200	0-2,000	A few drops to a teaspoonful.
II Moderately Toxic	**WARNING**	over 50 to 500	over 200 to 2,000	over 2,000 to 20,000	Over one teaspoonful to one ounce.
III Slightly Toxic	**CAUTION**	over 500	over 2,000 to 20,000	---	Over one ounce to one pint or one pound.
IV Relatively Non-toxic	**CAUTION**	over 5,000	over 20,000	----	Over one pint or one pound.

* Taken from the Pesticide Applicator Training Manual, Core Manual, Northeastern Regional Pesticide Coordinators.

Difficult terrain requires great care in use of mechanical as well as chemical products. A field of Fraser fir near Little Switzerland, N.C.

PESTICIDES AND TOXICITY

Know the relative toxicity of a chemical material **before** you use it. Many sources can help you determine this. The manufacturer is a good place to start.

These qualified sources can provide information which I strongly suggest you avail yourself to before you use a new and/or strange chemical.

A list of Poison Control Centers for New York State can be found in the "Addendum". That listing will inform you who the one is nearest you in case of emergency.

Toxicity is defined as the extent or degree to which a chemical substance is poisonous to humans and other animals. All pesticides must be toxic or poisonous to a certain extent in order to kill or cause injury to a target pest. Toxicity varies greatly among different pesticides, however, for each pesticide the level of toxicity is fairly uniform for a specific kind of group of animals, but it may vary considerably among different or unrelated species of animals. Persons using pesticides should at least have a general knowledge of the relative toxicity of the products they are using.

The toxicity of a particular pesticide is determined by subjecting test animals, usually, rats, mice and rabbits, to different dosages of the active ingredient in a pesticide product - that portion of the formulation which is toxic to the pest.

The toxicity of each active ingredient is determined by at least three methods: (1) oral toxicity, by feeding the chemical to test animals; (2) dermal toxicity, by exposing the skin to the chemical; and (3) inhalation toxicity, by making the test animals breathe vapors of the chemical. In addition, the effect of the chemical as an irritant to the eyes and skin is examined under laboratory conditions.

Toxicity is usually expressed as LD50 (lethal dose 50) and LC50 (lethal concentration 50). This is the amount or concentration of a toxicant (the active ingredient) required to kill 50 percent of a test population of animals under a standard set of conditions. Toxicity values of pesticides, based on a single dosage, are recorded in milligrams of pesticide per kilogram of body weight of the test animal (mg/kg) or in parts per million (ppm). LD50 and LC50 are useful in comparing the toxicity of different active ingredients in pesticides. The lower the LD50 of a pesticide, the greater the toxicity of the chemical to man and animals. Pesticides with high LD50's are the least toxic to man when used according to directions on the product labels.

Visualize 100 cages of rats, each having 1 rat in a cage. We are going to feed them a rodenticide to see how effective it is. To establish a lethal dose of 50, we will see how much rodenticide it takes to kill half the 100 rats in the test population, or, 50 percent of them. The weight of the quantity of rodenticide it takes to kill 50 percent of the rats is recorded as is the weight of the rats. The weight ratio given is in the metric system and states simply that it takes "X" number of milligrams of rodenticide to kill 50% of the rats, which weighed "y" kilograms. This could have been stated that it takes one ounce of poison to kill a one pound rat. However, LD/50 is always stated as milligrams needed to kill per kilogram of body weight.

When you look at an LD/50 chart, this weight ratio immediately tells you the toxicity of the poison. In the case of an LD/50 of 10, this means it only takes 10 milligrams of poison to kill 1 kilogram of the test animal, whether it is rats, insects, birds or whatever. If the LD/50 were 100, it takes more poison to kill the test animal and the poison is less toxic.

Some examples may help in discussing LD/50. Diazinon has been established as 108 milligrams per kilogram of body weight. Pyrethrin is less toxic then Diazinon. Boric acid is listed at 3000. Table salt (sodium chloride) is listed at 3320.

See the list that follows for some of our more common materials:

		Mg/Kg
PARATHION		13
DDVP (VAPONA)		62
*NICOTINE (55 mg cc)		90
DIAZINON		108
DDT		113
BAYGON		128
DURSBAN		163
*CAFFEINE (10%)		330
CHLORDANE	457 -	590
CARBARYL-SEVIN		500
*ASPIRIN (5%)		1200
MALATHION		1375
PYRETHRINS		1500
RONNEL		1740
BORAX	2660 -	5190
BORIC ACID		3000
*SODIUM CHLORIDE (salt)		3320
SILICA GEL (DRI-die)		3750
METHOXYCHLOR		6000
*ALCOHOL (absolute)		13,800

Pesticides which are classified as highly toxic or the basis of oral, dermal, or inhalation toxicity must have the signal words DANGER and POISON (in red letters) and a skull and crossbones prominently displayed on the package label As little as a few drops of such material taken orally could be fatal to a 150 pound person. Acute (single dosage) oral LD50's for pesticides in this group range from a trace to 50 mg/kg.

Pesticides considered as moderately toxic must have the signal word WARNING displayed on the product label. Acute oral LD50's range from 50 to 500 mg/kg. From one teaspoon to one ounce of this material could prove fatal to a 150 pound person.

Pesticides classified as either slightly toxic or relatively nontoxic are required to have the signal word CAUTION on the pesticide label. Acute oral LD50 values are greater than 500 mg/kg.

Despite the fact that some pesticides are considered to be only slightly toxic or relatively nontoxic, all pesticides can be hazardous to man, nontarget animals, and the environment if not used according to the instructions on the product label. Use the pesticide only as recommended by the manufacturer. As the applicator, you are legally responsible if a pesticide is misused in any way.

Acute oral and dermal LD50 values of some of the more commonly used pesticides are in the listings in the "Addendum".

TYPES OF FORMULATIONS

For your information and guidance, you should be as knowledgeable as possible about the nature of the chemical materials you might be handling. Some forms of a chemical material may be safer to you, easier to apply or even more effective, depending on the conditions and environment you have to work with. The different categories of pesticides will fit into one of the types described.

When the need for a pesticide arises, the objective is to deliver an effective amount of a suitable pesticide to the target pest. In some cases the pesticide may be a preventive treatment; in others it is curative. The pesticide formulation and equipment used must be suitable for the job.

A basic chemical or active ingredient, can rarely be used as originally manufactured. It is usually mixed with other substances to put it in a form that has good physical and handling properties and can be safely, easily, and accurately applied. This modification of the active ingredient into a mixture is called a pesticide formulation and is made up of active and inert ingredients. The final pesticide formulation is ready for use either as packaged or when diluted with water or other carriers.

Liquids

Emulsifiable Concentrates (EC): An emulsifiable concentrate is a liquid formulation of a pesticide that can be mixed with another liquid to form an emulsion. (An emulsion is one liquid that is dispersed, usually as very small globules, throughout another liquid). an EC usually contains 2 - 6 pounds per gallon of active ingredient. Water usually is the liquid with which an EC is mixed, but some EC formulations are made to be added to oil or other petroleum carriers.

Many active ingredients in pesticides are not soluble in water but are soluble in oils or other solvents. In an EC the active ingredient is dissolved in an oil or solvent and emulsifying agents and other adjuvants are added to the formulation so the EC can be mixed with water to form a "milky" emulsion. The emulsion can then be sprayed conveniently. Little agitation is required with EC's. Some crops are sensitive to the EC's of some insecticides so different formulations of the active ingredient (wettable powders or dust formulations, for example) may have to be used on them.

High Concentrate Liquids, Spray Concentrates. These formulations may be thought of as special EC formulations. They usually contain a high concentration of the active ingredient, as much as eight or more pounds per gallon. Most are designed to be mixed with water or oil and contain wetting agents, stickers, and other adjuvants. Ultra low volume (ULV) concentrates are designed to be used directly without further dilution and contain little but the pesticide itself.

Low Concentrate Liquids. These formulations are usually solutions in highly refined oils that contain low amounts of the active ingredient. Generally, they are designed to be used as purchased, with no further dilution. This type of formulation is often sold for use in controlling household pests, for mothproofing, or for use in barns as a space spray or a spray for livestock.

Flowables (F or L). Some active ingredients can be manufactured only as solid, or, at best, semi-solid materials. They usually have relatively low solubility in water or in other organic solvents. These pesticides are often formulated as flowable liquids. The active ingredient is very finely ground and suspended in a liquid along with appropriate suspending agents, adjuvants, etc. In this form the formulation can be mixed with water and applied. Flowables do not usually clog spray nozzles, require only moderate agitation, and in many ways can be handled as easily as EC formulations.

Solutions. Some active ingredients are completely soluble in water or organic solvents. In that original state they are liquids. The pesticide is formulated in an appropriate solvent or water and exists in the true solution, or molecular, state. Solutions properly prepared for special uses do not leave unsightly residues and will not clog spray equipment. Some of these formulations, however, can damage crops, so an alternative formulation may have to be used.

Aerosols. The active ingredient(s) in aerosols is in a formulation in a can under pressure. One or more pesticides may be in the same formulation. The propellant drives the formulation out through a fine spray opening. Usually the percentage of active ingredient(s) in an aerosol is very low. Convenience of use is the major advantage. Aerosols are sold mainly for garden and home use, not for agriculture use. Some are used in greenhouses, barns, etc.

Dry Formulations

Dusts (D). A dust formulation usually consists of the active ingredient mixed with talc, clay, powdered nut hulls, volcanic ash, or other such materials. The formulation is very finely ground to a fairly uniform particle size. Adjuvants are often added to ensure that the formulation will store well and handle acceptably when applied. Some active ingredients are formulated as dusts because in that form they do not cause phytotoxicity to the economic crop, whereas, an EC formulation might be quite phytotoxic to the crop. The percentage of active ingredient in a dust usually is low. Dusts are used dry, never mix them with water. Dust formulations are available for use on seeds, plants, and animals.

Granules (G). Granular formulations are dry formulations usually made by applying a liquid formulation to granules of clay or other porous materials such as corn cobs or walnut shells. The granules are prepared in advance to a standard size before the liquid formulation is applied. The liquid is adsorbed or absorbed (or both) on the porous materials. Additional adjuvants or conditioning agents may be added to granular formulations so they handle well. The percentage of active ingredient in granular formulations is lower than that of an EC but usually safer to apply than EC's or dusts. Granular pesticide formulations are most often used as soil treatments. They can be applied directly to the soil or over plants, since they do not cling to plant foliage, although they can be trapped in the whorls of some plants.

Wettable Powders (WP). Wettable powders are dry powdered pesticide formulations similar in appearance to dusts but unlike dusts in that they contain wetting and dispersing agents. Wettable powders are usually much more concentrated than dusts, containing 15-95 percent active ingredient (most formulations contain more than 50 percent). They are made to be mixed to form a suspension spray. Agitation is required in the spray tank to keep the formulation in suspension, since the formulation does not form a true solution. Because of the nature of the active ingredient, some pesticide products can be formulated into wettable powders but not into EC's. Good wettable powder formulations spray well and do not clog nozzles, but they are abrasive to pumps and nozzles. Most wettable powder formulations are less likely to damage sensitive plants (be phytotoxic) than are EC's. Wettable powders and EC's are the most widely used formulations.

Soluble Powders (SP). Soluble powders, like wettable powders, are dry formulations, but when soluble powders are added to water, they completely dissolve and form solutions. Agitation in the spray tank is sometimes required to get them into solution, but once in solution, they require no further agitation. The percentage of active ingredient in an SP usually is high. Compared to EC's and WP's, not many SP formulations are available.

130

Adjuvants or Spray Additives

Pesticides, whether emulsifiable concentrates or wettable powders, are formulated for general performance purposes under average conditions. For many jobs they perform satisfactorily, but there are also many situations where they fall short of the desired effect. For example, in very hard or soft waters, a formulation may have too little or too much emulsifier, with the consequent problems of difficulty in mixing or of excessive foaming. A formulation may evenly distribute a pesticide on the leaves of crops such as beans and potatoes satisfactorily, but on the waxy leaves of cabbage, cauliflower, or onions, the spray, instead of spreading as an even film over the leaf surface, may form small, round droplets. It then runs off of the plant and onto the ground, leaving no deposit to protect the plant. The addition of a surfactant to the spray tank will solve this problem. Recently it has been common to add to herbicides materials which improve their effectiveness by increasing their ability to wet and penetrate treated surfaces. A substance added to the spray mixture to aid or improve the performance of the main ingredient is an adjuvant.

Adjuvants may be added to the spray mixture to:

1) Improve the wetting of the foliage or the pest.

2) Change the evaporation rate of the spray.

3) Improve the ability of the spray deposit to resist weathering.

4) Improve the penetration, absorption and translocation of the pesticide.

5) Adjust or buffer the pH of the spray solution increasing the effectiveness and longevity of alkaline sensitive pesticides.

6) Improve the uniformity and amount of the deposit.

7) Improve the ease of mixing or compatibility of the spray mixture.

8) Increase the safety from spray injury to the crop.

9) Reduce the drift hazard to neighboring crops.

10) Improve physical properties of the mixture -- i.e., anti-foaming agents.

Depending upon their intended use, adjuvants are called emulsifiers, wetters, stickers, extenders, spreaders, deposit builders, film formers, buffering agents, thickeners, penetrants, foaming agents, anti-foaming agents, etc.

Adjuvants are highly active materials. In most cases, a very small quantity will have great effect. You should be careful to use only the amount recommended. Too much adjuvant may be just as bad as too little -- it makes little difference whether the pesticide runs off the foliage because it balls up or because it forms too thin a film on the foliage. Also, too much adjuvant may cause herbicide spray to lose some of its selectivity and injure plants normally tolerant of it.

Regulations require spray adjuvants, for use with pesticides, to be registered and carry an EPA number and either to be exempt from the requirement of a tolerance or to have a tolerance established.

Proper selection of the adjuvant for your job is of the utmost importance.

RECORD KEEPING

For most people, application of chemicals is a learning experience. You can best learn from these experiences if a record is kept every time a chemical application is made. It provides a basis for evaluation (success or failures) and for making corrections or improvements in the procedures. A form that could be used follows. You can make copies of this form and prepare a three-ring binder or folio to keep an ongoing record of your chemical activities.

Some chemicals tend to build up in plants and soils and can create a toxic situation. A record log provides some means of monitoring this. If a material did not work, you could check your record to determine why. A change in the time or rate of application, application technique, or chemical used, may be required. If the trees or seedlings were injured, well-kept records will help you determine what changes must be made to prevent additional problems in the future.

Appendix A contains a form sheet for your use.

SIMPLIFYING PESTICIDE CALCULATIONS
Larry J. Kuhns
AMOUNT OF FORMULATED PESTICIDES (FROM THE CONTAINER) NEEDED PER ACRE

FORMULATION	\multicolumn{9}{AMOUNT OF ACTIVE INGREDIENT PER ACRE}								
	1/2 lb	3/4 lb	1 lb	1½ lb	2 lb	3 lb	4 lb	5 lb	10 lb
1% Dust or Granule	50 lb	75 lb	100 lb	150 lb	200 lb	300 lb	400 lb	500 lb	1000 lb
4% Dust or Granule	12½ lb	18¾ lb	25 lb	37½ lb	50 lb	75 lb	100 lb	125 lb	250 lb
5% Dust or Granule	10 lb	15 lb	20 lb	30 lb	40 lb	60 lb	80 lb	100 lb	200 lb
10% Dust or Granule	5 lb	7½ lb	10 lb	15 lb	20 lb	30 lb	40 lb	50 lb	100 lb
14% Granule	3½ lb	5⅓ lb	7⅛ lb	10¾ lb	14¼ lb	21½ lb	28½ lb	35⅝ lb	71¼ lb
20% Granule	2½ lb	3¾ lb	5 lb	7½ lb	10 lb	15 lb	20 lb	25 lb	50 lb
25% WP	2 lb	3 lb	4 lb	6 lb	8 lb	12 lb	16 lb	20 lb	40 lb
40% WP	1¼ lb	1⅞ lb	2½ lb	3¾ lb	5 lb	7½ lb	10 lb	12½ lb	25 lb
50% WP	1 lb	1½ lb	2 lb	3 lb	4 lb	6 lb	8 lb	10 lb	20 lb
75% WP	⅔ lb	1 lb	1⅓ lb	2 lb	2⅔ lb	4 lb	5⅓ lb	6⅔ lb	13⅓ lb
80% WP	10 oz	15 oz	1¼ lb	1⅞ lb	2½ lb	3¾ lb	5 lb	6¼ lb	12½
86% WP	9 oz	14 oz	1¼ lb	1¾ lb	2⅓ lb	3½ lb	4⅔ lb	5¾ lb	11½ lb
10-12% EC 1.0 lb actual/gal	2 qt	3 qt	1 gal	6 qt	2 gal	3 gal	4 gal	5 gal	10 gal
15-20% EC 1.5 lb actual/gal	1⅓ qt	2 qt	2⅔ qt	1 gal	5⅓ qt	2 gal	10⅔ qt	13⅓ qt	26⅔ qt
25% EC 2.0 lb actual/gal	2 pt	3 pt	2 qt	3 qt	4 qt	6 qt	8 qt	10 qt	20 qt
2.67 lb actual/gal	1½ pt	2¼ pt	3 pt	2¼ qt	3 qt	4½ qt	6 qt	7½ qt	15 qt
40-50% EC 3.0 lb actual/gal	1⅓ pt	2 pt	2⅔ pt	2 qt	2⅔ qt	4 qt	5⅓ qt	6⅔ qt	13⅓ qt
4.0 lb actual/gal	1 pt	1½ pt	2 pt	3 pt	2 qt	3 qt	4 qt	5 qt	10 qt
57% EC 5 lb actual/gal	13 oz	1¼ pt	1⅔ pt	2½ pt	3⅓ pt	5 pt	6⅔ pt	8⅓ pt	16⅔ pt
60-65% EC 6 lb actual/gal	⅔ pt	1 pt	1⅓ pt	2 pt	2⅔ pt	4 pt	5⅓ pt	6⅔ pt	13⅓ pt
70-75% EC 8 lb actual/gal	½ pt	¾ pt	1 pt	1½ pt	2 pt	3 pt	4 pt	5 pt	10 pt

Example: You wish to apply a herbicide at the rate of 1 lb per acre. You purchased a 50% WP. From the table above you find that 2 lb of the 50% WP formulation are needed to provide the necessary dosage of 1 lb per acre.

Weight Conversion

16 ounces = 1 pound
454 grams = 1 pound

Area Conversion

43,560 sq. ft. = 1 Acre
1000 sq. ft. = 0.023 Acre

gallon (gal)	quart (qt)	pint (pt)	fluid ounces (fl.oz)	cups	tablespoon (tbl)	teaspoon (tsp)	milliliter (ml)
1	4	8	128	16			
	1	2	32	4			
		1	16	2	32		
			1	1/8	2	6	30
				1	16	48	240
					1	3	15
						1	5

The Pennsylvania Cooperative Extension Service

Characteristic	Sand	Loam	Clay	Peat/Muck
Adsorption capacity	Very low	Low	Moderate	Very high
Herbicide leachability	Rapid and deep	Moderate	Low	Almost none
Relative herbicide activity	High	Moderate	Moderate to low	Very low

Pesticide Labels

The information contained on pesticide labels has been called some of the most expensive words in all literature. This may well be true since the research, development, and registration procedures behind a label frequently cost the manufacturer 6 to 10 years time and 10 to 20 million dollars.

Before it is approved, every word on each label has been reviewed by several persons in the Registration Division of the Office of Pesticide Programs in the U.S. Environmental Protection Agency. No other product is more thoroughly tested before use.

Labels and Labeling

Whenever you purchase a pesticide, you also receive instructions that tell you how to use it. This information is referred to as the label or labeling. Label and labeling are very similar words but they don't have the same meaning.

The label is the information printed on or attached to the container of pesticides. This label does many things:

• To the manufacturer, the label is a "license to sell."

• To the state or federal government, the label is a way to control the distribution, storage, sale, use, and disposal of the product.

• To the buyer or user, the label is the main source of facts on how to use the product correctly and legally.

• The label is a way to tell users about special safety measures needed.

Labeling is all the information that you receive from the company or its agent about the product. Labeling includes such things as the label on the product and the brochures, flyers, and information accompanying the product or handed out by the dealer.

Why Read a Label?

The most important time spent in pest control is the time spent in reading the label. A pesticide is registered for use on specific crops for control of specific pests. The pesticide application is more likely to be successful in controlling the insect, weed, or plant disease if the directions for use on the label are read and followed. When label instructions are followed, you are virtually assured that the major possibilities of an accident are eliminated.

Amendments to the Federal Insecticide, Fungicide and Rodenticide Act passed in 1972 make it illegal to use any registered pesticide in a manner inconsistent with its labeling. Persons found guilty of using a pesticide in a manner inconsistent with its labeling may be subject to fine, imprisonment, or both. These amendments have elevated the status of the pesticide label to that of a legal document.

What Is on a Pesticide Label?

A pesticide label is required by law to contain certain information. An example of a typical label may be found on page 3 of this fact sheet. The numbers following the subheadings refer to locations on this label where the information may be found.

Trade (Brand) Name ①

Each pesticide manufacturer has a trade (brand) name for its product. If more than one company markets the same product, there may be several trade names for a pesticide. For example, both Lexone and Sencor are trade names for the same herbicide. Likewise, Lorsban and Dursban are trade names for the same insecticide.

Common and Chemical Names ②

In addition to a trade name, most pesticides have an official common name. It is an agreed-upon name for the active ingredient in the product. A pesticide sold under several trade names will always have the same common name. The common name for Lexone and Sencor is metribuzin and the common name for Lorsban and Dursban is chlorpyrifos.

The chemical name indicates the chemical composition of the active ingredient. Like the common name, it will be always the same for a particular pesticide. The chemical name for chlorpyrifos is 0, 0-Diethyl 0-(3,5,6-trichloro-2-pyridyl)-phosphorothioate.

Ingredient Statement ③

Every label must list what is in the product. The chemical that is toxic to the pest is referred to as the active ingredient and is given as a percentage of the formulation. It may be listed by either the common or chemical name. The inert ingredients (emulsifiers, solvents, carriers, etc.) do not need to be identified except by the percent of the formulation that they constitute.

Net Contents ④

The net contents indicates how much pesticide is in the container. The number will be expressed in gallons, pints, quarts, or other units of measure.

Name and Address of Manufacturer ⑤

The manufacturer is required by law to list its name and address on the label, so that the applicator will know where to call for information in case of an emergency.

Registration and Establishment Numbers ⑥

Two numbers must appear on every pesticide container: the registration number and the establishment number. The EPA registration number indicates that the product has been registered with the U.S. Environmental Protection Agency. The number is a code that identifies the manufacturer and the specific product label. The EPA establishment number appears either on the label or the container. It identifies the formulating facility that made the product. In case something goes wrong, the facility that made the product can be traced.

Use Classification ⑦

EPA is required by the amended Federal Insecticide, Fungicide and Rodenticide Act to classify pesticides for either general use or restricted use. In classifying a pesticide EPA considers:

• The toxicity of the pesticide.
• The way in which the pesticide will be used.
• The effect of the pesticide on the environment.

A *general use pesticide* is defined as one that will not harm the applicator or the environment to an unreasonable degree when used according to label directions. Pesticides classified for general use will be identified by the words "General Classification" appearing immediately below the heading "Directions for Use" on the label. General use pesticides are available to the general public for use according to label directions.

A *restricted use pesticide* is one that could harm the applicator or the environment even when used as directed by the label. Pesticides classified for restricted use will be identified by the words "Restricted Use Pesticide" at the top of the front panel of the label followed by the statement "For retail sale to and application only by certified applicators or persons under their direct supervision and only for those uses covered by the Certified Applicator's Certification." Restricted use pesticides must be applied by or under the direct supervision of a certified applicator. Through certification, an applicator demonstrates that he knows how to safely and properly use restricted use pesticides.

> Your State Cooperative Extension
> Service can inform you of restricted
> pesticides and requirements to
> become an applicator.

Pesticide products that have not yet gone through the classification process are considered unclassified and will have no general use or restricted use designation on their labels. They may be purchased and used according to label

directions by anyone. Amended FIFRA calls for the re-registration of all currently registered pesticides. These products will be classified when they are re-registered.

Directions for Use ⑧

Under the *Directions for Use* the manufacturer again indicates the use classification, which is followed by the statement, "It is a violation of Federal law to use this pesticide in a manner inconsistent with its labeling." The label lists only the registered (legal) uses of the pesticide. The directions for use also include the following:

• The crops, animals, objects or areas to be treated.
• The amount to use (per acre, per gallon of water, per 1000 sq. ft., etc.).
• The method of application and type of equipment.
• The timing and frequency of application.
• Specific limitations on reentry to treated areas.
• Limitations or restrictions on use to prevent any unreasonable adverse effects on the environment. This includes required time between applications or before harvest of the crop, crop rotation restrictions, warnings concerning use on certain crops, animals adjacent to water.

Precautionary Statements ⑨

The pesticide label contains certain precautionary statements to alert the applicator to hazards to himself, children, domestic animals, wildlife and the environment.

Signal Words and Symbols ⑩

Signal words are used on the label to indicate approximately how toxic the pesticide is to people. The signal words that follow are set by law. Each manufacturer must use the correct one on the label.

Signal Word	Toxicity	Apporoximate amount needed to kill the average person
DANGER	Highly toxic	A taste to a teaspoon
WARNING	Moderately toxic	A teaspoon to a tablespoon
CAUTION	Low Toxicity or comparatively free from danger	An ounce to more than a pint

All products must bear the statement **KEEP OUT OF REACH OF CHILDREN.** Products having the signal word **DANGER** on the label must also have the skull and cross-bones symbol and the word **POISON** printed in red in close proximity to it.

Statement of Practical Treatment ⑪

The labels for all highly toxic pesticides (signal word —**DANGER**) must give instructions for first-aid treatment in the case of accidental poisoning. Often labels for less toxic pesticides will also provide first-aid instructions. The practical treatment statements on the label are helpful to your physician. Take the label with you if you need to see your physician for the treatment of pesticide poisoning.

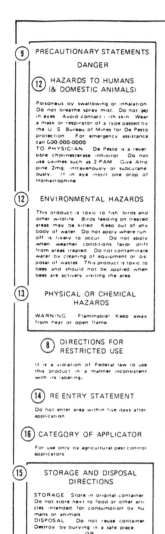

⑨ PRECAUTIONARY STATEMENTS

DANGER

⑫ HAZARDS TO HUMANS
(& DOMESTIC ANIMALS)

Poisonous by swallowing or inhalation. Do not breathe spray mist. Do not get in eyes. Avoid contact with skin. Wear a mask or respirator of a type passed by the U.S. Bureau of Mines for De Pesto protection. For emergency assistance call 600-000-0000.
TO PHYSICIAN: De Pesto is a reversible cholinesterase inhibitor. Do not use oximes such as 2 PAM. Give Atropine 2mg. intravenously or subcutaneously. If in eye instill one drop of Homatrophine.

⑫ ENVIRONMENTAL HAZARDS

This product is toxic to fish, birds and other wildlife. Birds feeding on treated areas may be killed. Keep out of any body of water. Do not apply where run off is likely to occur. Do not apply when weather conditions favor drift from areas treated. Do not contaminate water by cleaning of equipment or disposal of wastes. This product is toxic to bees and should not be applied when bees are actively visiting the area.

⑬ PHYSICAL OR CHEMICAL
HAZARDS

WARNING: Flammable! Keep away from heat or open flame.

⑧ DIRECTIONS FOR
RESTRICTED USE

It is a violation of Federal law to use this product in a manner inconsistent with its labeling.

⑭ RE ENTRY STATEMENT

Do not enter area within five days after application.

⑯ CATEGORY OF APPLICATOR

For use only by agricultural pest control applicators.

⑮ STORAGE AND DISPOSAL
DIRECTIONS

STORAGE: Store in original container. Do not store next to food or other articles intended for consumption by humans or animals.
DISPOSAL: Do not reuse container. Destroy by burying in a safe place.
OR
Contact State or Regional Federal Authorities for local restrictions on disposal.

---

⑦ **RESTRICTED USE PESTICIDE**

FOR RETAIL SALE TO AND APPLICATION ONLY BY CERTIFIED APPLICATORS OR PERSONS UNDER THEIR DIRECT SUPERVISION AND ONLY FOR THOSE USES COVERED BY THE CERTIFIED APPLICATOR'S CERTIFICATION.

①  **DE PESTO**

INSECTICIDE

ACTIVE INGREDIENT: *PESTOFF — 40.50%   ②
③ INERT INGREDIENTS: 59.50%
TOTAL: 100.00%

*TRI-SALICYLIC ACID ②

THIS PRODUCT CONTAINS 3.5 LBS OF PESTOFF PER GALLON
PESTOFF IS A REGISTERED TRADEMARK OF A-Z CORPORATION

KEEP OUT OF REACH OF CHILDREN
⑩ **DANGER — POISON**

⑪ STATEMENT OF PRACTICAL TREATMENT

IF SWALLOWED: Induce vomiting by giving a tablespoonful of salt in a glass of warm water. Repeat until vomitus is clear. Call a physician immediately.
IF INHALED: Remove to fresh air. Call a physician immediately.
IF IN EYES: Flush eyes with plenty of water for at least 15 minutes. Call a physician immediately.
IF ON SKIN: In case of contact, remove contaminated clothing and immediately wash skin with soap and water.

SEE SIDE PANEL FOR ADDITIONAL
PRECAUTIONARY STATEMENTS

⑤ MFG BY A-Z CHEMICALS
TOWN, STATE

ESTABLISHMENT NO. 00475-OK-1
⑥ EPA REGISTRATION NO. 1357-42

---

⑧ DIRECTIONS FOR
RESTRICTED USE
CONTINUED

ALFALFA: Alfalfa Weevil Larvae, Egyptian Alfalfa Weevil Larvae, Pea Aphid, and in New York state for Snout Beetle control. Apply the amount of De Pesto indicated in the chart, when feeding is noticed or when insects appear. Alfalfa Weevil Adult: Apply 1-2 pints per acre when insects appear. Lygus Bugs: Apply 2 pints per acre prior to bloom. Observe the indicated number of days after application before cutting or grazing. Do not apply more than once per season. Apply only to fields planted to pure stands of Alfalfa.

Pints of De Pesto Per Acre	Do Not Cut or Graze Within
½	7 days
1	14 days
2	28 days

MINIMUM GALLONAGE REQUIREMENT: Ten gallons of finished spray per acre with ground equipment, two gallons per acre with aircraft.

FIELD CORN: Corn Rootworms - Use 1½ - 2 pints of De Pesto per 13,000 linear feet (1 acre with 40 inch spacing). Apply, at planting, as a 7 inch band over the row by mixing with water or liquid fertilizers. When De Pesto is used with liquid fertilizers, mix in the following way making sure that the mixture is physically compatible. Premix 1 part of De Pesto with 2 parts of water. Add this premix to the tank of fertilizer along with rinsings from the premixing container. Maintain agitation in the tank after mixing and during application. Do not mix until ready to use.

SUGARCANE: Sugarcane Borer. Apply 1 - 1½ pints De Pesto per acre using ground or aerial equipment. Check sugarcane fields weekly, beginning in early June and continuing through August. Make first application only after visible joints form and 5% or more of the plants are infested with young larvae feeding in or under the leaf sheath and which have not bored into the stalks. Repeat whenever field checks indicate the infestation exceeds 5%. Do not apply within 17 days of harvest. Do not use in Hawaii.

④ NET CONTENTS ONE GALLON

Hazards to the Environment and Humans ⑫

When a pesticide is hazardous to bees, fish, or wildlife, the label will indicate the nature of the hazard and the precautions to take to prevent injury or damage to non-target species or to the environment.

The label also contains a statement of the human hazards and the routes of exposure together with a list of precautions and protective equipment to prevent accidents or injury.

Physical or Chemical Hazards ⑬

The label provides information about any fire, explosion or chemical hazards the product may have.

Reentry Statement ⑭

Some products will specify on their label how much time must pass before a pesticide treated area is safe for entry by a person without protective clothing.

Storage and Disposal Directions ⑮

The label provides information on proper storage and disposal procedures for the pesticide.

Category of Applicator ⑯

Some pesticide products may be limited for use to certain categories of commercial applicators.

When to Read the Label

A pesticide label should be read at least four times by the person using it.

1. *Before you purchase a pesticide,* read the label to determine:
   - If it is the right one for your pest problem.
   - If the site is on the label.
   - If it is too hazardous to use for your conditions.
   - If you have the right equipment to apply the pesticide.
   - If you need to be a certified applicator to purchase and use it.

2. *Before your mix the pesticide,* read the label to determine:
   - What protective equipment is needed.

- What the pesticide can be mixed with (compatibility).
- How much to use.
- How to mix it.

3. *Before you apply the pesticide,* read the label to determine:
   - Safety measures to follow.
   - Where it can be used (crops, animals, structures, etc.)
   - When to apply and what are the waiting periods for crops and animals.
   - How to apply and the rate of application.
   - Any special restrictions on its use.

4. *Before you store or dispose of the pesticide or the pesticide container,* read the label to determine:
   - Where and how to store.
   - How to clean or decontaminate and dispose of the pesticide container.
   - Where and how to dispose of surplus pesticides.

The pesticide label is your single most important source of information about the product. If you do not fully understand the information and the directions for use on the label, ask your pesticide salesman, vocational agriculture instructor, county Extension director, or university Extension Specialist to assist you in a correct interpretation.

Sheldon Anderson presenting Doug Drysdale of Egbert, Ontario, Canada with Anderson trophy for for the Grand Champion Concolor fir (at left) at Royal Agricultural Winter Fair in Toronto, Ontario, Canada - November, 1992.

PESTICIDE SAFETY

To protect man, animals, and the environment —

1. Read the label before each use. You'll be amazed at what you missed the last time you read it.

2. Observe all safety precautions. Wear protective mask and clothing, if directed on the label.

3. Avoid inhaling concentrated pesticide powders when filling the sprayer or duster.

4. Concentrated pesticides or mixtures or dusts spilled on skin should be washed off with soap and water immediately. Clothing wet with pesticides should be removed, skin washed, and clean clothing put on. Wash the contaminated clothing before using again.

5. Don't smoke or eat when using pesticides. Before eating or smoking, wash face and hands.

6. Wash hands and face, or better yet, take a shower after spraying or dusting and change to clean clothes. Wash contaminated clothes separate from family laundry before using again.

7. Another person in addition to the applicator should know the pesticide being applied — in case there is an accident.

8. If you feel ill when handling or spraying pesticides, stop right away. Don't try to finish the job. See a doctor and show him a label of the pesticide being used so that he can phone the Poison Information Center for the best treatment.

9. Avoid spray or dust drift to other crops, yards, streams, and ponds.

10. Do not rinse or wash spray tanks where rinse water will find its way into streams, ponds, or water supplies.

11. Store pesticides in original containers with original labels — out of reach of children, pets and livestock and away from food or feed. Keep in a locked storeroom or cabinet marked "Pesticides — Keep Out."

12. Never put pesticides in containers such as bottles, cans, cartons, bags, etc., which once had drinks or food.

13. Rinse metal, glass, and plastic containers with adequate water and pour into spray tank. Do it three times. Disarm the empty containers by puncturing them or breaking them so they cannot be used to hold drinks, food or feed.

14. Dispose of empty containers properly. Bury them at least 18 inches deep in a disposal area where the pesticides will not be washed into streams, ponds or water supplies.

Don't Use Pesticides If You Are Not Willing to Follow Safety Precautions.

THE ENVIRONMENT AND YOU

Tree growers, by necessity, are confronted with the need to use chemical materials that can be hazardous to them and their surroundings. You must be aware of possible dangers and act or respond accordingly. The previous section we hope provided some insight as to the nature of pesticides and their relative danger.

The level of potential danger is referred to as toxicity and is measured by relating one material to another.

We are all aware of environmental problems today. Polluted lakes, contaminated water and soil due to dumping, oil spills, acid rain affecting everything it contacts, chemical discharge into the air attacking the ozone layer and even radiation escaping from power plants are a few of many acute problems in our environment.

With all this, who needs any more problems? Awareness and preventative measures are crucial to everyone's welfare. We are including this special section because of the magnitude of the problems today and the necessity for taking precautions that avoid medical problems.

In a nutshell, it is all about safe handling, use, storage and disposal of chemical compounds. We cannot give intensive coverage of this subject but can only highlight some important aspects of it, the most important of all is that you must be fully aware that the use of chemicals could influence your health and longevity if improperly used. Always follow the manufacturers' instructions.

The chemicals we are referring to are designed to kill or control other living organisms. We, ourselves, are a living organism so it stands to reason that these materials could affect us, either short term or long term.

The impact of problems created in the past 50 years has resulted in legislation and creation of federal and state agencies to establish and enforce guidelines. The Environmental Protection Agency of the Department of Environmental Conservation can help you greatly..

To be aware of the potential danger of pesticides to ourselves and to our family is not enough. Circumstances, many beyond our control, make it mandatory that we comply with guidelines to protect others and the general environment. Laws are now being passed to insure safe conduct on everyone's part in regard to chemical use.

Pollution has become so bad in some areas of the world that the air, water, and food products are unfit for consumption by man or animal. Some of those areas are right here in the United States. We are all well aware of the threat by acid rain. This is a very visible effect of pollution that began as air pollution condensed out in the form of moisture and the polluted rain, fog, etc. attacked plants and structures alike. The soaring cancer figures, both incidence and death reflect pollution in its many forms.

139

All this points out why we must know what we are doing in the use of chemicals and how it affects everyone and everything around us. For this level of awareness to make a positive impact, basic knowledge and procedures must be followed. the best way to learn this is through the Pesticide Certification Program conducted by Cooperative Extension and/or other groups.

There are two parts to the program. One concerns the "private" applicator, the person or persons who work with or handle pesticides for their own business activity; the second category is "commercial". This involves people who handle and work with chemicals for others. An example would be a lawn care company. The requirements and certification they receive is more intensive than that of a private user of chemicals. Nonetheless, this program should be mandatory for every Christmas tree grower. Since every chemical is potentially harmful, background training is valuable. The cost in time and money is minor. Since most people reading this will be "private applicators", I am giving the procedures for this category. Persons who are or want to be commercial applicators should contact the D.E.C. or Cooperative Extension for detailed information.

The information that follows is specific to New York State but the steps and procedures are similar throughout the entire United States. Cooperative Extension usually conducts the training/test sessions. If in doubt, contact the Dept. of Environmental Conservation (DEC) through your State Capital. They may have an office nearby so consult your telephone book.

PRIVATE CATEGORY CERTIFICATION

Private applicators are people in the business of producing an agricultural commodity. Private applicators need certification if they use restricted pesticides in the production of an agricultural commodity.

The first step in the certification procedure consists of successfully passing the closed book basic "Core" examination based on information found in the Northwestern Pesticide Application Core Manual. This manual may be purchased from the Chemicals-Pesticides Program, Comstock Hall, Cornell University, Ithaca, New York 14853, or from your local county Cooperative Extension agent. The manual should be obtained and studied before taking the closed book exam.

At the time of the "Core" exam, private applicators will also answer ten additional questions concerning a crop or crops and pests capable of damaging the crop or crops in the commodity in which they wish to be certified. Study material for this portion of the examination is available from your county Cooperative Extension agent.

Private applicators are required to pass one such commodity examination to complete their certification. There are six such exams available: (1) field and forage; (2) fruit; (3) vegetable; (4) greenhouse and florist; (5) nursery, and (6) livestock and poultry.

140

Training for "Core" certification is available if desired, through most local county Cooperative Extension offices. Examinations may be given directly after the training session or 30 days after the training session depending upon the availability of training, scheduling and monitors, etc.

Arrangements for training and taking the examination should be made through the local county Cooperative Extension agent or the regional pesticide inspector. Verification should be made at that time to determine when exams will be given.

The core and commodity exams are given without a specified time limit. Full private applicators' certification requirements are met when applicants have successfully taken the core and a commodity exam.

Upon successfully passing the exam, private applicators will receive a notice for payment of fees. The cost at present is $15.00 for three years. An additional person on the same farm may be certified for $5.00 for three years.

Upon payment of the appropriate fees, the certified private applicator will be issued a certificate and identification card signifying the commodity he or she is certified in.

At the end of three years, it is necessary for the private applicator to renew his certification I.D. card. Notice will be sent by DEC and I.D. cards will be issued after payment of appropriate fees. I.D. cards must be renewed for an applicator's certification to remain valid. This will also enable the applicator to become recertified within the required six-year period based upon the date his first I.D. card was issued.

| SHEET NO. |
| YEAR |

-14 (6/77)

NEW YORK STATE DEPARTMENT OF ENVIRONMENTAL CONSERVATION
BUREAU OF PESTICIDES — ALBANY, NEW YORK 12233

CERTIFIED PRIVATE APPLICATOR
RECORD OF RESTRICTED PESTICIDE PURCHASE AND USE

ALL RESTRICTED USE PESTICIDES PURCHASED BY TRADE NAME AND EPA REGISTRATION NUMBER ON THE BACK OF THIS FORM.

NAME OF CERTIFIED APPLICATOR | CERTIFICATION I.D. NO.

ADDRESS

SEPARATELY BELOW ALL RESTRICTED PESTICIDES USED

NAME OF PESTICIDE AND EPA REGISTRATION NO.	CROP	TARGET	DATE(S) TREATED	APPLICATOR'S INITIALS

141

Most of you are not familiar with the classification of chemical products and/or the reasons for their specific handling recommendations. To help you understand this better, a form should be provided by your insurance carrier for the benefit of your fire department, personnel, as well as yourself. People outside New York state should consult their insurance carrier or local fire company jurisdiction to inform themselves of the appropriate procedures.

The New York State form is from The Office of Fire Prevention and Control. It is referred to as the "Hazardous Materials Report Form" (F100965-001 4/82).

The portion V where hazardous materials are listed shows the identifying symbols for each material category. The symbol on the container you purchase will correspond to one in this listing. This, therefore, serves to identify the category of material involved. Each category of material has its own care and handling procedure. The back sheet explains these categories. Read this over to familiarize yourself with them. When you purchase a material with a symbol on it that is unknown to you, consult this form or question your supplier.

Should a crisis or potential crisis be in evidence, immediate assistance is available from a number of sources. Your nearest poison control center should be contacted; other pesticide emergency response resources are:

PESTICIDE EMERGENCY RESPONSE RESOURCES

CHEMTREC   Spill cleanup information   1 (800) 424-9300

Pesticide Safety Team Network (PSTN)   1 (800) 424-9300

Pesticide Companies   (See Listing)

National Pesticide Telecommunications
Network (NPTN) US EPA & Texas Tech School
of Medicine   1 (800) 858-7378

Recognition and Management of Pesticide
Poisonings US EPA Office of Pesticide
Programs, Washington, D.C. 20460
EPA - 540/980-005

PESTICIDE POISONING CONSULTANTS:

Western States:
D. Morgan   Business -   (319) 353-5558
                      Home   -   (319) 338-8487

Eastern States:
S. Sandifer   Business -   (803) 792-2281
                      Home   -   (803) 722-7760
          =====================================

Chemical Manufacturers' Assn. -   1-800-262-8200
This toll-free number has been established to provide non-emergency health and safety info concerning any chemical-based product (toxicity, disposal, etc.) Mon-Fri 8 am to 9 pm EST.

PESTICIDE PRECAUTIONARY STATEMENT

Pesticides used improperly can be injurious to man, animals, and plants. Follow the directions and heed all precautions on the labels.

Store pesticides in original containers under lock and key—out of the reach of children and animals—and away from food and feed.

Apply pesticides so that they do not endanger humans, livestock, crops, beneficial insects, fish, and wildlife. Do not apply pesticides when there is danger of drift, when honey bees or other pollinating insects are visiting plants, or in ways that may contaminate water or leave illegal residues.

Avoid prolonged inhalation of pesticide sprays or dusts; wear protective clothing and equipment if specified on the container.

If your hands become contaminated with a pesticide, do not eat or drink until you have washed. In case a pesticide is swallowed or gets in the eyes, follow the first aid treatment given on the label, and get prompt medical attention. If a pesticide is spilled on your skin or clothing, remove clothing immediately and wash skin thoroughly.

Do not clean spray equipment or dump excess spray material near ponds, streams, or wells. Because it is difficult to remove all traces of herbicides from equipment, do not use the same equipment for insecticides or fungicides that you use for herbicides.

Dispose of empty pesticide containers promptly. Have them buried at a sanitary land-fill dump, or crush and bury them in a level, isolated place.

Note: Some States have restrictions on the use of certain pesticides. Check your State and local regulations. Also, because registrations of pesticides are under constant review by the Federal Environmental Protection Agency, consult your county agricultural agent or State extension specialist to be sure the intended use is still registered.

Christmas Tree IPM

by
Dr. Thomas A. Green

What is IPM?

Integrated Pest Management, or IPM, is an approach to growing a high quality product by maintaining insect, disease, wildlife and weed pests below economically damaging levels. Rather than attempting to eliminate all pests at all times, the IPM approach emphasizes managing crop production such that pests never cause more damage to the crop than the cost of controlling them.

Of course, this only makes sense. You throw money down the drain if you spray for a pest which is not severe enough to cause a loss greater than what you are spending to control it.

What are the benefits of practicing IPM?

Dr. Mike Raupp of the University of Maryland has done some pioneering work in ornamental crop IPM. Mike and his colleagues designed experiments where they set up an array of nursery plants suffering from varying degrees of pest damage. They then asked consumers how much they would pay for each plant. They determined that picture-perfect plants did not necessarily command a higher price than those with low to moderate levels of pest damage.

Therefore, we can conclude that the grower who keeps his or her crop covered with pesticide to prevent the least bit of pest damage is not likely to recover the cost of those sprays by charging a premium price. The grower who practices IPM, carefully sampling pest populations, and treating only when necessary to prevent damage that will actually impact the selling price, is most likley to end up with the highest profits at the end of the season.

What other benefits are available to IPM growers? A grower who practices IPM is much less likely to suffer from a surprise pest attack. IPM requires a familiarity with pest and symptom identification, life cycle information, and all possible control options. As the grower masters this knowledge, out-of-the-ordinary pests events will be more readily apparent and dealt with before they become pest disasters.

Using pesticides only when needed preserves beneficial insects. These "good bugs" are our allies in producing high quality crops. Insects which feed on mites and aphids are especially important in Christmas Tree production. In most years, mite and aphid pests are completely controlled by their own natural enemies, like lacewings, ladybugs, syrphid flies, and predatory mites. When we spray, needed or not, many of these beneficials are killed. This can release mite, aphid, and other pests from their natural control, requiring a special spray for these pests which would never have been a problem without the first spray! Beneficial insect populations can be supplemented with commercially produced beneficials when necessary.

Of course, we are all concerned about excessive pesticide use. An IPM grower can and should let his or her customers know what methods are being employed to keep pesticide use to a minimum. Some states have IPM certification programs for growers who demonstrate a commitment to ongoing training in and use of IPM methods. Showing your concern for your customers and the environment builds customer loyalty.

Responsible pesticide use through IPM benefits all growers. By treating only when needed, pest resistance to pesticides is delayed. If we all were to spray every week, needed or not, one of us is much more likely to encounter the pest which by chance has the right genes to survive the pesticide. This pest will reproduce and soon our sprays will no longer be effective in controlling serious pest outbreaks.

How do we practice IPM?

I like to think of IPM as a three-step process. Number one, we must become familiar with our pests and pest damage. What they look like, where to find them, and when to look for them. This is the only way to tell the good bugs from the bad, and when it's ok to have the bad bugs and when it's not. And how many is too many!

Pests and pest problems vary quite a bit from region to region. Pests in Pennsylvania are not all the same as those in the Pacific Northwest. It's important to track down information that's specific to your region.

Number two, once we know these things about our pests, we need to scout the crop regularly. First, gather the tools to do the sampling that's required to keep an eye on your crop. For Christmas Trees, your eyes are the best tools. You can help yourself out with a pocket hand lens, or a head-band mounted Optivisor. Other sampling tools include yellow sticky cards for adelgids and aphids. Use these only if you have a special problem with these pests.

Number three, consider all possible control options. Then you can make the best decision when your knowledge of pest biology, damage thresholds, and scouting results indicate control is needed. For example, weed pests can be controlled by herbicide application, mulch, cultivation, flaming, or mowing. And there are several herbicide options. You need to know which method will be the most cost-effective, and cause the least disruption of your management programs for other pests.

Overwhelmed? Relax. Establishing an IPM program is an ongoing process. Every little bit helps, start small and build from there. The following reference list gives some good sources to get you started. If you have a large enough operation, hiring a specialized IPM consultant may save you enough in pesticide costs to pay for the service.

Resources:

The Cooperative Extension Service
County or State University Office

These folks are the best! They are suffering from state and federal budget cuts, and they're doing their best in spite of it. The agent in your county or at your state University may not be specialized in Christmas Tree production and may not have the answer to your specific question. They will refer you to someone or some reference material to solve your problem.

Christmas Tree Growers Associations

There are a number of these across the country. Highly recommended if you are not already a member. These associations organize meetings and produce newsletters which may include information on IPM.

Cornell Christmas Tree Newsletter

Published every other week April through June, then every three weeks July through September for a toal of 10 issues. Focuses on what is happening in New York Christmas Tree plantings throughout the season. Tells you what to look for and when. How to time and target control measures if needed. $12 per year to Dr. George Hudler, Dept. of Plant Pathology, 315 Plant Science Building, Cornell University, Ithaca, NY 14853.

Ohio Christmas Tree Disease Control VideoTape

#CTD12 (VT31) Produced in 1987. $25 plus 3.50 postage to Extension Publications Office, The Ohio State University, 385 Kottman Hall, 2021 Coffey Rd., Columbus OH 43210-1044. (614) 292-1607. Also available are the **Christmas Tree Growers Handbook** (#CTGH NARE2), 114 page comprehensive management guide, $8 plus $3.50, and **Insect Pests of Christmas Trees** (#IPCT bull. 619) 21 pages of insect information, $2.00 plus $1.

Penn Pages

This is an on-line (computer-operated) service provided by the Pennsylvania State University. If you have a computer and modem, you can call this service and download a timely bulletin on Christmas Tree production. Information from the College of Agricultural Sciences, Penn State University, University Park, PA 16802. Phone (814) 865-2541.

The Christmas Tree Pest Manual

An excellent, though aging (1983), guide to Christmas Tree Pests, especially for North Central growers. Color photos of insect and disease pests and symptoms. $14 to the Superintendent of Documents, Government Printing Office, 710 N. Capitol St., Washington, DC 20402-9325. Document # 001-001-00641-6. Can be ordered by phone with a credit card, (202) 783-3238.

Northwest Christmas Tree Production Guide

As of February 1993, this guide is in the planning stage, projected printing date is late 1993. This publication will be put together by specialists in the Northwest, at the request of the Washington State Christmas Tree Grower's Association.

Pest Management Supply Inc., 311 River Dr., Hadley, MA 01035 (413) 549-7246 , FAX (413) 549-3930.

Features a full line of identification aids and sampling tools, including yellow sticky cards, magnifiers, sweep nets, beneficial insects. Free Catalog. PMSI has several hundred private consultants as customers. We may be able to help you with a referral to a qualified consultant in your area.

Thomas Green received his Ph.D. in Entomology from the University of Massachusetts. He founded Pest Management Supply Inc. in 1980 to provide one-stop mail-order shopping for growers of all crops who want to practice IPM. He welcomes your questions and comments!

Clothing selection and Laundering for pesticide applicators

Wearing the proper type of clothing can help pesticide applicators and mixer-loaders prevent accidental poisoning. Poisoning most often results from pesticides entering the body through the skin (dermal exposure) rather than through the lungs or mouth. Dermal exposure accounts for more than 80 percent of pesticide poisonings. Pesticides are absorbed through the skin on different parts of the body at different rates (fig. 1).

Symptoms of pesticide poisoning range from headaches and vomiting to unconsciousness and death. Dermatitis, a rash caused by a pesticide contacting the skin, is common and a major cause of missed workdays.

Your main defense against pesticide exposure is wearing proper clothing and protective equipment (fig. 2). Read and follow pesticide label directions and wear the protective clothing listed on the label. Choose clothing based on pesticide label requirements, personal preference, and type of work to be performed. Always meet the label's minimum requirements.

Protective clothing comes in several fabrics. They

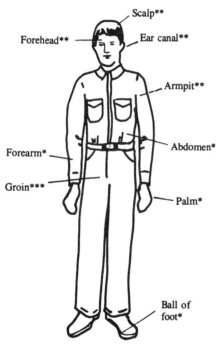

Absorption rates — *Medium, **High, ***Very High.

Fig. 1. Pesticides enter some parts of the body more readily than others.

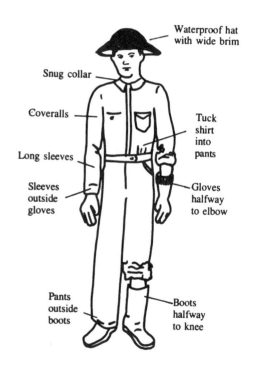

Fig. 2. Wear protective clothing correctly: shirt sleeves over gloves and pant legs over boots.

vary in chemical resistance, weight, strength, resistance to ripping and puncturing, response to temperature extremes, comfort, durability, and ability to be cleaned. Because no one material will protect you from all chemicals, you may need to have different clothes for different jobs.

Make sure the clothing you wear while applying pesticides is clean, dry, and free of holes. Cover all skin areas with appropriate clothing. Garments should allow freedom of movement. Batwing or raglan sleeves provide more freedom than conventional set-in sleeves.

Avoid swallowing pesticides, splashing them in your eyes, or spilling them on your body or clothing. Have the phone numbers of your local poison control center, doctor, ambulance, sheriff, and fire department ready for emergencies.

Pesticides fall into three toxicity categories:

- **Category I** pesticides are toxic and labeled with a skull and crossbones. They may be labeled with the words *danger* and *poison*.
- **Category II** pesticides are moderately toxic and are labeled with the word *warning*.
- **Category III** pesticides are slightly toxic and are labeled with the word *caution*.

Protective clothing

At a minimum, wear full-length pants and a long-sleeved shirt made from a tightly woven fabric when working with pesticides. Coveralls made of 100 percent cotton or a 65-35 cotton-polyester blend provide an extra layer of protection.

See Table 1 for clothing and equipment required for mixing, loading, and applying pesticides in various toxicity categories (i.e., caution, warning, danger) and with label statements. Since loading or mixing pesticides exposes you to spills, you may need different protection than when you apply sprays.

Fabric finishes for increased protection

Two renewable finishes help fabrics such as denim to resist absorption of pesticides into the fabric fiber. They are starch and fluorocarbon polymer. You can apply them to the lower pant leg to provide knee-to-ankle protection while applying pesticides.

A stiff starch finish traps the pesticide, reducing the amount of chemical that passes through the material. Starch also aids in cleaning because the pesticide washes away with the starch during laundering. Garments need to be starched after each laundering to maintain the added protection.

Fluorocarbon or soil-repellent finishes such as Scotchgard, Zepel, and Fybrite form a barrier that keeps pesticide out of the clothing. Reapply these finishes as needed, typically after four or five washings.

Disposable protective clothing

Disposable clothing is manufactured from a variety of lightweight, tear-resistant materials. Disposable fabrics, such as Tyvek fabrics, are made from non-woven, bonded fiber materials. When coated, disposable fabrics resist liquids. No Tyvek fabrics are effective against chlorinated hydrocarbons. Polyethylene-coated Tyvek is unsuitable for extended exposure to organophosphate pesticides.

Disposable coveralls should have elasticized wrists and ankles and flaps over the zipper. Make sure coveralls fit properly to avoid unnecessary wear and exposure.

Waterproof clothing

Waterproof clothing generally is made of fabric that has a waterproof coating or that is laminated to a waterproof material. The amount of protection depends on the waterproofing material. Gore-tex, latex rubber, PVC, neoprene, and butyl are common waterproofing materials. A new fabric, Comfort-Gard II, provides splash protection and yet breathes like cotton.

Avoid waterproof clothing that is lined with a woven fabric because the lining can become contaminated with pesticide. Instead, choose linings of a nonabsorbent material such as polyester.

Select fabrics resistant to the particular chemical being used. Look for strong, noncorrosive fasteners. Waterproof pants should be bib overall style so they overlap sufficiently with jackets. Select jackets with hoods for greater protection of head and neck.

Seams

Four types of seam are available for disposable and waterproof protective clothing. They are plain (sewn), bound, sealed (with liquid sealant or tape), and ultrasonic (heat sealed). For dry or granular pesticide applications, clothing with sewn seams gives adequate protection. A serged seam, typically produced with three interlocking threads, also provides adequate protection.

Clothing with bound seams performs well for working with liquids. Bound seams have a chemical-resistant binding over two layers of fabric that are sewn together. *Do not wear clothing with bound seams for extended contact with liquids.* Consider wearing clothing with sealed or ultrasonic seams for liquid pesticide applications during which the product may form pools on the garment.

Aprons

Aprons protect the front of the body during pesticide handling and mixing. Wear aprons in addition to other protective clothing, not instead of it. Choose an apron that has a wide bib to protect the chest. Choose one long enough to protect clothing. Aprons with sleeves are available.

Disposable aprons are made of thin plastic and can tear or puncture easily. Disposable aprons made of Saranex-treated Tyvek provide better protection.

Reusable aprons require regular cleaning and decontamination

Discard aprons with holes or tears.

Gloves

Waterproof gloves are an essential part of your protective equipment. Always wear them when working with pesticides. Never wear leather or cloth gloves because they absorb water and pesticides. Instead,

Table 1. Protective clothing and equipment requirements.

Summarized pesticide label statement	Mixer-loader Toxicity category		Applicator Toxicity category	
	I-II	*III*	*I-II*	*III***
Precautions should be taken to prevent exposure.	A, B, C, F, G, H, R *	A, B, C, F, G, H *	B, C, F, G, H, R *	B, C, F, G, H, R *
Protective clothing or protective equipment is to be worn.	A, B, C, F, G, H, R *	B, C, F, G, H, R *	B, C, F, G, H	C, F, G, H, R *
Clean clothing is to be worn.	C	C	C	C
Contact with clothing should be avoided.	A, B, C	B, C	B, C	C
Contact with shoes should be avoided.	B	B	B	B
Rubber boots or rubber foot coverings are to be worn.	B	B	B	B
Contact with skin should be avoided.	A, B, C, F, G, H	B, C, F, G, H	B, C, G, H	C, F, G, H *
A cap or hat is to be worn.	H	H	H	H
An apron is to be worn.	A	A		
Rubber gloves are to be worn.	G	G	G	G
Contact with eyes should be avoided.	F	F	F	F
Goggles or face shield is to be worn.	F	F	F	F
Avoid inhalation.	R	R	R *	R *
A respirator is to be worn.	R	R	R *	R *

 A daily change of clean coveralls or clean outer clothing. Wear waterproof pants and jacket if there is any chance of becoming wet with spray.

Disposable suits made of Tyvek can be used in some, but not all, situations. Uncoated Tyvek can be worn in place of coveralls or long-sleeved shirt and pants. It will not take the place of waterproof outer clothing. Tyvek that has been coated with polyethylene can be worn in place of waterproof clothing in some situations, but not with organophosphate liquids. The solvents in these pesticides will break down the polyethylene coating. Saranex-coated Tyvek suits can be used effectively with organophosphates. Neither uncoated nor Saranex-coated Tyvek adequately protects against chlorinated hydrocarbons such as methoxychlor.

 Waterproof apron made from rubber or synthetic material. Use for mixing liquids.

 Waterproof boots or foot coverings made from rubber or synthetic material.

 Face shield, goggles, or full-face respirator. Goggles with side shields or a full-face respirator is required for handling or applying dusts, wettable powders, or granules and during exposure to spray mist. Safety glasses with brow or temple protection may be worn if the label does not specify goggles or face shield.

 Waterproof, unlined gloves made from rubber or synthetic materials.

 Waterproof, wide-brimmed hat with nonabsorbent headband or hood if wearing a waterproof plastic rainsuit with hood attached.

 Cartridge-type respirator approved for pesticide vapors unless label specifies another type of respirator such as a dust mask, canister-type gas mask, or self-contained breathing apparatus.

*Use this equipment when there is a likelihood of exposure to spray mist, dust, or vapors.

**If the *Category III* pesticide application is being made in an enclosed area such as a greenhouse, or if the application consists of a concentrate spray of 100 gallons per acre or less in a grove, orchard, or vineyard, then use the protective equipment guidelines for *Category I-II* pesticides.

Source: Zavola, Melanie. 1991. The illustrated guide to pesticide safety. Instructor's edition. Univ. Calif., Div. of Agriculture and Natural Resources, Oakland.

wear clean, unlined gloves made from natural rubber, latex, PVC, butyl, neoprene, nitrile, or Silver Shield. Generally, latex is acceptable for dry formulations. Nitrile and butyl are adequate for most pesticides. Check the pesticide label for the proper glove material to use.

Choose gloves that reach the midforearm. For general work, wear protective clothing sleeves over the gloves. For overhead work, tuck sleeves inside the gloves.

Footwear

Unless you are prohibited by the label, you can wear leather when applying granular material and most category III (caution) chemicals. Leather can absorb pesticides and should not be used when there is a possibility of getting them soaked.

Wear unlined, chemical-resistant footwear when working with moderately and highly toxic pesticides. Unlined, chemical-resistant footwear is a sensible choice for all pesticide use. Common boot materials are neoprene, PVC, nitrile, butyl, and natural rubber or latex. Latex is effective only with dry formulations. Follow label directions as to the composition of your boots.

Protective boots should be calf high. Wear the legs of your protective pants outside the boots to prevent spray from getting inside. Rubber bands can seal pant legs around the outsides of the boots.

Choose a textured sole to provide adequate traction on wet surfaces.

Head protection

Take special care to protect your scalp, ear canal, and forehead. Select a wide-brimmed, waterproof hat that will protect your neck, eyes, mouth, and face. Plastic hard hats with plastic sweatbands are also a good choice. They are waterproof and cool in hot weather.

Avoid hats with fabric or leather sweatbands. Fabric sweatbands are difficult to clean, and leather ones cannot be thoroughly cleaned. Because they absorb pesticides, baseball caps offer little protection.

Eye protection

Always wear eye protection while mixing and loading pesticides; while cleaning, adjusting, or repairing contaminated equipment; during most applications; and whenever the label requires. Eye protection is available as goggles, face shields, or full-face respirators.

Goggles can be worn over eyeglasses. Goggles have elastic or rubber straps. Replace or wash straps when they become contaminated. Hoods help protect straps.

Face shields provide the best protection during pesticide mixing because they protect the face and eyes

from splashing liquids. Ones that wrap under the chin are best.

Do not wear contact lenses when handling pesticides. Chemicals can get behind the contact lenses and damage your eyes.

Respirators

When there is any risk of inhaling toxic pesticides, or when the label requires, wear a well-fitting respirator approved by the National Institute of Occupational Safety and Health, the U.S. Bureau of Mines, or the U.S. Department of Agriculture. Several types are available. Use the respirator recommended by the label.

Cartridge respirators are commonly used in pesticide application. Carefully follow directions and change the cartridge as recommended by the manufacturer. Disposable masks protect against some dusts but do not protect against liquid chemicals or vapors.

Fit is important. If you have facial hair or wear eyeglasses you may not be able to get a good seal. If you must wear corrective lenses, choose a full-face respirator specifically designed for corrective lenses.

Other considerations

- Have one or more sets of clothing to wear only while applying pesticides. Some pesticides are very difficult to remove from clothing. Even after laundering, they may remain in the fabric. Change clothing daily!
- If possible, remove contaminated clothing outdoors or in an entry. If you have used a granular pesticide, shake your clothing outdoors and empty pockets and cuffs. Place contaminated clothing in a plastic bag or plastic-lined box until laundering.
- Avoid wearing a wristwatch with a leather band or any jewelry made of leather. Once leather has been contaminated, it cannot be decontaminated.

Laundering recommendations

The cleaning of pesticide contaminated clothing raises many questions. What is the best method? What water temperature should be used during laundering? What about contamination of other clothing? Is one type of detergent better than another? This publication will help answer these and other questions.

Key words on all pesticide labels identify the toxicity of the products (Table 1). Use the key word as a guide when handling and laundering pesticide-contaminated clothing. Handling clothing contaminated with highly toxic chemicals requires more care than handling clothing contaminated with slightly toxic chemicals. However, all clothing contaminated with pesticides should be handled with care.

Table 1. Toxicity ratings of various pesticides.

Key word	Toxicity	Examples*		
DANGER POISON	Highly toxic/ concentrated	Avenge cyprex Counter Dinitro Di-Syston Dyfonate	furadan Guthion Hoelon methomyl paraquat	parathion supracide Temik Thimet Vendex
WARNING	Moderately toxic	Avadex diazinon dimethoate Lorsban		maneb Pydrin Roundup
CAUTION	Slightly toxic	Banvel Benlate captan 2,4-D Eptam		Glean malathion Pounce Sevin Treflan

*Toxicity of the pesticide may vary depending upon the formulated product. Use the key word as an indication of the toxicity level.

You cannot effectively launder clothing that has been saturated with pesticide mixture or that has received a spill of undiluted pesticide (concentrate). Pesticide concentrates have been known to stay in clothing even after 10 washings. Clothing contaminated with pesticide concentrates should be destroyed.

Wash contaminated clothing as soon as possible. It is much easier to clean fresh pesticide residues than to clean residues that have built up on the fabric or dried and set in the fabric. Clothing exposed to pesticides daily should be changed and laundered daily. *Always wear rubber gloves when handling contaminated clothing to prevent pesticides from entering your body.* Wash your gloves after each use and use them only for this purpose.

Store contaminated clothing in a separate container outside the living area of the house. A plastic bag or cardboard box lined with plastic will do.

Know when pesticides have been used so all clothing can be properly laundered. *Wash contaminated clothing separately from the family wash.* Pesticide residues move from contaminated clothing to other clothing when they are laundered together. If you often launder large amounts of clothing used in pesticide application, consider using a separate washing machine.

Wash only one or two garments in a single load. Wash garments contaminated by the same pesticide(s) together.

Prerinse contaminated clothing in the washing machine — twice, if possible — to help remove pesticide particles from the fabric. Prerinsing is especially good at dislodging particles of a wettable powder. Shirts, pants, coveralls, and underwear should be soaked in hot, soapy water for at least ½ hour as part of the prerinse procedure. Use any prewash product such as a solvent soak, prewash spray, or liquid detergent.

Washing in hot water (120° to 140°F) removes more pesticide from the clothing than washing in cooler water. Remember: the hotter, the better. Avoid cold-water washing! Although cold-water washing saves energy, it won't clean contaminated clothes.

Laundry detergents (phosphates, heavy duty liquids, or carbonates) are similarly effective in removing pesticides from fabric. However, heavy duty liquid detergents are more effective than others in removing emulsifiable concentrate pesticide formulations because of their oil-removing ability. Neither bleach nor ammonia has been shown to aid pesticide removal.

Launder using a full water level to allow the water to thoroughly flush the fabric. If your washer has a suds-saver system *do not use* it when laundering contaminated clothing.

Clothing worn while using a slightly toxic pesticide may be cleaned in one machine washing. However, at least three washings are needed for clothing contaminated with more-toxic pesticides, particularly if the clothing has a pesticide odor or a visible pesticide spot or stain.

After laundering, rinse the washing machine by running an empty load with hot water and the same detergent, machine settings, and cycles used for laundering the contaminated clothing. This is important because the washing machine may retain residues that carry over to later loads.

Line dry clothes to keep residues from collecting in the clothes dryer. Also, ultraviolet rays from sunlight help break down pesticides.

Renewable (temporary) protection

Two renewable finishes help fabrics resist pesticides and aid in cleaning. These finishes are starch and fluorocarbon polymer. They may be applied to the lower pant leg to provide knee-to-ankle protection.

A stiff starch finish traps the pesticide, thus reducing the amount of chemical that could pass through the material to the skin. Starch also aids in cleaning because the pesticide washes away with the starch during laundering. Garments need to be starched after each laundering.

Fluorocarbon or soil-repellent finishes such as Scotchgard, Zepel, and Fybrite form a barrier that prevents pesticide absorption and penetration. Reapply these finishes as needed, typically after four or five washings.

Waterproof protective clothing

Remove as much pesticide residue as possible from waterproof clothing by washing it with a hose and scrub brush out of doors. Wash in an area where the runoff will not cause contamination, such as a concrete pad or level, graveled driveway. Wash the clothing before removing it, if possible, to avoid contact between the contaminated clothing and your skin or clean clothing. Store the protective clothing in a clean plastic bag until it can be laundered.

To decontaminate the protective clothing, first soak it in warm, soapy water for ½ hour, then wash it in a washing machine using warm (not hot) water and liquid laundry detergent. Wash the garments separately from all other clothing to prevent contamination.

Hang up waterproof clothing to dry. Do not put it in a clothes dryer because the heat of the dryer may damage the waterproof finish. If the clothing is hung in direct sunlight, turn it inside out. This will prevent deterioration of the waterproof finish by the sun and help deactivate any pesticide remaining on the inside lining.

Goggles and face shields

Goggles and face shields should be washed in warm water and detergent. Use a soft brush, but do not rub or wipe the clear plastic lenses. Blot them dry and store them in a clean plastic bag. Check the headband to make sure it is in good condition.

Respirators

Discard cartridges, canisters, or filter pads after 8 hours of use, when breathing becomes difficult, or you notice pesticide odor. Wash the face piece with detergent and water, rinse it thoroughly, and let it dry in a well-ventilated area. Do not use alcohol or other solvents because they damage rubber and plastic. Store the respirator in a clean plastic bag.

Waterproof gloves and boots

Wash the outsides of waterproof gloves and boots with detergent and water before removing them. After removing them, wash them inside and out with detergent and water. Rinse them thoroughly and dry them in a well-ventilated area.

Storing safety equipment

Never use personal safety equipment for any other purpose. When not using it, keep it stored in a clean, dry place protected from temperature extremes and bright light. If possible, store safety equipment in resealable plastic bags. Light, heat, dirt, and air pollutants all contribute to the deterioration of rubber, plastic, and synthetic rubber products. *Never store protective clothing or equipment in an area where pesticides are kept.*

Keep household members safe

Follow these suggestions for reducing the chances of contaminating the family laundry and endangering family members:

- Whenever feasible, wear disposable protective clothing that can be destroyed after use.
- Wear clean protective clothing when working with pesticides. Wash contaminated clothing *daily*.
- Remove contaminated clothing at the work site and empty pockets and cuffs. Place clothing in a clean plastic bag until it can be laundered. Keep contaminated clothing separate from all other laundry.
- Remove and destroy clothing immediately if a pesticide concentrate spilled on it.
- Do not attempt to wash heavily contaminated clothing; destroy it and take it to an approved disposal site.

Destroying and disposing of pesticide-contaminated clothing

To properly dispose of pesticide-contaminated clothing, farmers and most private applicators can cut up clothing so that it unuseable and dispose of it in a landfill. Place clothing in a plastic bag to protect yourself and landfill workers.

Regulated generators of hazardous waste — applicators who generate 220 pounds of hazardous waste or 2 pounds of acutely hazardous waste annually — whose clothing is saturated with a formulation containing a U or P listed chemical as the sole active ingredient need to dispose of the clothing as a hazardous waste. If the clothing is saturated with a formulation containing more than one active ingredient, the clothing may not be considered a hazardous waste and could be disposed of in a landfill. If you have any questions, contact the regional office of the Idaho Division of Environmental Quality.

Always wear required protective clothing when working with pesticides.

Steps for washing pesticide-contaminated clothing

1. Keep pesticide-contaminated clothing separate from all other laundry.

2. Do not handle contaminated clothing with your bare hands; wear rubber gloves or shake clothing from a plastic bag into the washer.

3. Wash only a few items of clothing at a time so that the washing machine agitator can move the clothing freely during the wash cycle. Wash a medium-sized load in a large tub with a full volume of water. If your washer has a suds-saver system *do not use it* when laundering contaminated clothing. Do not combine clothing contaminated with different pesticides; wash them in separate loads.

4. Before washing, presoak clothing:
   - Soak clothing in a tub or automatic washer or spray them out of doors with a garden hose.
   - Apply prewash spray or liquid laundry detergent to soiled spots.

5. Wash garments in the washing machine, using the hottest water temperature, a full water level, and the normal (12 minute) wash cycle. Use the maximum recommended amount of liquid laundry detergent. Neither bleach nor ammonia seems to affect the removal of most pesticides. *Never* use both.

6. If garments had a pesticide odor or spots or stains before being washed, rewash them one or two times as in step 5.

7. Clean the washing machine before using it for other laundry by repeating step 5 using hot water, the full water level, the normal wash cycle, laundry detergent, *and no clothing.*

8. Dry laundry outdoors on a clothesline to avoid contaminating the automatic dryer.

9. If you wash a large amount of pesticide-contaminated clothing, consider using a separate washing machine for that purpose only.

MAJOR FOREST PEST MAMMALS AND BIRDS

Although they usually are considered to be desirable inhabitants of forest environments, some mammals and birds may seriously damage forest crops. Such damage often is overlooked or tolerated by landowners. Occasionally, however -- and particularly in forest nursery operations -- such damage may become economically significant and control measures are indicated. Conservation officers may issue permits to take wildlife whenever it becomes destructive to private property.

Deer

Deer feed mainly upon the buds and twigs of trees and shrubs. Resulting damage is easily distinguished from rabbit damage; deer have no upper front teeth, so must twist off the twigs, leaving ragged broken stubs. In contrast, the stubs left by rabbits look as though they had been formed by a single cut from a sharp knife. Deer browsing may kill or deform young trees through repeated browsing of twigs up to seven feet from ground level, plus additional heights depending upon snow depth. In large areas, such as forests, deer numbers must be reduced by harvesting sufficient animals; there are no repellents currently available which are economically suitable for use over wide areas. Small areas such as nurseries may be protected by deer repellent compounds sprayed upon the trees. The tops of nursery trees may be dipped in a thiram formulation to provide protection at the time of transplanting. Brush or spray applications may also be used; a more dilute solution may be used as a spray during the growing season. Compounds containing the ingredient thiram are also effective in repelling rabbits. This is most economically feasible for protection during months that nursery stock is dormant, or in Christmas tree plantations.

Rabbits

Cottontail rabbits are active year-round and feed upon the buds, twigs and bark of young trees in winter. The sharp, clean "slice" made when these animals clip off a terminal shoot looks as though it had been done with one stroke of a sharp knife.

Small areas of high-value trees such as nurseries may be fenced effectively against rabbits, using a tight chicken-wire fence of one-inch mesh. Commercial rabbit repellents may be sprayed or painted on young trees two feet higher than the snow is expected to drift. Frequent cutting of grass, weeds and brush in nursery areas and Christmas tree plantations helps to reduce the protective cover for rabbits. The tops of nursery trees may be dipped in a thiram formulation to provide protection at the time of transplanting. Brush or spray applications may be used; a more dilute solution may be used as a spray during the growing season. On larger areas, trapping may reduce rabbit numbers if several traps are used persistently. Box traps should be baited with apple or carrot. Where guns may be used safely, one of the most effective ways to reduce rabbit numbers is through shooting. A good rabbit hound will greatly increase hunting effectiveness.

Woodchucks

Woodchucks may occupy forest habitats, particularly woodland edges. They dig extensive burrows with two or three entrances, in which they hibernate during winter months. A mound of freshly dug soil at a burrow entrance, during spring months, identifies an actively used burrow. The bark of young trees in the vicinity of burrows may be severely damaged by chewing or clawing.

In April and May, woodchucks may be destroyed by fumigation of actively used burrows, with little danger to other valuable animals that sometimes occupy deserted "chuck" burrows. Special cartridges for gassing woodchuck dens are manufactured by the U. S. Fish and Wildlife Service and are sold through hardware and farm-supply stores. Avoid using them when fire hazards exist. Shooting and trapping are also effective. A skilled rifleman can control a local population of woodchucks within a few days. Number 1-1/2 or number 2 traps may be set at burrow entrances and concealed with a few leaves; they should be well-secured to prevent their being dragged into the burrow. Repeated control is necessary with all methods, as vacant burrows are quickly occupied by woodchucks from adjoining areas.

Field Mice

Field mice are among our most prolific and numerous mammals and are found wherever there is grass to feed upon. They construct networks of surface runways through the vegetation in summer and dig 2-inch-wide tunnels through snow in winter. During winters, particularly, they may gnaw bark from young trees. Usually this damage is not extensive enough in forest situations to warrant control. When such damage is extensive, mouse populations are usually very high. High mouse populations one year are usually followed by very low populations for the next several years, allowing forest regeneration to proceed without serious delay.

Zinc-phosphide treated grain baits are highly effective in reducing populations of these mice, but generally are economically feasible only on small areas which support high value trees, such as nurseries and Christmas tree plantations.

Tree seeds may be treated with thiram to protect them from damage by mice. This compound acts as a taste repellent.

Birds

Tree seeds may be treated with thiram to protect them from damage by birds through its action as a taste repellent.

Dormant terminal buds of small specimen trees may be protected against Pine Grosbeaks by small plastic sacks. Where serious damage is extensive, U. S. Game Management Agents may issue permits to kill migratory birds. Generally, shooting in the area where these bird flocks are feeding will move them to another feeding site.

Visitors at exhibit booth observing procedure for making an evergreen wreath. National Christmas Tree Growers Convention (a biennial meeting) Spokane, Washington - 1992.

BUSINESS CONSIDERATIONS

What does it cost to grow a Christmas Tree?

Too often the novice and experienced grower alike fail to search for a satisfactory answer to the question, "What are my chances for making a profit in growing and marketing Christmas trees?" In the past, the prospective tree grower has exhibited almost boundless enthusiasm over the financial returns from growing Christmas trees. Many have depended on this enthusiasm to carry them over all manner of obstacles and disappointments. Enthusiasm alone, however, is not a substitute for a careful assessment of the economics of growing Christmas trees.

The prudent person will attempt to evaluate the income potential of an enterprise as a basis for deciding to invest in it or not. For someone already actively growing trees, it is important that costs and returns be monitored constantly for the various specie and phases of the business as a basis for management decisions.

Most people continue with Christmas tree growing because it is enjoyable and satisfying, as well as profitable. Here we want to give you a basis for determining profitability or loss, whichever. Very few growers in the past ten years have experienced a "loss" on a year-to-year cash-in-pocket basis. Most growers have never really analyzed it on the basis that will be shown in this chapter.

Several key factors have contributed to the "success" which many have enjoyed in recent years. Some of these are:

1. Undersupply.

2. An inflationary economy.

3. Trend to choose and cut (fewer middlemen).

4. Technological changes:
    a. Better Machinery (small tractors, shearing equipment, etc.)
    b. Better and more selective chemicals (herbicides, insecticides, etc.)
    c. Higher quality planting stock (select seed sources, faster growing, etc.)

This section requires careful attention because Factor No. 1 (shortage of trees) may undergo a drastic change in the next ten years. Many people believe there may still be a shortage of high quality trees. That's why it is essential that new or old growers, alike, must make quality foremost.

A grower must take into consideration all costs. All expenditures include time, equipment and value of your land (or leasing costs). Also, income that would have accrued if invested in some other venture and for the same period (a money market account could be one option).

Schedule F of the 1040 Tax Form does not take into consideration expenses such as time and land value. You should place a value on your time just as if you had to hire the work done. A work log or complete "diary" of activities should be kept. Guesses are not good enough!!!

Since, even under the new tax laws, Christmas trees are taxed as capital gains (see section on Income Tax), the cost of seedlings and planting, fertilizer, lime, and land improvements must all be capitalized.

If your land and buildings have joint use with some other crop, then use only the costs that are applicable to your Christmas tree venture.

You need to determine land, building and equipment costs. (Land cannot be depreciated, however). Include improvements of the land to the value, i.e., cost of drainage, tile, brush clearing, etc. When arriving at a value of your buildings, figure interest on this value. Value of equipment should be treated likewise, less one-year depreciation. (You should be keeping a depreciation schedule for all your capital items).

Your labor will include:
- (Your own actual time spent)
- Site preparation (capitalized if hired)
- Planting time
- Application of pesticides
- Liming and fertilizer time
- Mowing (not capitalized)
- Shearing (not capitalized)
- Surveying/Inspection of areas
- Equipment/Machinery repair
- Bookkeeping/Records
- Travel time (to and from farm, trips to meetings and conventions, etc.
- Other activity specific to your situation

Expenditures are many - they include hired help, planting stock, fertilizer, pesticides, various supplies, equipment parts, fuel, vehicle operation costs, association dues and subscriptions, legal and professional fees, licenses, taxes, utilities, interest, and banking costs. Extra costs may include consulting fees, costs of preparing transplant beds, machine hire, cost of special clothing, barter income and many other items too numerous to mention.

All these costs of items can be expensed on a year-to-year basis. Obviously, many dollars are going out but nothing coming in. It becomes apparent that the true return on your investment can only be calculated after the fact, i.e., until all the costs have been recorded and all the trees from the first year have been cut and sold, you will not know what your profit/loss figure is. Since most growers plant each year, the true cost picture really gets fuzzy after a few years, especially due to replanting, interplanting, etc. You can project costs and returns using the examples that follow.

While true costs are the best guide in evaluating your operation it is essential that some projection be calculated, if for no other reason than to find out if you are "on the right tract". Some growers actually chart their field on quadrille (graph) paper and take a physical survey every year as to survival, condition of the trees, etc. This also gives you the opportunity to see where seedling replacement may be necessary. (See field layout). The first year survey (in the fall) may not be an accurate guide since that particular plant has not gone through the winter (a complete growing season). It will give you an indication, however. If area size or total numbers are large you might walk a row in three or four different places and note the dead or missing trees. Divide the number of trees missing into the number of trees in the row. This gives the percentage of loss.

After all is said and done, we still haven't taken into consideration things like:

A.   A severe winter causing snow/ice damage to trees.

B.   Insect infestation that got out of control - (Gypsy Moth Quarantine such as in Northern New York State with Scleroderris Canker).

C.   Failure to sell trees that were ready for sale; costs rise sharply when salable trees are carried over into the next season.

D.   Glut of trees (reduces income projection by 50%?)

E.   Shifting consumer preference to other kinds of trees.

F.   Fire in the plantation.

G.   Health failure - requiring hiring of labor. (This is the reason why you must calculate your time value).

H.   Work load becomes excessive and a partner comes into the business.

I.   Heavy losses - localized in plantation or occasional in occurrence.
     1. Deer browsing.
     2. Mice girdle a portion or a whole field of trees.
     3. Herbicide injury - complete or partial loss.
     4. Bad planting year - 50% loss, or planting stock deteriorated before planted, etc.

It is necessary to make a series of assumptions regarding future expenses and anticipated returns to obtain an estimate of probable income. Sometimes growers avoid this kind of analysis because they do not have enough confidence in their ability to make good assumptions. They are fearful of error. Indeed, the risk of substantial error has to be admitted. It cannot be entirely avoided because expenses and future income must necessarily be estimated. The estimate of probable income cannot be better than the assumptions made of costs and returns.

160

Table 1 gives information on practices, costs, and returns which is the basis for calculations in the analysis for Scotch pine and white spruce. The data are representative of current practices, but again growers are advised to use their own experience where it differs from the examples.

Tables 2 and 3 show analysis of costs, returns and net incomes for Scotch pine and white spruce through one crop rotation. The procedure should appeal to new and experienced growers alike because it is a way of evaluating the ongoing tree farm business as well as the venture under consideration.

Though the assumed values for costs, returns, and other data are generally representative of local experience, you should be cautioned that costs, selling prices, and practices differ from the sample cases. In such cases, the grower should substitute cost and return figures that best fit your own situation.

Basic Data for Scotch Pine and White Spruce
Cost/Return

Table 1.

	Scotch Pine	White Spruce
Rotation including 1 yr. fallow time	9 yrs.	11 yrs.
Spacing	6 x 6 (1210 trees/acre)	5 x 5 (1 7 4 0 trees/acre)
Area in Lanes and Roads	10%	10%
Net trees per acre	90% of 1210 = 1090 trees	90% of 1740 = 1566 trees
Survival	85% of 1090 = 926 trees	85% of 1566 = 1331 trees
Planting Stock	2-0	3-0
Shearing labor	$4.50 per hr.	$4.50 per hr.
Interest rate	14%	14%
Stumpage price/6-7' trees	$10.00	$12.00
Surviving trees sold	80% of 926 = 741 trees	80% of 1331 = 1065 trees
Lime cost-includes spreading (2 ton/acre)	$30.00/ton	$30.00/ton
Fertilizer 20-10-10	$6.00/50 lb. bag	$ 6 . 0 0 / 5 0 lb. bag

Note: The land value and site improvement costs along with taxes should be prorated over the number of trees in ground since these costs are real whether you plant 1,000 trees or 10,000 trees. If 10,000 trees were planted, these fixed costs would amount to 1/10 of cost per 1,000 since the same amount of cost was spread over 10 times as many trees.

Other references for cost analysis of Christmas trees growing are:

"Costs and Returns in Christmas Tree Management", Research Report No. 155, Michigan State Univ. Agr. Exp. Station, E. Lansing, Michigan. 1972.

The tabulations in Tables 2 and 3 are on the basis of 1 acre of plantation. Income from tree sales assumes the sale of 7-foot trees on the stump. Each cost and return is capitalized at 14 percent compound interest to the end of the crop period.

Table 2. Costs and Returns for Scotch Pine Christmas Trees on a 9-Year Production Period

	Basis	Interest[1] factor	Capitalized the end of 9 years
Management costs & taxes	$80 each year	16.0853	1,286.82
Interest on $700 land value	Annual	2.2520	1,576.40
Cost of stock	$120 per M x 1,090 = $131	3.2520	426.01
Stock shipping cost	$5.00	3.2520	16.25
Planting cost	$120 per M x 1,090 = $131	3.2520	426.01
Weed control at planting	$30	3.2520	97.56
Later weed control	2nd year $30	2.5023	75.07
Later weed control (herbicide)	3rd year $30	2.1950	65.85
Later weed control (herbicide)	4th year $30	1.9254	57.76
Later weed control (mowing)	5th year $50	1.6890	84.45
Later weed control (mowing)	6th year $50	1.4815	74.08
Fertilizer (material & labor) Limed prior to plant - 2 Ton/acre @ $30	1st year $60	3.2520	195.12
6 oz. fertilizer/tree(926 trees)	3rd year $42	2.1950	92.19
8 oz. fertilizer/tree(926 trees)	6th year $55	1.4815	81.48
Spraying for insect control	Annually $10	13.2328	132.33
Shearing	3rd year 4¢/tree x 926 = 37.04 2.1950		81.30
	4th year 5¢/tree x 926 = 46.30 1.9254		89.15
	5th year 10¢/tree x 926 = 92.60 1.6890		156.40
	6th year 12¢/tree x 926 =111.12 1.4815		164.62
	7th year 12¢/tree x 926 =111.12 1.2996		144.41
	8th year 15¢/tree x 679 =101.85 1.1400		116.11
Cleanup for next crop	8th year $25	1.1400	28.50
Trees sold and returns received	7th year 1/3 = 247 x $10.00 = $2,470.00	1.4815	3,659.31
	8th year 2/3 = 494 x $10.00 = $4,940.00	1.2996	6,420.02
Total accumulated returns			10,079.33
Total accumulated costs			5,467.87
Net income for one crop	In 9 years		4,611.46

[1] Interest factor is based on 14% compound rate of interest and appropriate time period.

Table 3. Costs and Returns for White Spruce Christmas Trees on an 11-year Production Period.

	Basis	Interest[1] factor	Capitalized to the end of 11 years
Management costs & taxes	$80 each year	23.0445	1,843.56
Interest on $700 land value	Annual (rent)	3.2262	2,258.34
Cost of Stock	$150 per M x 1,570 = $235.50	4.2262	995.27
Stock shipping cost	$5	4.2262	21.13
Plant cost	$120 per M x 1,570 = $188.40	4.2262	796.22
Weed control at planting	$30	4.2262	126.79
Later weed control (herbicide)	2nd year $30	3.7072	111.22
Later weed control (herbicide)	3rd year $30	2.1950	65.85
Later weed control (herbicide)	4th year $30	2.8526	85.58
Later weed control (mowing)	5th year $50	2.5023	125.12
Later weed control (mowing)	6th year $50	2.1950	109.75
Later weed control (mowing)	7th year $50	1.9254	96.27
Later weed control (mowing)	8th year $50	1.6890	84.45
Later weed control (mowing)	9th year $50	1.4815	74.08
Later weed control (mowing)	10th year $50	1.2996	64.98
Fertilizer (material & labor) 4 oz/tree @ 12¢ lb. (20-10-10)	3rd year 250 trees/hr. = 62.21	2.1950	136.55
8 oz/tree @ 12¢ lb. (20-10-10)	5th year 200 trees/hr. = 126.46	2.5023	316.44
Spraying for insect control	Annually $10	19.3373	193.37
Shearing	4th year 3¢/tree x 1,331= 39.93	2.8526	113.90
	5th year 4¢ tree x 1,331= 53.24	2.5023	133.22
	6th year 6¢/tree x 1,331= 79.86	2.1950	175.29
	7th year 10¢/tree x 1,331=133.10	1.9254	256.27
	8th year 12¢/tree x 1,331=159.72	1.6890	269.77
	9th year 12¢/tree x 710= 85.20	1.4815	126.22
	10th year 15¢/tree x 355= 53.25	1.2996	69.20
Cleanup for next crop	11th year $25	1.1400	28.50
Trees sold and returns received	8th year 1/2 = 355 x $12.00 = $4,260.00	1.6890	7,195.14
	9th year 1/3 = 355 x $12.00 = $4,260.00	1.4815	6,311.19
	10th year 1/3 = 355 x $12.00 = $4,260.00	1.2996	5,536.30
Total accumulated returns (sale of trees)			19,042.63
Total accumulated costs			8,677.34
Net income for one crop	In 11 years		10,365.29

[1]Interest factor is based on 14% compound rate of interest and appropriate time period.

RECORD KEEPING

No matter what business you are in, keeping a record of what you are doing, and have done, is necessary. It is more essential with Christmas tree growing because you have at least six years before a crop comes to market, and usually much longer.

You cannot remember all the details regarding everything you have done over a six, eight, ten year period, or longer. You must keep some form of record as a basis for writing off your costs on Schedule F (Farming) of your federal tax return. This includes amortization and depreciation schedules and others.

We have records of all customer seedling purchases since we offered planting stock for sale many years ago. This has enabled us to check seed sources if a customer specifies the year the stock was planted. It can help you to construct your records if you have started planting but haven't kept any records.

As suggested in the section on Site Preparation; make a careful sketch of your farm. Make it coincide with your soil map. If necessary, enlarge it using one of the newer copy machines. After you have all the basic information shown, such as road frontage, boundaries, roadways in plantation, etc., make several copies of it.

Every spring planting should be recorded on your map. After several years we take one each of the original maps and record all the prior information on the one map. We also include notes about planting conditions and procedures, what is accomplished each day, work hours and all cost information. This information is kept in a notebook or three-ring binder for that year. It becomes a running record year to year.

A diary or log of your entire year's operation (events, dates, etc.) should be kept. We make notations re weather conditions (rain, snowfall, temperatures, etc.). Every area is different. Records at the Buffalo airport weather station do not provide much clue as to the actual events here in Elma, New York, 20 miles away, or 40 miles away at our Cattaraugus County location on Blue Hill.

While we have given you considerable data in our book as to tree growth, etc., you will still want to record your own data, since your conditions will be different from ours.

Each tree area could have its own cost basis since years to harvest time, pesticide spraying, mowing, fertilizing, etc. may be different from every other area on your farm, regardless of the nature of the operation. French Scotch take about two years longer to come to market than East Anglia; (our experience) however, the workload may not prove to be any greater than for the other, since much less shearing is required on the French.

The actual time and cost figures whether for mowing, shearing, fertilizing, etc. should be recorded including your own hours "on the job". Even if you do not place a dollar value on your efforts (which you should), it serves to remind you how much of your time has gone into the enterprise.

164

"An Economic Analysis of Choose and Cut Christmas Tree Production In Maryland", Dept. of Agr. and Resource Economics, Univ. of Maryland, College Park. 1985.

"Growing Christmas Trees In The South", General Report SA-GR 5, USDA Forestry Service, Atlanta, Ga. 1980.

You will be able to monitor the wholesale value of your trees from year to year by talking with other growers and wholesale tree buyers. If the market value of trees drops, you may want to reevaluate your cultural procedures and cash outlay to see where you might enact cost-cutting measures. Without records you cannot know what you are doing.

All this suggests a tougher road for Christmas tree growers in the future. All the more reason to investigate the investment potential very carefully under your own specific set of circumstances.

More on tax implications follows:

Return on Investment - Capital Gain/Investment Credit/Depreciation

Following the 1986 federal tax law changes, Christmas trees (like timber) no longer received advantageous capital gains treatment. That is, all tree income became ordinary income.

Until 1986, Christmas trees on the stump had received up to 60% exemption from taxation and that was after the amortized costs had been deducted. Simply, Christmas tree growing for an ambitious, healthy individual was rewarding income profit wise. Today it is not.

Not only do you have to carry land preparation and planting costs on the books until the trees are harvested, but you are then taxed on the full amount.

The investment credit that encouraged investment in equipment and structures was also done away with.

Of course, as this tolerable tax scenario changed, the overall cost of growing trees went upward. Property taxes, cost of goods and services, local and state sales taxes and state income taxes all went up in most areas of the country.

During the 1980's, trees planted for Christmas trees exceeded expected harvest estimates by three to one. As I am writing this now in 1992, the market has been reflecting this excess production by way of lower prices both wholesale and retail, and in increasing numbers of trees unsold both in the field and at the cut tree lot.

When you factor in this recent market climate, many areas of the country afford very poor return for wholesale growing of Christmas trees. Retail marketing of the quality trees you grow, especially when sold "cut your own" continues to provide a reasonable return on the investment, with intelligent and prudent cultural and business management.

In the highly competitive marketplace, you must learn the tax laws that impact on your business. Rent instead of buying, contract labor instead of hourly employees, dug instead of cut trees are some of the many options you have.

Most forms explain the tax laws in brief. If you need clarification, or more detailed information, contact the IRS information center and your respective state office of taxation and finance. Federal IRS offices and listing of some of the available publications follows. Write for the ones that will affect you.

For clarification of existing laws and background of legal procedures, you should consult the current tax book by Vernon L. Bowlby, C.P.A. entitled "The Tax Planning Manual For Tree Growers - Under The 1986 Law", 1986-87 edition. For information or cost contact: Bowlby Publishing Co., Inc., 310 N.W. 5th St., Corvalis, Oregon 97330. See ads in tree journals/bulletins also.

Mr. Bowlby has a newsletter with update of his tax activity and decisions as they affect the tree growers. He conducts seminars in various cities around the country. Trade magazines and associations will keep you informed or you can write to him at the above address.

If you have an accountant or other tax preparer they should acquaint themselves with the contents of Mr. Bowlby's book.

It is evident from inquiries we have received in recent years about tax rulings that IRS personnel in offices around the country, sometimes, lend their own interpretation of the statutes, or they are simply not acquainted with the nuances of the tax laws governing Christmas trees.

The IRS does have a publication No. 225 entitled "Farmers tax Guide". Two simplified publications (free) by IRS are #920 about tax changes and #946 explaining business related changes. Booklet No. 225 Farmer's Tax Guide will be very helpful also. Other helpful leaflets are:

```
# 51 Agricultural Employer's Tax Guide
#378 Fuel Tax Credits
#527 Rental Property
#529 Miscellaneous Deductions
#534 Depreciation
#587 Business Use of Your Home
```

If local sources do not have these forms, write to:

```
IRS Distribution Center
P. O. Box 25866
Richmond, VA  23260
```

Further, the gain or loss to the taxpayer is an amount equal to the difference between the fair market value of the standing timber as of the first day of the taxable year in which the timber is cut, and the adjusted basis for depletion. The timber is carried on the taxpayer's books (capitalized), and that cost basis reduces the amount received from the sale of the timber as far as taxes are concerned.

A fair market value of the tree "on the stump" is usually less than the retail price. The customer pays you on your lot, i.e., wholesale value vs retail value. The amount you receive over that fair market value on the stump (as of the first day of the year in which it was cut) is income (less expenses) and must be considered ordinary income for taxation purposes.

For example, on December 31st you determined from your retail lot sales/receipts that you sold 800 trees. You determined from wholesale prices of the prior year that your trees on the stump had a value of $10.50 each. From your capitalized-cost-record (costs accumulated over the life of those trees) you calculated "cost-per-tree" at $1.50. Your adjusted cost basis of each tree is, therefore, $9.00 each. This total figure is treated as capital gains and is recorded on Schedule D and Form 4797. (Your Schedule F should have a notation that might read like this: "Capital gain income from Christmas trees ($7200) has been recorded on Schedule D in keeping with IRS code Section 631A".) (Most of our sales are as wholesalers, where we do our own cutting and, therefore, we use 631B). Using your retail sales receipts, say, $17,500 (includes sales of wreaths and all other items, etc.), the income computation would look like this:

Total Receipts - $17,500

Less (on the stump value)
Transferred to Schedule D - $ 7,200
                             $10,300 Gross Income to
                                     Schedule F

Less all costs of Retail
Lot Operation (Advertising,
tools, utilities, extra
help on three busy weekends,
etc.   - $ 2,300 Itemized on Sched F
                             $ 8,000

The $8,000 represents net farm income which appears on Schedule F. This figure is transferred to Form 1040. Since format of Form 4797 and Schedule D will probably be changed with the new tax law, we are not going to show any forms here.

There are two elections that can be made in terms of qualifying for long-term capital-gains-treatment. They are the IRS code Sections 631A and 631B. 631A pertains to growers who cut their own trees while 631B pertains to sale of trees on the stump.

The holding period requirements for these provisions are now different.

Holding period for 631A:

A.   The grower must own the timber or rights for more than six months before sale.

B.   The grower must own the timber or cutting contract rights on the first day of the tax year in which the cutting occurs (calendar or fiscal year).

The current situation of a "choose and cut" operator is that the rule 631A election would govern his business. (IRS code of 1954). What that rule states is that in the taxpayer's taxable year the cutting of timber (for sale or use in the taxpayer's trade or business) during the year by the taxpayer who owns, or has a contract right to cut the timber (may not own the land, etc.). If he owned the land or has a contract right for the appropriate holding period beginning the first of the year, then this is considered a "sale or exchange" and is given capital-gains-treatment. Depreciation Schedule, Form 4562 is used to record Capitalized items.

Although the investment climate is shrouded in black clouds, there may be a silver lining sometime in the future. Christmas trees remain a capital-gains property, the same as timber. Some people think some capital-gain exclusion may be granted again in the future. In the meantime, Christmas tree plantings have to be capitalized as in the past. Costs of planting stock and labor costs for planting are capitalized and not expensed. Land preparation and improvement, including fertilizing and liming prior to planting, has to be capitalized. Liming, fertilizing, herbiciding costs (materials and labor), mowing, shearing and shaping and other costs relating to cultural practices can be expensed annually by using Schedule 1040 as we said earlier. Equipment and buildings can be depreciated. These schedules necessitate the use of long Form 1040 in your tax preparation. (You can still use a joint return status).

Costs for replanting of seedlings (due to losses) must also be recorded in the capitalization record.

Before you start your harvesting, and receive income, you will have to make an election as to how you want to run your business for tax purposes. You should review the IRS rulings at that time and decide how you want to conduct the sale of your trees.

Any trees removed from the ground with roots intact is no longer considered "timber". The proceeds from its sale (wholesale or retail) is considered ordinary income. The tree becomes "timber" when it is over six years of age from seed and severed from its roots. Technically, its "birthday" is the day the seed germinates.

Investment credit for Christmas tree growers for forestation or reforestation was excluded by IRS Regulation 1.194-3 adopted December 15, 1983. Prior to that a 10% credit had been available. Provision is still available, however, to timber growers.

As a farm labor employer you must comply with a variety of state and federal regulations. Guideline information is being presented here for federal and New York State employers. For more detailed information or interpretation, consult the appropriate state and federal office or an attorney.

The Social Security Act covers farm employees (including family members other than a spouse over the age of 21) who were paid $150 or more in cash wages during a calendar year for cash pay on a time basis. Cash wages are defined as the total wages paid before payroll deductions but do not include the value of meals, lodging or farm produce an employee receives.

All employers must file year-end Social Security reports on hired help by January 31 (Federal Form 943). If federal income taxes are withheld, they are reported on this form. If taxes are deposited with the Internal Revenue Service (IRS) before the end of the year, the deadline for filing the form is February 10. To complete Form 943 properly, the employer must have an identification number and the Social Security number of every farm employee.

Family Members

For Social Security (FICA) tax purposes, children under the age of 21 who work for their parents and individuals who work for a spouse are not covered even if they are paid regular wages. If the business is a partnership or corporation, however, these family members are subject to FICA taxes (unless the employee is the son or daughter of a partner.

"Month-end-check" Guide

Farm employers must either withhold employees' Social Security taxes and add the farm's share or pay both the employer's and employees' share. If the employer pays the employees' share, it becomes subject to income taxes but is not considered cash wages. If the combined total of withholding and employer's contributions for all employees equals $500 or more at the end of the month, the employer must deposit the total amount at a Federal Reserve bank or authorized commercial bank by the 15th of the following month. If less than $500 has accumulated at the end of a calendar quarter, the employer is required to deposit the total amount at the end of the following month. In either case, Federal Depository Receipt Form 511 should be used if income tax is withheld from employees. Social Security and income withholdings should be added together to determine whether $500 has accumulated. If total accumulated withholdings equal $3000 or more on the 3rd, 7th, 11th, 15th, 19th, 22nd, 25th or last day of the month, they must be deposited within three banking days.

Tax Statement to Workers

Employers are required to provide each employee with a statement by January 31 indicating wages reported to the Federal Internal Revenue Service and the New York State Tax Bureau and the amount of Social Security taxes that have been withheld. Copies of forms W-2 (federal) and IT-2101 (state) or SS-14 can be used for this purpose.

The intent of the law is for employees to pay their own share of the Social Security tax. Each state is different as you will want to contact your state department of labor for rulings and filing procedures.

FEDERAL INCOME TAX

The Tax Reform Act of 1986 made sweeping changes in the federal income tax law. Most of these changes do not radically affect the withholding and reporting requirements of farm employees. However, because there are different methods now being used to calculate individual tax liability, it is important that employers and employees use only up-to-date forms and instruction booklets in tax reporting.

Many of the changes in the federal tax law take effect sometime in 1987 or later. It is essential, therefore, to get updated information each year.

The Internal Revenue Service has permitted employers to withhold taxes on wages of agricultural workers since January 1, 1971. Although withholding is not required on wages of farm workers, it is a service that many farm employees need and appreciate.

To have income tax withheld an employee must submit a written request to his or her employer. No form is necessary. The request should contain the name, address, and Social Security number of the employee and the name and address of the employer. The W-4 is a simple card used to claim withholding exemptions.

Accepting the written request and W-4 from an employee and commencing to withhold taxes indicates voluntary agreement on the employer's part. To terminate the agreement, the employer or employee must give written notice 30 days before the desired termination date. The following section discusses procedures for depositing withholdings.

Farm employers are responsible for providing each employee with an annual information return and for filing a statement with the government indicating payments of any amount (including the cash value of payments not made in cash) made to farm employees during the year for salaries, fees, or other compensation for personal services. Federal Form W-2 is used for this purpose and must be distributed to employees by January 31 and sent to the New York State Department of Taxation and Finance and the Social Security Administration by February 28.

Working Students may be subject to withholdings. Under the tax law, individuals are not subject to withholding of federal income tax if they paid no tax in the previous year and they do not anticipate being liable for any federal income tax in the current year. Students who work part time or during the summer frequently meet these criteria. Such students should fill out Form W-4E, Withholding Exemption Certificate, and give it to their employers. These forms can be obtained from district offices of the IRS. Students who follow these procedures will not have to wait to receive refunds.

IRS Publications

Listed below are the numbers and titles of selected IRS tax publications. The list includes all the publications referred to in the chapters of this book, as well as others that might be of interest to you. A full list can be found in Publication 910, *Guide to Free Tax Services*. If you only need to order *tax forms and publications* and do not have any tax questions, call 1–800–TAX–FORM (1–800–829–3676).

General Guides
1 ..... Your Rights as a Taxpayer
17 ..... Your Federal Income Tax (an income tax guide for individuals)
334 ..... Tax Guide for Small Business
509 ..... Tax Calendars for 1992
553 ..... Highlights of 1991 Tax Changes
595 ..... Tax Guide for Commercial Fishermen
910 ..... Guide to Free Tax Services

Employer's Guides
15 ..... Circular E, Employer's Tax Guide
51 ..... Circular A, Agricultural Employer's Tax Guide

Specialized Publications
349 ..... Federal Highway Use Tax on Heavy Vehicles
378 ..... Fuel Tax Credits and Refunds
448 ..... Federal Estate and Gift Taxes
463 ..... Travel, Entertainment, and Gift Expenses
501 ..... Exemptions, Standard Deduction, and Filing Information
502 ..... Medical and Dental Expenses
503 ..... Child and Dependent Care Expenses
504 ..... Tax Information for Divorced or Separated Individuals

505 ..... Tax Withholding and Estimated Tax
510 ..... Excise Taxes for 1992
521 ..... Moving Expenses
523 ..... Tax Information on Selling Your Home
524 ..... Credit for the Elderly or the Disabled
525 ..... Taxable and Nontaxable Income
526 ..... Charitable Contributions
527 ..... Residential Rental Property
529 ..... Miscellaneous Deductions
533 ..... Self-Employment Tax
534 ..... Depreciation
535 ..... Business Expenses
536 ..... Net Operating Losses
537 ..... Installment Sales
538 ..... Accounting Periods and Methods
541 ..... Tax Information on Partnerships
542 ..... Tax Information on Corporations
544 ..... Sales and Other Dispositions of Assets
547 ..... Nonbusiness Disasters, Casualties, and Thefts
550 ..... Investment Income and Expenses
551 ..... Basis of Assets
554 ..... Tax Information for Older Americans
556 ..... Examination of Returns, Appeal Rights, and Claims for Refund
559 ..... Tax Information for Survivors, Executors, and Administrators
560 ..... Retirement Plans for the Self-Employed
561 ..... Determining the Value of Donated Property
583 ..... Taxpayers Starting a Business
584 ..... Nonbusiness Disaster, Casualty, and Theft Loss Workbook
586A ..... The Collection Process (Income Tax Accounts)
587 ..... Business Use of Your Home
589 ..... Tax Information on S Corporations
590 ..... Individual Retirement Arrangements (IRAs)

594 ..... The Collection Process (Employment Tax Accounts)
596 ..... Earned Income Credit
909 ..... Alternative Minimum Tax for Individuals
911 ..... Tax Information for Direct Sellers
915 ..... Social Security Benefits and Equivalent Railroad Retirement Benefits
917 ..... Business Use of a Car
925 ..... Passive Activity and At-Risk Rules
926 ..... Employment Taxes for Household Employers
929 ..... Tax Rules for Children and Dependents
936 ..... Home Mortgage Interest Deduction
937 ..... Business Reporting (Employment Taxes and Information Returns)
946 ..... How To Begin Depreciating Your Property
1544 ..... Reporting Cash Payments of Over $10,000

Spanish Language Publications
1S ..... Derechos del Contribuyente
179 ..... Circular PR, Guía Contributiva Federal Para Patronos Puertorriqueños
556S ..... Revisión de las Declaraciones de Impuesto, Derecho de Apelación y Reclamaciones de Reembolso
579S ..... Cómo Preparar la Declaración de Impuesto Federal
586S ..... Proceso de Cobro (Deudas del impuesto sobre ingreso)
850 ..... English-Spanish Glossary of Words and Phrases Used in Publications Issued by the Internal Revenue Service

---

How to Get IRS Forms and Publications

You can order tax forms and publications from the IRS Forms Distribution Center for your state at the address below. Or, if you prefer, you can photocopy tax forms from reproducible copies kept at participating public libraries. In addition, many of these libraries have reference sets of IRS publications which you can read or copy.

If you are located in: **Send to "Forms Distribution Center" for your state**

Alaska, Arizona, California, Colorado, Hawaii, Idaho, Montana, Nevada, New Mexico, Oregon, Utah, Washington, Wyoming

Western Area Distribution Center Rancho Cordova, Ca. 95743-0001

Alabama, Arkansas, Illinois, Indiana, Iowa, Kansas, Kentucky, Louisiana, Michigan, Minnesota, Mississippi, Missouri, Nebraska, North Dakota, Ohio, Oklahoma, South Dakota, Tennessee, Texas, Wisconsin

Central Area Distribution Center P.O. Box 9903 Bloomington, IL 61799

Connecticut, Delaware, District of Columbia, Florida, Georgia, Maine, Maryland, Massachusetts, New Hampshire, New Jersey, New York, North Carolina, Pennsylvania, Rhode Island, South Carolina, Vermont, Virginia, West Virginia

Eastern Area Distribution Center P.O. Box 85074 Richmond, VA 23261-5074

Foreign Addresses—Taxpayers with mailing addresses in foreign countries should send their requests for forms and publications to: Forms Distribution Center, P.O. Box 25866, Richmond, VA 23289; Forms Distribution Center, Rancho Cordova, Ca. 95743-0001, whichever is closer.

Puerto Rico—Forms Distribution Center, P.O. Box 25866, Richmond, VA 23289

Virgin Islands—V.I. Bureau of Internal Revenue, Lockharts Garden, No. 1A, Charlotte Amalie, St. Thomas, VI 00802

Employees have a Tax Responsibility which most of us are familiar with. Every citizen or resident of the United States, whether an adult or a minor, who was paid $5,550 or more in the 1991 taxable year must file a return. In the case of married couples filing joint returns or a "single" return, the amount is $10,000 and $2,150 respectively. These numbers will probably change with each succeeding year, and/or as the federal statutes change.

Farm employees are required to file and pay a declaration of estimated income tax (Form 1040-ES) if their income from sources not subject to withholding was $500 or more and they expect their tax liability on these earnings to be $500 or more. The tax may be paid in four equal installments. Some employees have been penalized for not filing estimates. Once an employee has filed Form 1040-ES, the IRS will automatically send additional forms and information, including payment vouchers.

A single dependent child employed on a farm must file an income tax return if his or her gross income was $3,560 or more, unearned income was $500 or more, or self-employment income was $400 or more during the tax year. Unearned income includes interest, dividends, and trust income. Self-employment income includes money from the sale of livestock and produce owned or raised by the child.

STATE INCOME TAX

In general, New York State's income tax laws are the same as the federal laws. Tax rates are different and state forms are usually required, but the basic principles and many of the procedural requirements are the same. Each state is different so you will want to contact a state office near you for information.

A New York state employee who wishes to have state income tax withheld should submit a written request to his or her employer along with a completed Form IT-2104. If the employer chooses to withhold, no other action is necessary. Withheld dollars for taxes should be sent to the Income Tax Division with Form IT-2101-BNS. If less than $600 is withheld semiannually, the employer is required to file twice annually - before January 31 and before July 31. If between $600 and $7,500 is withheld semiannually, the employer must file on or before the 15th day of the month, except in December when the due date is January 31. If between $7,500 and $35,000 is withheld, semiannually, returns must be filed twice monthly, and if more than $35,000 is withheld, quarter-monthly.

Employers must file information returns with the New York State Tax Department indicating the salaries of all farm employees who earned $600 or more during the calendar year. State Forms IT-2102 and IT-2103 are used for this purpose. A copy of Federal Form W-2 may be substituted for State Form IT-2102. These forms must be filed by February 28. Individuals must file a New York State income tax return if they are required to file a federal income tax return. Again, the terms and conditions in each state is different so contact your state labor department.

Additional information may be needed. Detailed descriptions of an agricultural employer's obligations under the federal tax laws may be found in IRS Circular A, **Agricultural Employer's Tax Guide** (Publication 51). See also Farmer's Tax Guide (IRS Publication 225). Contact your area Social Security Administration office for additional information.

WAGES must be paid to employees "weekly and not later than seven calendar days after the end of the week in which the wages are earned" or in full every two weeks. Deductions other than legal withholdings and deductions made with the employee's permission for the employee's benefit, such as health insurance premiums, are prohibited. Agricultural workers may be paid by check without special permission. Any questions or violations pertaining to wages should be directed to the New York State Department of Labor. See address listing. Find out what conditions must be met in your state.

The Federal Wage-Hour Law stipulates that the current federal minimum wage for most agricultural employees is $3.35 per hour. Full-time students, who may not work more than 20 hours each week while school is in session, may be paid a special minimum wage of 85 percent of minimum wage or $2.85. Overtime pay is not required for agricultural employees. Check with the federal office nearest you as this may have changed since this writing.

Students are frequently employed to help plant, shear, and do other cultural activities, so this information should be helpful regarding "full-time" students.

Workers who are full-time students, regardless of age, may be employed by retail and service employers, farmers, and colleges and universities at rates no less than 85 percent of the minimum wage otherwise applicable. They may work no more than 20 hours in any work week, however, except during vacations, when they may work up to 40 hours. To hire a full-time student, an employer must obtain a Full-Time Student Certificate from the U.S. Department of Labor. A certificate will be issued after the Department of Labor has determined the following: that full-time students are available for employment granting the certificate is necessary to prevent curtailment of opportunities for their employment; granting the certificate to more than six students will not substantially reduce the probability of employment for persons other than those employed under the certificate; and granting the certificate will not result in other employees, including students, receiving reduced wages.

The federal certificate covers full-time students of any age whereas the state certificate deals with youth under 18, regardless of their student status. Also, the state Youth Rate Certificate permits an employer to hire an unlimited number of youth, whereas, the federal Full-Time Student Certificate, as a rule, permits no more than six full-time students to be hired and their hours cannot account for more than 10 percent of the employer's total man-hours of labor. An employer covered by both laws must comply with both standards. See the section entitled "Youth Employment" for more details.

For details about coverage requirements, exemptions, employer allowances and certificates required for employment of handicapped workers, contact your nearest Department of Labor (see address listing).

New York State Farm Minimum Wage Law

An employer who is covered by the federal Wage-Hour Law is also covered by the state Farm Minimum Wage Law and must comply with both laws. Currently, the basic minimum wage under both laws is $4.25 per hour as of Juanuary 1, 1992.

The minimum wage rate for youth under 18 years of age is lower than for adults (see table). To pay at this lower rate, the employer must obtain a Youth Rate Certificate from the commissioner of labor and keep it on file for six years after employment is terminated. These certificates may be obtained from New York Department of Labor district offices. A Youth Rate Certificate permits the employer to hire any number of young workers. Youth under 16 must also have work permits. These permits may be obtained by the employee from the local school office. Employers are responsible for checking to see that each young person has a work permit. An employer covered under the federal Wage-Hour Law needs to obtain a federal Full-Time Student Certificate as well as the state certificate. Full-time students may work no more than 10 percent of their employer's total man-hours of labor. For additional information, contact Employment Standards Administration, U. S. Department of Labor, 1515 Broadway, New York, NY 10036

Minimum Wage Requirements and Allowances For New York State Farms
(Rate per hour unless otherwise indicated)

	As of 1/1/92
General Minimum Wage	$4.25
Farm Minimum Wage	$4.25
Youth under 18 (certificate required):	
Harvesting	
First Harvest Season	$3.60
Second Harvest Season	$3.80
Third or more Harvest Season	Basic Min.
Nonharvesting	
First 300 hours	$3.60
Second 300 hours	$3.80
Under 16 (farm work permit required)	$3.20

Allowances can be made for meals at $1.70 per meal. Lodging allowances are also made. Contact your State Labor Office for details about this as well as other aspects of state law not covered here. Persons in other states and/or farms in other states should contact your respective state department of labor.

INSURANCE

Workers' Compensation Insurance

Coverage

The New York State Workers' Compensation Law covers most employees. Some special coverage provisions and/or exemptions apply to farm laborers, volunteers, domestics, chauffeurs and teenagers. Your state labor department will inform you of the terms and conditions in your state.

Farmers in New York State must purchase workers' compensation insurance if their cash wage payments to farm employees totaled $1200 or more in the previous calendar year. Insurance must be purchased from a private carrier or the State Insurance Fund for 12 months beginning April 1. Larger employers find it profitable and are permitted by the Workers' Compensation Board to self-insure.

The $1200 annual payroll rule applies to only four farm classifications, general farms (0006), fruit farms (0007), vegetable or berry farms (0031), and poultry farms (0034). Other businesses classified as nursery (0005), florist, cultivating and gardening (0035), landscape gardening (0042), tree pruning and spraying, custom work (0106), and stores (8001) are not subject to the $1200 payroll rule. These businesses must provide workers' compensation coverage regardless of their annual payrolls.

Farm Family Workers

An employer's spouse or child under the age of 18 is considered an employee if his or her services are provided under an "express contract for hire". An "express contract for hire" is a legal term used to distinguish a situation in which a person is a hired worker from one in which a person does an occasional chore or odd job for pay. The farmer's 16 year old son who works as a hired hand, whether full time during school vacations or part time during the school year, is considered an employee, for example, whereas children who help out occasionally in the barn or perform tasks for which they are paid by the job are usually considered casual laborers.

To determine which situation applies to your family members, ask yourself the following three questions:

- Am I paying a regular wage for the work being done?

- Is my family member performing tasks I would hire an outsider to do?

- Do I have an understanding, or an agreement, with this person (even an oral one) that tasks will be performed for compensation?

If the answer to all three questions is yes, the services are clearly being performed under an express contract for hire and workers' compensation laws apply. If you are still not sure of the nature of the relationship and your legal obligations contact the Workers' Compensation Board.

One grower I talked with recently about market conditions said "It took us a while to realize our business wasn't growing trees, it's selling trees".

Almost anyone who has sold Christmas trees just one year has come to that realization. This being fact, you might ask why not write a book just about selling? (marketing). Much has and continues to be written, but growing the trees comes first.

Marketing must be tailored to each grower/retailer's situation, which is comprised of many factors. We can only present here some ideas, suggestions and guidelines. "Addendum to Basics of Growing Christmas Trees" presents many ideas and case histories. You will want to learn all you can about how to sell your trees.

Some additional comments follow by Gregory Passewitz, who is involved with natural resource development for the Ohio Cooperative Extension Service. His thoughts are appreciated.

Monterey pine is featured at Jackie and Larry Cavaletto's "cut-your-own" tree farm. The train ride is the highlight of the visit for young and old alike. They encourage picnicking and a life-size nativity scene features real animals.

CONSIDERATIONS IN MARKETING CHRISTMAS TREES

Gregory Passewitz
Leader, Natural Resources and Small Business
Community and Natural Resource Development
Ohio Cooperative Extension Service

Marketing is the most important aspect of any successful business. Without a market, the finest product you have to offer will not turn a profit. Marketing is a matter of selling your product, your service, and yourself to the prospective buyer...and so it is with Christmas trees.

Today and in the foreseeable future, the marketing aspect of the Christmas tree industry will be taking on even greater importance. Surveys made by the National Christmas Tree Association show that the gap between the number of trees planted and the number of trees sold continue to widen. In 1974, for every tree sold, 1.1 were planted; 1983, 2.6 trees were planted for every one sold, and in 1987, 3.1 trees were planted for everyone sold. What is even more alarming is the distribution of the market share. The percentage of households having a natural tree declined from 36 percent in 1978 to 31 percent in 1981, to 26 percent in 1986. During the same period, artificial tree households increased from 40 percent to 47 percent.

In spite of these findings, opportunities still exist for Christmas tree growers to capture a portion of the market lost to artificial trees.

How can a grower accomplish this? By making an outstanding effort at selling quality trees. At the outset, the grower must realize before the first seedling is planted that marketing trees is not just s single activity that occurs between Thanksgiving and Christmas Eve. In fact, marketing is a strategy and an activity that should be an integral part of the total business from planting to harvesting.

Marketing Options

Generally, there are three methods of marketing your trees. You may choose to wholesale the trees at the farm to a buyer, who in turn will retail the trees. Second, you may decide to retail the trees yourself. This can be done on the farm as pre-cut or choose-and-cut trees, or the retail operation could be located off the farm at a suitable location. A third option is a combination of retailing and wholesaling. No matter how you choose to market your trees, an accurate inventory is essential. Not only will this develop a schedule of trees available for market, but it will also create a planting schedule to perpetuate the business. At least two or three years prior to harvest, the grower should begin to establish possible market outlets. An inventory should be taken that reflects species, tree heights and quality.

Selling Trees Wholesale

Starting with wholesaling, let's now look at some of the specific factors involved in each marketing method. As you will see, many of these factors are interrelated. The layout of your wholesale operation has to be considered carefully. Two specific items to consider include access roads and loading areas. Remember, you will be selling trees in quantity, which will require sufficient room to operate equipment and load trees. As a grower, you have several options on how to sell your wholesale trees. They include:

1. Sell trees by the block. The buyer pays a pre-determined lump sum and either the grower or buyer cuts and bales the trees. Delivery by the seller is optional.

2. Sell the trees by the piece on the stump. Buyer selects the trees to be cut and either the buyer or grower cuts and bales the trees. This option encourages the practice of taking the best trees and leaves the grower with only the poorer quality trees.

3. Another option is for the grower to select, cut, and bale the trees. Buyer will pick up the trees at roadside or seller may deliver.

4. Consignment is another option but is rarely used. The grower assumes the risk that the seller will be able to move the trees. The seller has everything to gain and nothing to lose.

Retail Marketing

If trees are sold at a city lot, location is of prime importance. The lot should be close to a well-traveled road, have adequate parking, security, enough elbow room to do business and be in a neighborhood conducive to good sales. In setting up a city lot, the grower enters into direct competition with established businesses. Also, the rental or purchase of a lot may be a sizeable investment compared to the total value of the trees. Some costs to be considered include: transportation of trees to lot, lights, fixtures including signs and tree posts, advertising and labor including your own labor. Trees must be sold to cover these costs before a profit can be realized.

The location of the retail farm lot is also important. The most successful farm lots are usually located within 20-30 miles of a metropolitan area although customers will travel up to an hour if they feel you lot is meeting their needs. If farms are further away, the grower has to be more innovative to entice the customer to visit the farm. In addition, the roads to the farm have to be accessible and clearly marked.

Layout - The layout of the retail lot is very important regardless of whether it is a city or farm lot. At a city lot, the seller is somewhat bound by the dimensions of the lot. However, he can set up a customer flow pattern that invites the customer to shop the entire area and to display the trees to their best advantage. In a farm situation the trees should be close to the parking lot or a series of all-weather lanes. This permits the grower or "cut your own" customer to carry the trees short distances and complete sales quicker. The rows should not be more than 15 or 16 deep. Trees on steep slopes are not ideal for "cut your own" customers. If only certain blocks or trees are to be cut by the customer the grower has to limit the sales area. This can be done by roads, signs, fences, or employees.

Parking - Adequate parking is a major consideration in selling trees. If customers cannot reach the retail lot due to parking conditions, a sale will be lost. In developing a parking area, especially for farm sales, a two-way or circular one-way traffic pattern is desirable. Parking lots and roads should be all-weather if possible. The location of the parking lot should be central to the main sales area and have controlled access to the trees. In other words, have only one exit for trees to leave the lot with one or two people manning this exit. To determine how much parking is needed is difficult. The more items you have to sell, or if you have a "cut your own" operation; the longer the customers will generally stay...perhaps as long as two hours.

Another rule of thumb is: given an even flow of customers, the seller can estimate about fifteen parking spaces for every ninety to one hundred buyers. If you sell half of your trees on a December weekend, the seller will need to have parking to accommodate this peak period. An acre with 90 degree diagonal parking will accommodate between 75-100 parking spaces, allowing for lanes in the lot.

Customer Relations - Customer relations is that aspect of business management concerned with how customers feel about a place of business - its personnel, product, and service. A christmas tree retail lot that feels the customer is the most important person is heading in the right direction for good customer relations. A successful customer relations program, is designed to meet the needs and wants of the customer.

Usually a customer's first impression of your business is made by the appearance of the lot and the employees who greet him. Your employees' face-to-face contact with the customer, impressions they make and image your lot presents will begin to shape the customers' attitudes to your attitudes to your business. To strengthen customer relations, your employees need to:

1. Have knowledge about the trees being sold.

2. Know how to approach the customer.

3. Greet the customer.

4. List the features and benefits of the product.

5. Know how to counter some sales resistance.

6. Develop an effective selling technique.

7. Know how to close a sale.

In addition, a tidy lot that conveys conscientious upkeep will help bring back customers. For on-farm selling, a grower can make this experience even more enjoyable and meaningful--especially when a family is involved. Wagon rides for cut-your-own customers can be an enjoyable experience. A shelter that has a warm fire, a cup of coffee or hot chocolate are also nice extras. All of these are personal experiences for your customers that build good relations. The opportunities are unlimited. Always remember, work very hard to get the customer to your business location--but the key to business success is to bring the customer back again.

Advertising - The offering of a **quality** product is **your most important asset** and good customer relations and customer comments to others can be a help in getting and keeping customers. Advertising is needed, especially in the first couple of years while the business is getting established. All advertising campaigns must start with market identification. The market the Christmas tree grower wants to reach must be identified geographically and demographically. Then, the grower must carefully segment the target market to focus on how best to advertise, reach and influence it. In reaching and selling the target market, Christmas tree retailers must carefully balance their advertising reach and frequency. **REACH** is the number of people that see or hear the ad. **FREQUENCY** is the number of times they see or hear it. For example, television may have the best reach; but radio and newspaper may be more practical for frequency.

Below is a list of some commonly used advertising methods and their associated pros and cons. As you can see, there are many ways to reach your potential customers.

Pros and Cons of Different Advertising Methods

Media	Types	Advantages	Disadvantages
Newspaper	Morning, Evening, Sunday	Common to everyone; bought to be read; good for ads	No selective readership, short life
Radio	AM, FM	Low cost, selective listenership	Short life, listeners have limited attention
Television	Local	Low cost per exposure, selective, highly visible	High cost, viewers may ignore the message
Outdoor signs	Display, posters, billboards	Low cost, repetition	Short and simple message

There are many other advertising methods. Organizations may sell tickets for 1 or 2 dollars off a tree when purchased at the lot. Another common method is coupons redeemable at the time of purchase. In advertising you are limited only by your inventiveness and imagination. Many growers have overcome severe location adversities by effective advertising and selling quality trees. It depends on each individual situation. No one method will work for everyone. Your success in the Christmas tree industry will depend not only on how well you grow the tree, but the effort you make to market it.

Remember, all the trees in the world won't help if you can't sell them. You begin by growing or buying a quality tree and then sell this quality, along with good service and yourself at a fair price.

MARKETING AND HARVESTING AS A WHOLESALER

TO MARKET - "TO OFFER FOR SALE; TO FIND A PURCHASER FOR". If we knew there would always be more customers than trees, this chapter could be omitted. Buyers would flock to your door. That may not be the case, so some serious planning and effort should be undertaken early - as early as right now! Don't wait until your trees are large enough to cut and then wonder what you are going to do with them. That will be too late.

First, you should know that grade standards have been set up as with most other agricultural products. These standards are given on the page that follows. Marketing and harvesting is a crucial part of the wholesale grower's business. Simply, it's pay day! It is the day you have been working towards for 6, 8, or maybe 10 years or longer.

Develop contacts with established tree retailers in advance of your first harvest. Encourage tree buyers to come out to your plantation and see the trees during the summer and fall prior to harvest. Most larger buyers are contacting growers early in the year, as early as June.

WHAT PRICE SHOULD I GET FOR MY TREES? You should get a "feel" of the market. That includes supply vs demand within 100 miles of your area, value relative to quality, approximate prices other growers are asking and other market information. The general market conditions and specific prices from the prior year provide a very good guide. If you learn that more trees are coming onto the market, then there will be a downward pressure on prices. Buyers are acutely aware of the supply and demand situation. Even if you do not make a sale you will have learned something from a prospective buyer. Talk to buyers.

New York State Department of Agriculture and markets publishes a recap of prices of the prior season by regions around the state. Other states have information available. Many Michigan growers actually mail out a price list in late summer. Get your name on their mailing lists.

At the summer meetings of the various state tree growers associations, buyers are there to discuss their needs and price ideas Prices relate to quality so you will have to benchmark to compare your quality with other growers. Large buyers have most of their needs contracted for, usually from their regular suppliers, early in the year. Do not wait until October or November to line up your buyers. A buyer's loyalty should be developed for business in future years. The more you learn about the buyer's needs, the better for you in establishing an ongoing business. In recent years we have become much more market-oriented, however, we try to fit the trees available to buyer's needs. For example, a low income area tree lot has a limited capacity for high priced trees. These customers simply cannot afford to pay high prices so they will go elsewhere. The buyer will lose money and blame you for his failure. It is a two way street in the buyer/seller relationship, especially if your buyer is new in the business.

By mid and late summer most of your tree areas will be mowed, the trees will be sheared and ready for viewing by the buyers. Many of your buyers will be those you sold last year and you may have several more that contracted you previously. If you have several thousand or more trees to sell and/or the demand for trees in your immediate area (50 mile radius) has been filled, you will have to put the word out farther from home. If trucking costs are $1.00 per mile, the farther from home, the less you will get for your trees. (You may not be paying the freight directly but your tree price will have to be competitive (or a little better) than in the area where the trees are going.) Of course, quality plays a big part and you must have good-to-excellent quality to interest buyers far from home.

There is a tendency for choose and cut operations to do a poorer cultural job, hence, when the time comes that they need to wholesale trees, they don't fare as well as they could.

As the size of plantations got larger the practice by the grower to pre-tag trees became established Sometimes smaller growers let the buyer tag his own trees. A special pricing arrangement might be worked out that requires that they take 200 trees from a particular area, all at one price or on a split price basis depending on size and quality. In the pre-tagged plantation, two grades are usually available (sometimes three). For example, blue tagged trees may be classified as premium and red tagged as #1 quality. The buyer can tour your farm and decide what he wants to buy. If the buyer wants 250 premium trees and 250 #1's the order can be consummated by a signed contract with a deposit given by the buyer. Occasionally, a buyer will buy sight unseen based on your reputation. See example of contract in Appendix A. You can write up your own contract which may contain stipulations that tell how you want to operate. Since our wholesale farm is in the ski country, we state in our contracts that all trees must be removed from the plantation by Thanksgiving weekend. (The county does not keep the road open after December 1st). Any such terms of sale must be stated in your agreement with the buyer. You must have a complete "meeting of the minds" in your wholesale dealings to be confident the deal will be consummated with both parties satisfied. Of course, many deals are closed with an exchange of cash at harvest time. We prefer to have our trees sold early and thus avoid speculation in the market.

Trees are sold "on the stump". We have always shown the cut/baled/roadside charge separately on the contract form. This way there is no doubt about the value of the tree that coincides with your capitalized cost. Any excess of the cut/baled/roadside costs will be reflected on Schedule F as regular income (not capital gains) with your actual costs getting recorded on the expense portion of the form.

We do not permit a buyer to cut and bale his own trees. At an early point in time we found it created more problems than it solved. In this day and age, the liability factor is reason enough. Inadequate equipment, inexperienced help, inclement weather conditions, insufficient knowledge of field conditions, delays and interruptions of all kinds, and lack of control on our part are additional reasons why we conduct the entire harvest ourselves with our own personnel.

Additional problems must be worked out if you harvest from several locations and/or you are not staying on the premises when the harvest is underway; theft is a serious problem for some growers. Once trees are cut and baled they should be kept under surveillance.

"Banding" fertilizer around young tree

Near killing frost-injury (Austrian pine)

Severe winter snow damage to Douglas fir

A deer "rub" on fraser fir

MARKETING CHOOSE AND CUT

In a Choose and Cut business you benefit twice. You get a return on your investment from growing a tree and you get a retailer's profit through sale directly to the user. There is no middle man and you can control the marketing factors. In fact, it offers you an opportunity to engage in allied activities that can be very profitable. The gift and/or ornament shop, wreaths/roping, firewood, live trees and the sale of other products can all contribute to the income producing objective.

A Choose and Cut business is not without problems. Every business is conducted differently depending on the physical layout, degree of involvement, size of the operation, manpower available, weather conditions, etc. One grower's problem may be different from your's. We will discuss some of the common problems.

First of all, adequate parking space is essential. The larger your operation (the more customers), the more parking space needed. Off-road parking is necessary. Narrow roads, obstacles along shoulders and potential injury to occupants due to other vehicles are several reasons why off-road parking is needed. The more time a customer spends at your plantation, the more parking space you will need. The turnover time is lengthened.

The larger the crowds, the greater need for traffic control; also, a one way entrance and departure road may be needed. Even this roadway should be two lanes so that one vehicle can always be kept moving.

If vehicles are allowed onto the plantation itself, then a whole traffic pattern and procedure must be developed and maintained. Solutions to problems must be anticipated. Flat tires, getting stuck in the mud or snow, engine failure, etc. are all possible problems. The more activities offered, the longer the turnover time at your plantation. Your rules and procedures can be tailored to reduce the turnover time.

A gift shop and/or any other activity will extend the visitation time. A heated snack shop serving hot chocolate, cookies, etc. will add to the staying time. A wood-burning stove adds to the atmosphere or any other means of creating a warm welcome environment can prove more profitable to the "Choose and Cut" business. Making wreaths, roping, selling bough material, fresh arrangements from natural greens and gift shop items are all primary items a tree buyer may purchase.

Most "Choose and Cut" businesses have a high "repeat customer" trade from year to year. These people know what you have to offer and are usually prepared to spend more money than just the price of a tree. You will develop services and products to take advantage of this "annual family event".

The longer the customer stays at your location, the greater the need for additional facilities. Those might include lavatories, warm-up room, (stove, etc.) and a food/snack shop. Large operations might sell between 2,000 to 5,000 trees in one season. Some may sell more than 1,000 trees in any one day. These numbers create much demand on all the available facilities. Careful consideration to all aspects of the marketing and merchandising program must be made.

Security of the lot, protection from theft, traffic control and medical help may all be needed as your operation grows. Hiring of trustworthy personnel may present a problem, too.

The characteristics of your clientele will help to determine how you operate. If you are on the outskirts of a good-sized city or town your customers are readily at hand and do not usually rely on some of the extra services. They are in proximity of their own facilities. However, children are a big part of this event so their special needs must be kept in mind.

Some Choose and Cut operators don't wait until December to sell trees. They open their plantation to visitors in late summer/early fall and allow customers to pre-tag their trees. This procedure offers definite advantages. Guaranteed advance sale! (They leave a deposit and they take the pressure off the December visit.) Some people simply prefer to visit the plantation when the weather is nice. (See pictures.)

This summer/fall visitation must be managed carefully. You cannot permit people to wander in whenever they feel like it. Again, the activity must be supervised; also, you do not want people in the plantation when shearing and other activity is in progress.

Another sales element is that many pre-cut tree sales will be made at your plantation. Some people want a tree and would rather pick out one that is already cut. Some growers tell me they sell as many pre-cut trees as they do choose and cut. This works out well when a distant area of the plantation is inconvenient for choose and cut. Also, a good pre-cut business might permit operating a wholesale business from another less accessible or less suitable retail location.

Many growers set up a lot and start to develop a retail business years ahead of the time their own trees are ready. In fact, many of you reading this may already be involved with a retail business and tree growing can augment that activity. All of the principles of your present business activity will help you in the tree growing activity.

From an operational standpoint, the way you want to develop the retailing operation will dictate many practices you employ in the plantation. The cultural needs of replanting, mowing, shearing, spraying, etc. still have to be done so you will develop operational procedures accordingly. For example, in a field of trees the best trees will get sold and the poorer ones will remain. This requires decisions on how to develop the poorer trees and, perhaps, when to give up on a particular tree. Obviously, the better your cultural practices and techniques, the more trees will get sold thus resulting in more profit for you. Poor quality trees due to poor cultural practices will definitely hurt your business. Your competition will be pushing you to do a better job.

To stimulate your thinking about how you might actually want to operate, some ideas follow:

Upon entering the plantation a ticket might be given out. If you supply saws, a blue ticket would be given to the saw borrower. A white ticket might mean they have their own saw. (NO CHAIN SAWS ALLOWED.) An instruction sheet with tree varieties and prices would be included. If trees are being sold "per foot of height", then marking stakes may be placed in the plantation just for marking purposes. One grower I know has permanent stakes which also serve as bird perches. (Deters birds from perching on the leaders of trees, especially when they are in the soft stage and breaking or bending the leader.) The attendant in the field might actually cut the tree (or assist in the cutting) when the tree has been selected. This avoids possible injuries and eliminates high stumps that would have to be cut again before mowing.

Some plantations use tractor and wagon or even a sleigh. The tree is usually brought back to the barn or checkout area. It can be sized, if not already done in the field, and payment taken.

Other items, supplies, ornaments, wreaths, boughs, etc. may be paid for separately. A talk with a real live Santa Claus and a candy cane may be provided sometimes, at no extra charge, simply as a drawing card and to promote good will. Frequently the tractor and wagon is part of the outing. Whatever you do, make it fun. You will have a customer for many years to come, and it provides free advertising (the best kind you can get).

Pricing of the trees deserves a little more discussion here. How you want to do it is entirely up to you. Some growers have one price for any tree no matter what its size and quality. This procedure encourages people to take a tree larger than they need and penalizes the small tree buyer. This might be compensated, however, by offering smaller pre-cut trees. (Might be from another area that you want to clear but not open up to the public.)

Some growers price the tree according to height at time of checkout. Different tree varieties might be priced differently to accommodate the budget of your customers.

Pre-pricing of trees may be suitable on the pre-cut tree lot, but not satisfactory in the field. Switching of tags, loss of tags, etc. has discouraged most growers from field tagging. The pre-tagging in the field during the late summer and fall has worked well for many growers. The pre-tagged trees are usually cut before the plantation is opened up to the general public. The pre-tag customers can simply pick up their tree which can be baled ahead of time. The pre-tagged trees can be placed alphabetically in a secure place near the checkout area. The tag will bear a number which also appears on the receipt given to the customer at the time of tagging. A deposit on the tree is an essential step in the pre-tag procedure.

Hours of operation must be determined. Most growers are open from the Thanksgiving weekend right up until Christmas. The first weekend you are open can be a big one. Many people want their choice of the best quality tree.

They sometimes lose sight of the fact that a tree cut four weeks or so before Christmas may not be a very fresh one by the time Christmas rolls around.

On a year-to-year basis, the selling price or "market" will vary. You will have to be mindful of the market factors and respond accordingly. Any oversupply will probably result in reduced prices. A new retail lot in town, especially if it has high quality trees, can reduce your sales. Another choose and cut business in the area will surely give you competition. It can be crucial if you are in a limited market area. Be aware of such eventualities. They will guide your decision making. (You may want to wholesale some of your excess trees or open a lot in a nearby city, etc.) As the buying season approaches, you know what you have to sell and you have a "feel for the market", your initial pricing policy can be set. You may have to change it, however. If good size Douglas Fir are in short supply, you may get more for them. Market considerations can go either way. In brief, know your competition and market conditions. Just the tone of the economic conditions in your area will affect your customers actions, too.

The management of your lot may be made easier by working with a local group as a fund raising activity. Their activity may range from actually running your tree lot to selling baked goods in your shop. Many times a donation can be worked out if members of a particular group agree to patronize your lot. Many groups need funds and they provide an excellent source of help and product sales. These groups may be Boy Scouts, Girl Scouts, Kiwanis, Lions Club, 4H, local school band groups, church groups and many others too numerous to mention. Take advantage of these opportunities.

Housekeeping and sanitation in the fields and on the grounds is essential to continued good business. Clean surroundings establish a precedent the same way dirty/messy surroundings do. Litter can cause accidents and mechanical problems sooner or later. Hazards that lead to accidents can result in high insurance payments, far and beyond what they should be. Most places provide trash cans and/or barrels. Keep them emptied so that garbage does not accumulate around them.

In the fields all obstacles should have been removed before allowing the public to enter. The general terrain of a "U Cut" area can be hazardous to the children. Avoid or correct any such situation. High stumps are the biggest problem. Wise operators make sure that all stumps are cut within 1" of the ground. The high stump situation can result in serious problems when snow covers the fields. The attendant/attendants on the lot should walk their areas at the beginning of the next day to be sure all stumpage is removed. Doing this daily is best because a snowfall at night or late afternoon darkness can hide the problem Also, high cut stumps may encourage others to do the same thing. Cutting above the bottom whorl, for example, will result in a smaller tree to the buyer and possible loss of income to you. (A well-shaped, full tree all the way to the ground is the best way to avoid high cuts.)

Be mindful of the critical part weather plays in your operation. Good December weather favors choose and cut operations more so than a regular retail cut tree lot. Two bad weather weekends can ruin your business for that year. This is especially true of plantations that are a long way away and/or are difficult to reach. Also, your policies and procedures must be made more flexible to allow for exceedingly bad weather. A very bad weather year could result in 50% or more loss of normal business.

One very important management factor, sometimes overlooked or not given the proper attention, is the actual inventory of your merchandise. I mean trees! It is essential to know what you have to sell. In the late summer and early fall we inventory all our fields and take a count of all the trees that are of harvestable size. This is all recorded on paper, by area and specie. It will be critical to you because you must know what you have to sell and it also provides basis for projecting income. It will serve as a signal to limit or restrict tree sales from a specific area to avoid overcutting. It may even dictate the length of your season since, if you sell too many one year, you may have very few the next year.

When we survey our fields we take a "guesstimate" of what may be forthcoming the following year and also the year after that. Again, if your projections show a lean harvest two years hence, then you may want to curtail sales in the current year to try to stretch the supply. Although you can purchase cut trees from someone else, it is always more profitable to sell your own.

The idea that people go out to the country to get a lower price is not necessarily the case with Christmas Trees. At the farm you have a better selection, better quality, a fresher product and a pleasant family experience. Many people are willing to pay a premium price for this!

Some extras, essential on a tree lot:

-Many hand saws (SANDVIK type works best).
-Twine.
-Rain gear/boots (on loan).
-A baler - (at least a hand baler with vexar), twine works
 fine too.
-Nursery marking pens.
-Tags, if only to mark reserved trees.
-Flagging Tape/Ribbon - To mark a tree even if a customer
 decides on another tree.
-Snappies - Auto trunk lid tie-downs.
-A tree shaker or hard ground or concrete area where trees
 can have loose needles and chaff removed.

Additional Items to sell:

-Tree Stands.
-Tree Skirts to cover stand around tree.

Additional items to sell (continued)

-Tree Removal Bag.
-Candle Rings for a table decoration (made with natural
 greens, of course).
-Candle-Holder Yule Log.
-Pine Cone Wreaths, Pine Cone Christmas Trees and other cone
 decorations.
-Wreaths and sprays.
-Roping.
-Boughs/Branches for Decoration on Mantles, Etc. (Douglas
 Fir, Fraser, Balsam, Holly, Boxwood, Bayberry and others).

Give-Away items to promote business:

-A tag or card telling how to care for the Christmas tree.
-Coloring Books for kids.
-Candy Canes/Peppermint Sticks, Santa Claus Suckers,
 balloons, etc.
-Pens, Pencils or other advertising specialties.
-Christmas Stick-ons (Santas, Christmas Trees, etc.).

A couple of references that follow plus a few others from
your nearest public library should provide many more ideas for
marketing and merchandising products.

Christmas Magic by Margaret Perry
Doubleday & Co. Garden City, NY 1964
L of C # 64-17295

Treasury of Christmas Crafts & Foods
Better Homes & Gardens
Meredith Corp. Des Moines, Iowa 1980
L of C # 79-55159

Gorden Anderson, a tree grower near Cleveland, Ohio, tells
about his experiences:

A GOOD CHOOSE & CUT YEAR
by Gordon Anderson, Kirtland, OH

The ingredients for a good year are: ideal weather, a
seller's market and a good crop. we enjoyed all three during
our Cut-your-own Christmas Tree sales at Creawood Forest in
Kirtland, Ohio.

They say a Pacific high pressure area was responsible for
the weather. We were given cold and relatively dry air from
Canada rather than our usual warm and moist air coming up the
Mississippi Valley. The success of a Cut-your-own operation is
more dependent on good weather than a regular retail lot. If
the weather is cold and wet on the two selling weekends of
December, you have lost a season.

In 1974, we had 19 inches of heavy, wet snow that fell in
early December, and stayed for the season. The heavy snow,
laying in the trees, distorted their shapes and restricted our
sales. In wet seasons, with the traffic on the farm roads and
in the fields, it is difficult to keep the trees from mud. It
is rather disheartening to see a beautiful tree, that is going
into someone's own living room, covered with mud.

This year, our fields were frozen dry for the entire sales period. Add to this, a few light snow flurries. This put the customer into the spirit of Christmas and makes for a very pleasant situation.

There are a few things going for a cut your own operation. It is hard to say which is the most important, but I believe it is the knowing of getting a fresh cut tree. Every retail lot in the country advertises "fresh cut", no matter when the trees were cut. I have had customers come in from the field, very happy, with a tree of lower quality than they could have got from our pre-cut selection. It was fresh - they knew it was fresh.

The family, going to the farm, selecting and cutting a tree of their choice, is an experience that many are willing to pay for. In many cases, it is the desire for the old fashion, the traditional and the back to nature movement.

No pre-cut sales lot will ever be able to display the selection of trees, as a cut your own sales. Because of handling problems, the tree in the field is shown at its best.

Whatever the reason may be, for the last number of years, the demand has been greater than the supply. The artificial tree has been around long enough that it will give us no surprise. The shortage of natural trees, the difficulty of finding a quality tree, will encourage some to buy the artificial.

There is no satisfaction greater than looking over a field and seeing a "good" crop. In Christmas trees, it takes a long time, 8 - 12 years. The right selection of stock, on the right site. Good growing years with adequate moisture. Protection from the competition of grass, weeds and brush. You have had no fires. Insects and diseases have been controlled or absent.

Beyond having a healthy plant with foliage that has good color, it is the shearing crew that makes your trees. You have only one chance a year to make your trees, it cannot be treated as just another chore. I am much happier with the boy that shears 200 salable trees than the boy that does a half-hearted job on 400 trees.

Preparation for the sales season really starts with an inventory in late summer. The objective of our inventory is to give us the number of trees by specie and height class. It is important to know how many 10' Scotch Pines you have to move that year. It is also important to know how many 5' white pines you have that will be 7' in two years.

We have experienced the problem of over cutting. The penalty for over cutting is that you are forced out of the market until you can grow new stock. In our case it only took a couple of years to be back, but we lost our momentum, we lost our customers, and it took a little time to build back up again.

It is desirable to have continuous production of a known product. So that your spruce customer can come each year and be able to purchase his 8 foot spruce. The customers will adjust to the crop to some degree, if the quality is there.

On October 1, we start tagging and pricing the trees that will be offered for sale. A plastic zap tag is marked with a waterproof magic marker. The tag is placed slightly inside the foliage so it will be protected when the tree is dragged in. The tag is also stapled to make it difficult to attempt to switch price tags. All price tags are on the south side of the tree. The uniform placement of the tags makes it easier for the customer to find and they are also looking at the best side of the tree.

Other pricing techniques have been used: flat price - "X" dollars per foot or "X" dollars per tree of customer's choice. Neither method is very sophisticated. You lose control of your customer. We love our customers but do not want them telling us what trees they will cut.

In selling at a flat price you cannot get a premium price for your premium trees. Your customers can wander the entire farm, even looking at the landscaping on your front lawn. If you are selling Scotch Pine, some one will wander into your block of Blue Spruce and insist it is a Scotch Pine. The first 50% of your customers get a fair deal - then you or they are stuck with the poorer quality trees.

If you sell by the foot, you have the same problem of control of the customer. Other tricks the customers will play is to break the leader out, so he doesn't have to pay for that top six inches or cut the top out of a large tree. The last year we sold by the foot was the year someone cut the top six feet out of a twelve foot powder Blue Spruce.

In pre-pricing the trees for sale, you can control where the customers will cut. It gives the opportunity to thin out the trees that are too close for full development. It is possible to get the premium price on the premium trees, and also to put a lower price on the number two's. With the right price you can sell about anything.

The customers will cut about 70% of what you have pre-priced. What is left is scattered. You will make mistakes on pricing. If you want to sell a thousand - pre-price twelve or thirteen hundred trees.

It is difficult to know on October 1 what the retail prices will be in December. On a retail lot you can get "the feel" of prices as you make a few sales. You can check other lots so that you will have a good idea if trees are in long or short supply. Be high enough in your original pricing. It will be easier to announce a discount than to try to ask for more.

The reason for the early start is that it is usually warm and dry. It is difficult to write on wet tickets, difficult to attach tags with gloves on. it can be "gotten out of the way" before working on wholesale orders, going deer hunting, etc.

Once the selling season starts, we place a cashier in the parking lot - at the edge of the field. Instructions are given and saws picked up at the cashier's booth. We are very firm that a cut tree must have a price ticket attached to it when brought in for payment. A visible sign is posted at the information booth showing prices we would charge for an unticketed tree. It is about double the price that we have on our pre-priced trees.

Once the rules have been made and explained to the customer, we do everything possible to make the experience as pleasant as is possible. Most problems arise because of a lack of understanding and a lack of communication.

We have been involved in a sales program that has worked well for us. A number of years ago the Seniors at our High School wanted to sell trees. They ran into many problems locating good trees, displaying, staying all night to watch the trees, etc. The following year we offered them the opportunity to sell tickets which we would redeem on the purchase of a tree. The tickets sold for a dollar and we would redeem them for a dollar at the time of purchase of a tree.

This worked well for both of us. On a given night in early December, the class canvassed the entire town. They raised their money – with no cash investment and with only one night of effort. Boys and girls could both be involved.

We do like our Police. We are on a busy route through town. Our entrance and exit are somewhat hidden and a safety problem Primarily for safety, somewhat for the convenience of our customers on busy weekends, we hire two policemen to direct traffic in and out. It doesn't hurt a bit for the officer to block traffic so a customer can make an easy entrance. Two officers on the road does attract a little attention and does slow traffic down. There seems to be a bit more of a security problem these days. I use the officers for an escort to make a deposit at the end of a busy day and I hope many people are watching.

Labor, equipment and materials are very expensive. It is imperative to be as efficient as possible in their use. We have frustrations – one example is the rather simple task of hauling trees in from the field. The employees just cannot bring in a good load. Mostly they are underloaded. They just throw a few trees on and are content in driving back and forth to the field. They can be very busy – but not producing.

> He who has a thing to sell
> And goes and whispers in a well
> Is not so apt to get the dollars
> As he who climbs a tree and hollers.

The search is on for just
the right tree.

Baling the tree is fun
and makes it easy to
transport and mount in
stand.

Wholesale harvest in progress.
Tractor, wagon, and high-speed
compression baler with a five-
man crew works best.

"Sky" and Joan Weller
R.D. #4 Box 236A
Washout Road
Scotia, New York 12302
Tel. (518) 393-2052

SKY VIEW ACRES TREE FARM

Sky View Acres Tree Farm is a small Christmas tree operation located in the Glenville Hills of Schenectady County. It is operated by Schuyler "Sky" and Joan Weller. The name of our farm came from my nickname "Sky", from the beautiful view we have overlooking the Mohawk River Valley, and from the eighty fine <u>acres</u> that we own.

As a youngster I wished that my father would allow me to sell Christmas trees in the back yard of our home in Scotia, New York. It wasn't until many years later, when my wife and I built a home on her father's farm, that I began to realize my <u>boyhood</u> <u>dream</u>.

In the late 1950's my father-in-law decided to sell his dairy herd and give up farming. He didn't want his fields to grow back to brush so he started planting pine trees. Each year he bought a 1,000 or so trees from New York State and planted them (not with Christmas trees in mind) but as a reforestation project. We didn't start thinking seriously about growing Christmas trees until 1975.

After getting permission to plant trees on the farm for the purpose of selling them for Christmas trees, we called in a state forester to advise us on what kinds of trees would grow best on our land. Since our ground is a hard clay soil, and not well-drained in many areas, his advice was to plant mostly Norway and White spruce trees along with Douglas fir, Balsam fir and Scotch pine.

We placed an order with the state and the first week in May, 1976 we picked up 3,500 seedlings from the Saratoga Tree Nursery. We were on our way to becoming Christmas tree farmers (we thought)!

At that time our method of planting was following 4-foot stakes, spaced 50 or so apart, in what we thought was a straight line. We used a shovel to make the opening in the ground, placed the tree in the left-hand corner of the opening and sealed it shut with our foot. Then we paced off approximately 6 feet for the next tree keeping the 4-foot stakes in sight for the rows. We planted Christmas tree planting stock this way for several years. All this time we didn't realize the importance of soil tests, mowing the fields, and using herbicides and pesticides. As a result only a few hundred trees survived from the 1,000's we had planted.

194

We weren't discouraged, however, and in 1978 we joined the New York Christmas Tree Growers' Association. This was a step in the right direction. We have learned a great deal from the members, consultants, and the many special speakers we have heard at the meetings. We have also made a lot of wonderful friends. We now purchase our seedlings from private nurseries to assure getting the quality and seed sources conducive to a successful Christmas tree operation. We have purchased planting lines with beads marked on the line every 6 feet. Now we are sure we are planting in straight rows in both directions. Our other method of planting proved disastrous. We were unable to mow until the trees were tall enough to see and the mowing turned out to be a "labor of love" since the trees didn't end up in straight rows.

We still found that in our soil the survival rate of planting bare root seedlings was poor so in the spring of 1982 we initiated another planting method. We purchased 1-gallon pots and planted each seedling in a pot. For our soil mixture we used equal parts of sand, soil, peat moss and perlite. We watered them regularly with 20-20-20 fertilizer. The following spring we purchased a 6-inch auger for our tractor. We marked the rows to be planted, drilled the hole, tapped the tree out of the pot and planted it in the hole. We carried extra soil with us to be sure the tree was planted without any air holes. Starting the seedlings in the pots gave the seedlings a chance to develop a better root system before transferring them into a field area.This method of planting has worked the best for us; however, it is a much slower process: another "labor of love".

We are still faced with many problems such as, wet areas, areas that cause frost pockets, insects and predators like mice, deer, etc. We have given up trying to grow Fraser and Balsam fir because of the deer problem. We have reverted back to growing the species the state forester advised many years ago and i.e. spruces, Douglas fir and Scotch pines.

In the late 1970's we started to mow around some of the trees my father-in-law had planted and we found them to be near saleable size. We pruned them and opened up our farm for a "Choose N' Cut" operation. Since we only had a few trees available we didn't advertise. Our business grew by word-of-mouth.

The fall of 1979 we converted the old milk house into what we call our "shop" and "warm-up" room. We serve coffee and hot chocolate while our customers warm up around the wood stove and, of course, there are candy canes for the children. We find that they are the ones who bring the parents back the next Christmas season.

Joan started making wreaths for sale in 1979. We sell them plain and decorated at the farm. One of our local hardware stores retails some of our wreaths, also. The wreath sales have developed into an integral part of our business.

Every year our "Choose N' Cut" tree business grows and our own supply of saleable trees is inadequate. In 1986 we decided to purchase ready-cut trees to augment our own supply. The project was well received and each year we increase the number of trees we purchase. We only purchase from growers that we know from the New York State Christmas Tree Growers Association. That way we are assured of quality and fresh-cut New York State grown trees.

There is so much more to Christmas tree farming (true of any business) than most people realize. The concensus of opinion , generally, is that you plant the trees, wait ten years or so, cut them and collect money. Not so. Every month of the year there is a job waiting to be done; also, there is MUCH to be learned. We are learning all the time. What works for one grower may not work for another. For us, what started as a part-time project has turned into a full-time job. BUT!: Joan and I really enjoy our Christmas tree farm. It is our wish that one or more of our children will also. We love working with Mother Nature and meeting Her challenges. Although the jobs are endless, so, too, are the rewards. A good wife (if it weren't for Joan there would be no tree farm), acreage to plant on, and a lot of hard work, but, nevertheless, the formula for making a <u>boyhood dream</u> become a reality.

Wreaths and floral decorations provide a second-
income product using natural materials.

MARKETING - RETAIL LOT (CUT TREES)

Some growers are engaged in cut tree retailing, just as they are in wholesaling and choose and cut. As stated earlier, most choose and cut businesses do an excellent cut tree business so the hints that follow should be helpful.

For those of you who may want to try your hand at selling Christmas Trees in advance of growing them, these suggestions will be helpful.

The marketing and merchandising suggestions offered earlier could apply to a cut tree retail lot. A live Santa Claus, hot chocolate, free balloons for the kids and many other ideas can be employed on the cut tree lot. Many customers stopping at a retail lot spend much less time than at a choose and cut plantation. This does not preclude the sale of all the other decorative and sundry items, however.

Whether operating a "Choose and Cut" business or a regular pre-cut retail lot, advance notice of your intentions to have trees available can be made known by a sign. As soon as Halloween is over, your sign should go up.

Here are some helpful hints in setting up and operating a successful pre-cut retail lot:

Trees should be displayed carefully so as to insure their appeal and stimulate a quick buying decision on the part of the buyer. Trees attached to posts in an upright position best display the shape, fullness and quality of the tree, as well as any possible faults.

Proper lighting is necessary as winter daylight is short and supper hour and early evening sales can contribute greatly to your overall sales. Keep the lot tidy. Don't leave branches or allow butts of trees to lay around. Keep the main traffic areas of your lot free of snow and ice also. Many people will enter your lot without proper footwear.

Don't put all the choicest trees out on the lot all at once. Feed trees onto the lot so as to have a fresh selection for as long as possible.

Display the best trees along the road where passing traffic can see them. That will prompt many potential buyers to stop. Gaps or poor sides of a tree should be placed against the post so the tree shows well.

Poor quality or damaged trees can be displayed in a "bargain" or "Charlie Brown" area and priced accordingly.

Some lots pre-price their trees, others don't. You can decide this as you get a feel of customer response. Many people like to dicker over the price of a tree. Our own experience has been not to put a price tag on the trees.

Don't miss an opportunity to sell a little poorer tree at a little lower price. A perfect tree will sell itself.

Offer assistance to a tree buyer. They need to have a quality/price idea, or the price of one tree variety versus another.

Many retail tree lots have natural looking trees, not colored. Most tree varieties (Norway spruce, E. white pine, Douglas fir, balsam and Fraser firs) usually have good color. Poor colored Scotch, Austrian or white pine might warrant the use of colorants. Colorants are usually either a deep green or a blue-green. Poorer quality and off color trees might prompt you to flock some of those poor quality trees. White, green, red, blue are colors frequently used. There is a limited market for flocked trees however.

Potted and balled and burlapped trees can expand your sales considerably. The preparation of these trees can and should be done well in advance of the opening of the lot.

Wreaths, roping and additional bough material should be available to increase your dollar volume. You can easily learn how to make your own wreaths and decorative materials. Wreath buyers tend to buy early so as to have their decorations (usually on a door or chimney of the house) visible throughout the season. They should be available right after the Thanksgiving weekend.

Clear and clean up the entire tree lot as soon as all trees are sold or as soon after Christmas Eve as possible. Many eyes see your lot and the impression you give will influence sales in the future.

=======================================

The greater the number of trees to harvest the earlier the harvest should start. Weather becomes a highly unpredictable factor.

We do no cutting until we have had two "hard" frosts. That is, the temperature goes down to the 22 degree mark and stays there for six hours. This may occur two nights back to back or it may occur a week or so apart. This "sets" the needles on the tree. It sends the tree into a secondary stage of dormancy. A light frost on a couple nights is not adequate because a few warm days can bring the tree out of dormancy.

Occasionally, we will have a lingering summer and it may be late October or early November before these frosts occur. Some growers are forced to cut trees to meet deadlines. The order of cutting coincides with "keeping" characteristics, Scotch, Austrian, Red, White Pines followed by Douglas Fir, Balsam, Fraser, Concolor and other true firs. Spruces are last with Blue Spruce, White Spruce and Norway in that sequence. It is the last week in November when we cut spruce. Air temperatures should be 32 degrees and rising as we like to have the sap running up into the tree.

We try to avoid working in very bad weather. Freezing temperatures slow you down and make baling difficult. Damage to trees can be great. Colds, sore throats, etc. can cripple the work crew and make future productivity costly.

We work with a two to five man crew. One cuts, another pulls trees to the aisle where the tractor, wagon and baler are to move down the field. The third man operates the baler, the fourth feeds trees into the baler, and the fifth loads onto the wagon or truck and moves the "train" along. (See Picture)

When organized and all equipment is operating smoothly, 500 or more standard size trees can be cut, baled and secured in a day. All the factors of manpower, equipment, weather, etc. will govern how many you can do in a day.

Don't cut any more trees than can be baled and moved that day. In fact, we do it in stages so that trees are not left out and unbaled. Trees should be moved to the collection or sizing yard so that snow and theft problems are avoided. We try to load out an order as soon as trees are ready. You need the close cooperation of your customers to do this. They must understand how you operate and avail themselves accordingly. If you live away from the premises, you may have to move the cut trees to a secure place in the field or to a neighbor's yard or provide some form of surveillance. These same precautions should be followed by the retailer.

To have a smooth harvest operation, the preparation must be completed ahead of time. Equipment must be serviced and ready, saws (chain saws) sharpened and serviced, gasoline mixture made up, stump treatment ready, chains for tractor, twine, ropes, towing chain and all other foreseeable items ready or anticipated and arrangements made. Even the best of plans can go bad, but you will learn other bitter and costly lessons if the essentials are not provided for. Oh yes, remember Christmas Tree growing (and harvesting) is fun!!

High-speed compression balers are great but for some trees getting them home the "old-fashioned" way is best.

Where To Go For Additional Help

Few industries have highly-qualified people more willing to assist one another than Christmas Tree growers. Although this may be due partly to the diverse nature and variable factors unique to this undertaking, it is also characteristic of the people involved and, usually, dedicated to this activity. They become "hooked" on Christmas Tree growing both for profit and pleasure and many are willing to help the "newcomer".

The following are a few sources of help. The more sources of assistance you are aware of, the better your chances of growing high-quality trees profitably.

Cooperative Extension Service. They are countrywide (see listing) and are present in practically every County of every State in the country. They are an "extension" of your State's University and their purpose is to guide and serve you in many home and farm (city and rural) activities, including those of a horticultural nature. There is a modest fee to join and receive newsletters, bulletins, and notices of activities. Your membership is a "must".

Suppliers/growers of plants (planting stock) have been an excellent source of guidance. They are dedicated, hard-working people who know a lot about what other growers are doing and what problems may occur. Also, they are aware of the marketing trend in the industry since they have to be planning as much as five years ahead. Their time is valuable since they usually have a work load that far exceeds time available to them-so prepare your questions and be brief when consulting them.

Tree Grower Associations. (See listing). These are usually by State, but several of the very best include several states, i.e., Northwest Christmas Tree Growers' Assn. They all hold meetings to discuss common problems and plan other activities. "Winter" meetings provide sessions that discuss general subjects such as insect/disease management, tax and legal aspects of tree growing, sales and marketing activities, etc. "Summer" meetings, of most associations,are at growers' plantations. Here you can gain more "input" about tree growing and cultural practices from experienced people in the industry. Like most Associations they have a quarterly "Journal or Bulletin" that includes valuable subject material, supplier ads, classifieds, and industry concerns, in addition to a marketing program. The strongest effort has been to combat the artificial tree.

Product/Equipment Suppliers. There are products on the market that you will need to acquire to perform the functions of growing Christmas Trees (both good and poor products). Suppliers generally relate the favorable features of their product or piece of equipment but do not mention the limitations, problems, durability, serviceability, costs (after the initial sale), and other aspects that you may encounter later. Product/equipment suppliers, however, are helpful and knowledgeable and they are essential in the Christmas Tree-growing enterprise. Other tree growers are a source of guidance regarding which products best suit your needs. Investigate before you buy!

"Addendum to Basics of Growing Christmas Trees" has 60 pages of product suppliers. You will find this very helpful for requesting literature and evaluating products. A brief list of "catalog" (mail order) suppliers is included in the Appendix. These catalogs list, picture, and price most of the products you will need. Write for them. They are usually free.

Publications and Books. In addition to the Association bulletins, journals, and University publications (through Cooperative Extension), many books are available on general as well as specific subjects. Book stores and publishers' listings are key sources. These books are usually written by "experts" in their field, thus providing in-depth discussions. They provide excellent long-term reference material. Larger city/county libraries have extensive reference material, both in book and periodical form. They also have government publications such as Forestry Service reports and studies. Do some research by visiting libraries in or near your vicinity. Your nearest college/university library usually has specialized and extensive material that can be very helpful.

Christmas Trees magazine, Editors-Charles and Sally Wright, P.O. Box 107, Lecompton, Kansas 66050, Tel. (913) 887-6324, is a quarterly publication of interest to all growers. It contains information on many subjects. Many tree grower associations provide a subscription to this publication as part of their membership. Take time to regularly read the written word. You will be rewarded by becoming a better tree grower.

Consultants/Professional Services. Some long-time tree growers offer their services as consultants. Established, as well as new growers, can get valuable assistance from these "pros". However, do some research and preliminary work first, i.e., soil tests, soil fertility, slope and drainage considerations, knowledge of adaptable tree types, income objectives, etc.

Most consultants work on a day or half-day basis with a fee plus expenses, usually travel/mileage compensation. Some will work on an hourly basis, particularly if the problem has been identified,etc. More growers should avail themselves to the knowledge and judgment of consultants who are generally successful growers with a lifetime experience with forestry. This is a vital step that pays for itself many times over. Just avoiding a problem or bad decision can save you many years of living with a non-productive and costly situation.

Other Tree Growers. Last, but not least, your fellow grower (who becomes your friend) can be very helpful since you probably have common problems and "two heads" are usually better than one. Another tree grower who is nearby (a competitor) may not be willing to assist you.

Help from a fellow grower will take many forms from basic discussion about chemicals and where to find something to sharing time and equipment. In some areas of the country this is carried to the ultimate by the formation of a marketing co-op or marketing association. This is in addition to the State Association and is, sometimes, a regional organization.

In the last few years, some marketing groups have evolved but more will be needed, possibly as a result of new growers like you, since many of the "old guard" are comfortably entrenched in "doing their own thing."

APPENDIX A

CONVERSION TABLES

Customary to Metric
(approximate to within 2%)

When You Know	Multiply by	To Find	Symbol
inches	25	millimeters	mm
inches	2.5	centimeters	cm
feet	0.3	meters	m
yards	0.9	meters	m
fathoms	1.8	meters	m
miles	1.6	kilometers	km
square inches	6.5	square centimeters	cm^2
square feet	0.093	square meters	m^2
square yards	0.84	square meters	m^2
acres	0.4	hectares	ha
square miles	2.6	square kilometers	km^2
cubic inches	16.4	cubic centimeters	cm^3
cubic feet	0.028	cubic meters	m^3
cubic yards	0.76	cubic meters	m^3
ounces (fluid)	30	milliliters	mL
pints	0.47	liters	L
quarts liquid	0.95	liters	L
gallons	3.8	liters	L
pints	0.55	liters	L
quarts dry	1.1	liters	L
bushels	35	liters	L
bushels	0.035	cubic meters	m^3
avoirdupois ounces	28	grams	g
avoirdupois pounds	0.45	kilograms	kg
short tons (2000 lb)	0.91	metric tons	t
long tons (2240 lb)	1.0	metric tons	t

(Fahrenheit temperature — 32) x 0.56 = Celsius temperature

Metric to Customary
(approximate to within 2%)

When You Know	Multiply by	To Find
millimeters	0.04	inches
centimeters	0.4	inches
meters	3.3	feet
meters	1.1	yards
kilometers	0.62	miles
square centimeters	0.155	square inches
square meters	10.8	square feet
square meters	1.2	square yards
hectares	2.5	acres
square kilometers	0.39	square miles
cubic centimeters	0.06	cubic inches
cubic meters	35	cubic feet
cubic meters	1.3	cubic yards
milliliters	0.034	ounces (fluid)
liters	2.1	pints liquid
liters	1.06	quarts
liters	0.26	gallons
liters	1.8	pints
liters	0.9	quarts
cubic meters	28	bushels dry
grams	0.035	avoirdupois ounces
kilograms	2.2	avoirdupois pounds
metric tons	1.1	short tons (2000 lb)
metric tons	1.0	long tons (2240 lb)

(Celsius temperature x 1.8) + 32 = Fahrenheit temperature

CHEMICAL INDEX (herbicides)

Common Name	Trade Name	Manufacturer
acifluorfen	Blazer	BASF
asulam	Asulox	Rhone-Poulenc
BAS 514 (Quinclorac)	Impact	BASF
BAS09002S	----	BASF
benefin	Balan	DowElanco
bentazon	Basagran	BASF
chlopyralid	Stinger	DowElanco
chlorflurenol	Break-Thru	Andersons
crop oil concentrate	Booster	BASF
2,4-D	Formula 40	DowElanco
2,4-D/triclopyr/clopyralid	XRM-5202	DowElanco
2,4DP-P	----	BASF
2,4-D/MCPP/dicamba	Trimec	PBI-Gordon
DCPA	Dacthal	Fermenta
dicamba	Banvel	Sandoz
diclobenil	Casoron	Uniroyal
diquat	Diquat	Valent
Chlorimuron (DPX 6025)	Classic	DuPont
ethofumesate	Prograss	Nor-Am
Fatty acid salts	Sharpshooter	Mycogen
fenoxaprop	Acclaim	Hoechst-Roussel
fluazifop-p	Fusilade 2000	ICI Americas
glyphosate	Roundup	Monsanto
imazaquin	Scepter	American Cyanamid
imazethapyr	Pursuit	American Cyanamid
isoxaben	Gallery	DowElanco
isoxaben/oryzalin	Snapshot	DowElanco
isoxaben/trifluralin	Snapshot TG	DowElanco
MCPA	MCPA Conc.	Rhone-Poulenc
MCPP-P	----	BASF
metolachlor	Pennant	Ciba-Geigy
MON 15151, 04, 75	Dimension	Monsanto
MSMA	Daconate 6	Fermenta
napropamide	Devrinol	ICI Americas
Norflurazon	Solicam	Sandoz
oryzalin	Surflan	DowElanco
oryzalin/benefin	XL	DowElanco
oxadiazon	Ronstar	Chipco, Rhone-Poulenc
oxyfluorfen	Goal	Rohm & Haas
oxyfluorfen/pendimethalin	Scott's O.H. II	O.M. Scott
paraquat	Gramoxone	ICI Americas
pendimethalin	Pre-M, Stomp	Lesco, Cyanamid
prodiamine	----	Sandoz
S-3182	----	O.M. Scott
sethoxydim	Poast	BASF
simazine	Princep	Ciba-Geigy
simazine/metolachlor	Derby	Ciba-Geigy
triclopyr/clopyralid	Confront (XRM-5085)	DowElanco
triclopyr/2,4-D (amine)	Turflon II Amine	DowElanco
triclopyr/2,4-D (ester)	Turflon D	DowElanco
triclopyr amine	Turflon Amine	DowElanco
trifluralin	Treflan	DowElanco
trifluralin/benefin	Team	DowElanco
X-77	X-77	Valent

AL - Alabama: Cooperative Extension Service, Auburn University Auburn, Alabama 36849

AR - Arkansas: Cooperative Extension Service, 1201 McAlmont, University of Arkansas, Box 391, Little Rock, Arkansas 72203

CA - California: Limited-Scale Agriculture Programs, ABS Extension, University of California, Davis, CA 95616

CN - Connecticut: University of Connecticut, Dept. of Agricultural Publications, U-35, Room 223, 1376 Storrs Rd., Storrs, CT 06268

FL - Florida: Editorial Department, G022 McCarty Hall, Institute of Food and Agricultural Science, University of Florida, Gainesville, Florida 32611

GA - Georgia: Division of Ag. Communication, College of Agriculture, University of Georgia, Athens, GA 30602

HA - Hawaii: Publications and Information Office, Krauss Hall 108, University of Hawaii, 2500 Dole Street, Honolulu, Hawaii 96822

IA - Iowa: Publications Distribution Center, Printing and Publication Building, Iowa State University, Ames, Iowa 50011

KS - Kansas: Hyde S. Jacobs, Cooperative Extension Service, Extension Agricultural Programs, Umberger Hall, Manhattan, Kansas 66506

MA - Massachusetts: Robert W. Martin, Dept. of Agri. and Res. Economics University of Massachusetts, 201 Draper Hall, Amherst, Massachusetts 01003

MD - Maryland: Farm Institute, Cooperative Extension Service, The University of Maryland Eastern Shore, Princess Anne, MD 21853

ME - Maine: Information and Publications Editor, Cooperative Extension Service University of Maine at Orono, Orono, Maine 04469

MI - Michigan: Susan Kindinger, Cooperative Extension Service, 11 Agriculture Hall, Michigan State University, East Lansing, MI 48824

MN - Minnesota Extension Service, Communication Resources Distribution Center, University of Minnesota, Minneapolis, Minnesota 55455

MO - Missouri: George W. Enlow, Lincoln University, Cooperative Extension Service, 900 Moreau Drive, Jefferson City, MO 65101

MS - Extension Information, Mississippi Cooperative Extension Service, Mississippi State University, Mississippi 39762

MT - Montana: Montana State Univeristy, Bozeman, Montana 59715

NC - North Carolina: Agricultural Communications Department, Box 7603, North Carolina State University, Raleigh, North Carolina 27695-7603

ND - North Dakota: Duane R. Berglund, Cooperative Extension Service, Box 5437, NDSU Station, North Dakota State University, Fargo, ND 58105

NE - Nebraska: Agricultural Communications, University of Nebraska-Lincoln
Lincoln, Nebraska 68583-0918

NH - New Hampshire: Henry W. Corrow, Jr, Extension Editor, Taylor Hall
Durham, N.H. 03824

NJ - New Jersey: Cooperative Extension Service, Publications Distribution Center
Cook College, Rutgers University, P.O. Box 231, New Brunswick, NJ 08903

NM - New Mexico: Agricultural Information Dept., Drawer 3AI, New Mexico
State University, Las Cruces, New Mexico 88003

NV - Nevada: Alice M. Good, Agricultural Information Office, College of
Agriculture, University of Nevada-Reno, Reno, Nevada 89557-0004

NY - New York: Cornell Distribution Center, 7 Research Park, Ithaca, NY 14850

OH - Ohio: Publications Office, Cooperative Extension Service, 2120 Fyffe Road
Columbus, Ohio 43210-1099

OK - Oklahoma: Central Mailing Services, Oklahoma State University, Stillwater,
OK 74078

OR - Oregon: Cooperative Extension Service, Oregon State University, Corvallis,
Oregon 97331

PR - Puerto Rico: Jorge Luis Leon, University of Puerto Rico, Agricultural
Extension Service, Darlington Building, Mayaguez, PR 00708

RI - Rhode Island: Publications Office - C, Room 10 Woodward Hall, University
of Rhode Island, Kingston, RI 02881-8004

SC - South   Carolina: Public   Service   Publications,Dept.   Agricultural
Communications, 103 Fike Center, Clemson University, Clemson, SC 29631

SD - South Dakota: Agricultural Communications, South Dakota State University,
Brookings, SD 57007

TN - Tennessee: Extension Mailing Room,Institute of Agriculture, P.O. Box 1071
Knoxville, Tennessee 37901-1071

TX - Texas: Dept. of Agricultural Communications, Texas A&M University,
College Station, Texas 77843

UT - Utah: Extension Publications Officer, Utah State University, Logan, Utah
84322-5015

VT - Vermont: Rick Wadkernagel, University of Vermont, 178 South Prospect
Street, Burlington, Vermont 05401-1020

WA - Washington: Bulletin Office, Cooperative Extension Service, Cooper
Publications Bldg., Washington State University, Pullman, WA 99164-5912

WI - Wisconsin: Jerry McGee, Publications Editor, College of Agri. and Life
Sciences, Cooperative Extension Service, University of Wisconsin-Madison
Madison, Wisconsin 53706

PRODUCT SUPPLIERS WITH CATALOGS (PARTIAL LIST)

Ben Meadows Co., P. O. Box 13633, Station K, 1423 Dutch Valley Pl. N.E., Atlanta, GA 30324, 1-800-241-6401

Campbell Tree & Land Co., Inc., Wautoma, WI 54982, 414-787-4653

Farber Bag & Supply Co., 8733 Kapp Drive, Box 78, Peosta, IA 52068-0078 (Tools, sprayers, tree & landscape items, burlap, etc.), 1-800-553-9068 or 1-800-228-7527, in Iowa 1-800-942-4610

Forestry Suppliers, Inc., Box 8397, 205 W. Rankin St., Jackson, Miss. 39204, 1-800-647-5368

E. C. Geiger, Box 285, Rt. 63, Harleysville, PA 19438, 215-256-6511

Good-Prod. Sales, 825 Fairfield Ave., Kenilworth, NJ 07033, 201-245-5055

International Reforestation Suppliers, 2100 W. Broadway, P. O. Box 5547, Eugene Oregon 97405, 1-800-321-1037

Kelco Industries, Box 160, Milbridge, MA 04658, (tools, supplies), 1-800-343-4057

The Kirk Company, Grower Products Division, R.R. 3, Box 590, Wautoma, Wisconsin 54982, 1-800-252-KIRK, (414) 787-3317, FAX (414) 787-3509

A. M. Leonard, Inc., 6665 Spiker Rd., Piqua, OH 45356, (general supplies), 513-773-2694, 1-800-543-8955

Nasco Farm & Ranch, 901 Janesville Ave., Fort Atkinson, WI 53538, 414-563-2446

North Star Evergreens, Inc., Box 253, Park Rapids, MN 56470, 218-732-5818

SAJE, Inc., 6392 Portland Road, N.E., Salem, OR 97305, (Shears, Tools, Supplies & Clothing for Tree Growers), 1-800-354-4565 or 503-390-6705

D. H. Shelton & Sons, 635 84th Lane N.W., Coon Rapids, MN 55433, 612-571-8700

Sterling Bag Co., Foot of Fisher Rd., Lackawanna, NY 14218, (Vexar, burlap, tools, general supplies), 716-826-1991

Sun-Rise Supply, Co., Inc., Route 2, Box 300E1, Bassfield, MS 39421, 601-736-2148, or 1-800-777-2148

TSI, Inc., P. O. Box 151, Highway 206, Flanders, NJ 07836, 201-584-3417

Teufel Nursery, 12345 N.W. Barnes Road, Portland, OR 97229, 503-646-1111

Veldsma & Sons, Inc., P. O. Box 6, Forest Park, GA 30050, 404-361-8814 or 1-800-458-7919

Note: "Addendum to Basics of Growing Christmas Trees" also published by Treehaven Evergreen Nursery contains more than 60 pages of listings arranged by subject.

PARTIAL LIST OF CHEMICAL PRODUCT MANUFACTURERS

AMERICAN CYANAMID COMPANY, Agricultural Div., P. O. Box 400, Princeton, NJ 08540

BASF WYANDOTTE CORP., Agricultural Chemicals Div., P. O. Box 181, 100 Cherry Hill Rd., Persippany, NJ 07054, 201-263-3400, Emergency Tel. 201-263-0200

CHEVRON CHEMICAL COMPANY, Ortho Division, 940 Hensley Street, Richmond, CA 94801

CIBA-GEIGY CORP., Research and Development Dept., Agricultural Div., P. O. Box 11422, Greensboro, NC 27409, Emergency Tel. 919-292-7100

DIAMOND SHAMROCK CHEMICAL CO., Commercial Development, Agricultural Chemicals Div., 1100 Superior Avenue, Cleveland, OH 44114

DOW CHEMICAL USA, Agricultural Products Dept., P. O. Box 1706, Midland, MI 48640, 517-636-1000, Emergency Tel. 517-636-4400

DREXEL CHEMICAL CO., P. O. Box 9306, Memphis, TN 38109, 901-774-4370

DU PONT COMPANY, Biochemicals Dept., Wilmington, DE 19898, Emergency Tel. 302-774-2421

E. I. DU PONT, Agricultural Prod. Dept., Walker's Mill, Wilmington, DE 19898, 1-800-441-7515

ELANCO PRODUCTS CO., Lily Research Laboratories, P. O. Box 708, Greenfield, IN 46140

FARMLAND INDUSTRIES, P. O. Box 7305, Kansas City, Missouri 64116

GULF CROP PROTECTION PRODUCTS, Gulf Oil Chemicals Company, P. O. Box 2900, Merriam, Kansas 66201

HOPKINS AGRICULTURAL CHEMICALS CO., Box 7532, Madison, WI 53707, Emergency Tel. 214-931-8899

ICI UNITED STATES, INC., Biological Research Center, Agricultural Chemicals Div., P. O. Box 208, Goldsboro, NC 27530

MAGNA CORPORATION, P. O. Box 33387, 7505 Fannin Street, Houston, TX 77033

MILLER CHEMICAL AND FERTILIZER CORP., P. O. Box 333, Hanover, PA 17331, Emergency Tel. 717-632-8921

MOBAY CHEMICAL CORP, Agricultural Chemicals Div., P. O. Box 4913, Kansas City, KA 64120, Emergency Tel. 816-242-2000 (days), 816-242-2582 (nights and weekends)

Partial List of Chemical Manufacturers (continued)

MONSANTO COMPANY, Market Development Department, 800 N. Lindbergh Blvd., St. Louis, MO 63167, Emergency Tel. 314-694-2194 (days), 314-694-1000 (nights)

NOR AM AGRICULTURAL PRODUCTS, INC., 350 West Shuman Blvd., Naperville, IL 60566, Emergency Tel. 312-961-6500

ROHM AND HAAS COMPANY RESEARCH LABS, Norristown and McKean Roads, Spring House, PA 19477

SANDOZ, INC., Crop Protection, 480 Camino del Rio South, San Diego, CA 92108, Emergency Tel. 714-436-0217

STAUFFER CHEMICAL CO., P. O. Box 760m Mountain View, CA 94042

THOMPSON HAYWARD CHEMICAL CO., P. O. Box 2382, Kansas City, KA 66110, 913-321-3131

UNION CARBIDE CORPORATION, T. W. Alexander Drive, P. O. Box 12014, Research Triangle Park, NC 27709, Emergency Tel. 304-744-3487 (collect) spills, poisonings 212-551-4785 (days) 914-946-0646 (nights)

- -

CANADIAN CHRISTMAS TREE ASSOCIATIONS

President:
Richard A. Lord
Lord's Forestry Enterprises, Ltd.
P.O. Box 204
Bridgewater, N.S. B4V 2W8

British Columbia:
Eric Rasmussen
Box 2426
Canyon View Road
Invermere, B.C. VOA 1KO

Manitoba:
Bruce MacLeod
1074 Dorchester Avenue
Winnipeg, Manitoba R3M OS3

New Brunswick:
Vince Cormier
NBCTG Co-op Ltd.
R.R. #10
Fredericton, N.B. E3B 6H6

Nova Scotia:
William Stewart
NSCTGA
R.R. #3
St. Andrews, N.S. BOH 1XO

Newsletter:
Roch Dufresne
192 Rang VII
Arthabaska, Quebec G6P 6S2
(819) 357-7064 (819) 758-0589 (FAX)

Ontario:
Art Murcott
OCTGA
P.O. Box 339
Brooklin, Ontario LOB 1CO

Prince Edward Island:
John MacRae
PEI CTGA
R.R.#1
Charlottetown, P.E.I. C1A 7J6

Quebec:
Christian Morin
APANQ
340, Rang des Chutes
Ham Nord, Quebec GOP 1AO

Saskatchewan:
Gordon McKay
Box 1551
North Battleford, Saskatchewan
S9A 3W1

NATIONAL CHRISTMAS TREE ASSOCIATION, INC.

STATE ASSOCIATION CONTACTS

State	Contact
Alabama	James Frye, Rt., 13, Box 371-B, Jasper, AL 35501, 205/221-2214
California	Sharon Burke, California Christmas Tree Growers, 1451 Danville Blvd., #102, Alamo, CA 94507, 415/837-7463
Connecticut	John Olsen, RFD 1, Box 329, Voluntown, CT 06384, 203/376-2370
Florida	Debra Arnold, 3325 Treiman Blvd., Dade City, FL 33525, 904/583-3647
Georgia	Sonny Strickland, Rt. 1, Box 462, Moultrie, GA 31768, 912/941-5786
Illinois	Stephanie Brown, RR 1, Box 255, Simpson, IL 62985, 618/695-2784
Indiana	John R. Seifert, SEPAC Box 155, Butlerville, IN 47223, 812/458-6978
Inland Empire	Patti Wright, East 14009 Nixon, Spokane, WA 99216, 509/928-4905
Iowa	Chuck Young, 410 W. Madison, Knoxville, IA 50138, 515/842-2030
Kansas	Tony Delp, Rt. 2, Box 174-A, St. John, KS 67576, 316/549-3273
Louisiana/Mississippi	Kevin Steele, 56459 Dollar Rd, Angie, LA 70426, 504/848-2403
Maine	Albert Gondeck, RD #2, Box 1792, Turner, ME 04282, 207/225-3031
Maryland	Carville M. Akehurst, P.O. Box 314, Perry Hall, MD 21128, 301/256-5595
Massachusetts	H. Peter Wood, P.O. Box 375, Greenfield, MA 01302, 413/774-4200
Michigan	Laurie Dornbush, 2098 Butternut, Okemos, MI 48864, 517/347-1010
Mid-South	Richard Winslow, Proctors Hall Rd., Sewanee, TN 37375, 615/658-5117
Minnesota	Jim & Gen McCarthy, P.O. Box 130307, St. Paul, MN 55113, 612/633-0873
Missouri	Maryls Doerflinger, 10226 Lane, Kansas City, MO 64134, 816/763-8754
Montana	Linda McHenry, 385 Lake Blaine Road, Kalispell, MT 59901, 406/755-2783
Nebraska	Sandra Wade, RR 1, Box 119, Colon, NE 68018, 402/443-5308
New Hampshire/Vermont	Pam Dwyer, RD 1, Box 470, Wolcott, VT 05680, 802/888-2783
New Jersey	Charles A. Dupras, Box 29, River Road, Mays Landing, NJ 08330, 609/625-2307
New York	John B. Webb, 2947 E. Bayard Street Ext., Seneca Falls, NY 13148, 315/568-5571
North Carolina	Patricia Thiel, P.O. Box 1937, Boone, NC 28607, 704/262-5826
North Dakota	Northeast District Forester, Rt. 1, Box 1, Walhalla, ND 58282, 701/549-2441
Northwest	Bryan Ostlund, P.O. Box 3366, Salem, OR 97302, 503/364-2942
Ohio	Judith Humphrey, 1115 Branch Rd., Medina, OH 44256, 216/725-6188
Pennsylvania	Melissa Piper Nelson, 44 Cessna Drive, Halifax, PA 17032, 800/547-2842
Rhode Island	Jane Durning, 70 Burdickville Road, Charlestown, RI 02813, 401/364-7599
Rocky Mountain	Linda Staley, P.O. Box 1465, Monument, CO 80132, 719/481-4946
South Carolina	Marvin Gaffney, 1433 Fire Tower Road NE, Orangeburg, SC 29115, 803/533-0133
Texas	Alton L. Buehring, 424 American Bank Plaza, Corpus Christi, TX 78475, 512/881-8031
Virginia	Katherine Ward, HCR 60, Box 41-T, Deerfield, VA 24432, 703/939-4646
West Virginia	Gene Bailey, HCR 72, Box 36, Camp Creek, WV 25820 304/425-5928
Wisconsin	Virginia Mountford, 213 Pierce Street, Arlington, WI 53911, 608/635-7734

National Christmas Tree Association
611 East Wells Street
Milwaukee, Wisconsin 53202-3891
414/276-6410

210

PESTICIDE APPLICATION RECORD

Date	Field	Applicator	Pest	Chemical and Formulation	Amount Used	Area Treated	Gal. of Water	Comments on application (equipment, weather, pest size or density, etc.)

APPENDIX B - LOOSE ITEMS

Taper Gauge

Seedling Price List

Book Order Form